Y0-EHY-505

300-5
9

American Literature
A World View

PS
92
.W25

American Literature

A WORLD VIEW

by Willis Wager

NEW YORK
New York University Press

LONDON
University of London Press Limited
1968

47558

© 1968 by New York University
Library of Congress Catalog Card Number 68-29434
Manufactured in the United States of America

Acknowledgments

An excerpt from "Words for the Wind, I" is quoted from *Words for the Wind* by Theodore Roethke, Copyright © 1955 by Theodore Roethke, by permission of the publisher, Doubleday & Company, Inc.

Passages from "The Waste Land" and "East Coker" are quoted from *Collected Poems 1909-1962* by T. S. Eliot, Copyright 1930, 1939, 1943, 1950 by T. S. Eliot, Copyright 1934, 1935, 1936, 1952, by Harcourt, Brace and Company, Inc., by permission of the publishers, Harcourt Brace & World and Faber and Faber Limited.

Two lines from "Reporting Back" in *Traveling Through the Dark* by William Stafford. Copyright © 1962 by William Stafford. By permission of Harper & Row, Publishers.

An excerpt from "The Bridge" from *Complete Poems & Selected Letters & Prose of Harte Crane* by Harte Crane. Copyright 1933, 1958, 1966 by Liveright Publishing Corp. Permission by LIVERIGHT, Publishers, New York.

Passages from "A Route of Evanescence" and "Safe in Their Alabaster Chambers" reprinted by permission of the publishers and the Trustees of Amherst College from Thomas H. Johnson, Editor, *The Poems of Emily Dickinson*, Cambridge, Mass.: The Belknap Press of Harvard University Press, Copyright 1951, 1955, by The President and Fellows of Harvard College.

CONCORDIA COLLEGE LIBRARY
BRONXVILLE, N. Y. 10708

Passages from "New Hampshire," "The Pasture," "Fire and Ice," and "A Boundless Moment" quoted from *Complete Poems of Robert Frost*. Copyright 1923, 1939, © 1967 by Holt, Rinehart and Winston, Inc. Copyright 1951 by Robert Frost. Reprinted by permission of Holt, Rinehart and Winston, Inc.

An excerpt from "For John Kennedy His Inauguration" from *In the Clearing* by Robert Frost. Copyright © 1961, 1962 by Robert Frost. Reprinted by permission of Holt, Rinehart and Winston, Inc.

Lines from "Hypocrite Auteur" by Archibald Macleish reprinted from *Collected Poems 1917-1952* by Archibald Macleish by permission of Houghton Mifflin Company, publishers.

Lines from "Astigmatism" by Amy Lowell reprinted from *The Complete Poetical Works of Amy Lowell* by permission of Houghton Mifflin Company, publishers.

Excerpts quoted from Ezra Pound, *Personae*. Copyright 1928, 1954 by Ezra Pound. Reprinted by permission of New Directions Publishing Corporation and Faber and Faber Limited, publishers.

Lines from "Sacramental Meditations, Second Series, Meditation Three" reprinted from *The Poetical Works of Edward Taylor*, edited by T. H. Johnson (Copyright Rockland 1939; Princeton University Press 1943) by permission of Princeton University Press.

Excerpt from "Tamar" by Robinson Jeffers reprinted from *The Selected Poetry of Robinson Jeffers*, Copyright © 1924 by Peter G. Boyle reprinted by permission of Random House, Inc.

Excerpt from *The Grapes of Wrath* by John Steinbeck. Copyright © 1939 by John Steinbeck, reprinted by permission of The Viking Press, Inc.

Introduction

Now in the late twentieth century a world approach to American literature is more feasible than ever before, thanks to Carbon 14 analysis; and, since World War II, such an approach has been needed more than ever before. At one time, perhaps, intelligent people could dismiss America, Africa, and most of Asia as not having had any history till Europe brought it to them, and could even dismiss most of the European past, too, as having been "*pre*historic." But no one can today.

By the time of the Middle Stone Age in Europe (perhaps by 7500 B.C.), Mongolian peoples had migrated to the Americas via the Bering Strait — and their descendants today are known as the American Indians. Meanwhile, migrations from the Central Asiatic area were streaming into Europe — particularly of tribes that spoke languages usually referred to as Indo-European. From Asia the Indians-to-be were moving eastward and the Indo-Europeans westward. Soon there were to be, in a manner of speaking, Indians right and left. By the time the Mediterranean peoples were at their height, so also were the Pacific peoples: the Romans ruled in Eurasia, the Han in China, the Mayans in America. By the fifteenth century the Incas had a considerable empire in Peru, and the Aztecs in Mexico, with the ruins of the Mayan realm in between.

Extant is the text of a complete Inca drama, the *Ollantay*, in Quechua. Though written down later, it originally seems to have been performed shortly after the resignation of the Inca Pachacuti in 1471. Ollantay, a trusted general, has fallen in love with Pachacuti's daughter. Discovering that she is pregnant, Pachacuti throws her in prison. Ollantay flees, but is treacherously taken prisoner. Before he can be brought to justice, however, the old ruler has been succeeded by his son, who is as gentle as his father had been harsh and who releases his sister and makes Ollantay viceroy of Cuzco. Though the heroine here reminds one a little of Shakuntala, the *Ollantay* is much less sophisticated than the Sanskrit drama. We know that the American Indians, like the Eastern Asiatics, were great lovers of drama — a feature of American life by no means extinct in our present century of movies, radio, and television. Some twentieth-century readers have found the *Ollantay* too sentimental for their taste and have questioned its antiquity. Naturally, whenever anything oral is transcribed, it is changed. But the *Ollantay* was not Christianized as was, say, *Beowulf*.

From the Mayan area in the highlands of Guatemala, there remain two sizable works which — though also written down after the Conquest — undoubtedly go back to times before Columbus. One is the sacred book of this people, the *Popol Vuh*, which contains much the same type of material as *Genesis* and Homer — heroic exploits, creation of man from an ear of corn, establishment of human sacrifice, enumeration of early leaders and tribes. Man is here in close communion with nature and — as in Homer — there are scenes of great laughter. The other is *Rabinal Achi* [The Man from Rabinal], a dance-drama leading up to a human sacrifice: with a great deal of incantational repetition, it has about it the lapidary quality of Gertrude Stein's *Three Lives*. The central figure, a captive, moves step-by-step with the somnambulistic inevitability of a character in a Kafka novel to the climax — heart excision.

From ancient Mexico there is a rich literature that can be read today with more assurance of authenticity than that from areas farther south. Written down in the sixteenth century by Spanish scribes were Aztec hymns and sayings (some as old as the thirteenth century) and extensive bodies of Aztec legendary and historical accounts. Some of this material has literary interest, for example an Aztec poem composed by a ruler of Telzcoco, Nezahualcoyotl [Famishing Coyote], who died at eighty in 1472. This poem has been translated into English prose thus:

> All the earth is a grave, and naught escapes it; noth-ing is so perfect that it does not fall and disappear. The rivers, brooks, fountains, and waters flow on, and never return to their joyous beginnings; they hasten on to the vast realms of Tlaloc, and the wider they spread be-tween their marges the more rapidly do they mould their own sepulchral urns. That which was yesterday is not today; and let not that which is today trust to live tomorrow.
>
> The caverns of earth are filled with pestilential dust which once was the bones, the flesh, the bodies of great ones who sat upon thrones, deciding causes, ruling assem-blies, governing armies, conquering provinces, possessing treasures, tearing down temples, flattering themselves with pride, majesty, fortune, praise, and dominion. These glories have passed like the dark smoke thrown out by the fires of Popocatepetl, leaving no monuments but the rude skins on which they were written.

A good example of mid-sixteenth-century literary Aztec is Bernardino de Sahagun's account of the Spanish Conquest. As late as the nineteenth century Maximilian was issuing procla-mations in Aztec as well as in Spanish, since he wished to make himself out to be the Indians' friend.

In the more northern regions there has, of course, been a great deal of recording of Indian material such as the tribal chronicle of the Delawares, the *Walum Olum*, preserved in an early-nineteenth-century manuscript. In the early nine-teenth century Henry R. Schoolcraft brought out several vol-umes; and in 1945 Paul Radin published the Winnebago ritual drama, *The Road of Life and Death*.

The American Indian languages are by no means dead. Their literature, now covering centuries, is hardly to be ignored. And if it is not American, what is? If literature is influenced by natural environment, how can there help being a relationship between American-Indian and American-European literature? And in the normal sequence of three stages that most literatures pass through — oral, written, printed — is not the literature of American Indian origin the first?

Contents

American Literature

A World View

From Letters
I. to Memoirs
Columbus to Franklin

Others besides Asiatics reached America before the fifteenth century. There may have been some from Africa — from the Nile, from Carthage, from the West Coast. It has become increasingly clear that there were some from Europe. Excavations carried on in northern Newfoundland from 1961 to 1963 by Norwegian archaeologists have revealed the foundations of seven buildings that give a Carbon 14 dating of around the tenth century. Scandinavian sagas of the eleventh and twelfth centuries refer to Norsemen as having crossed the ocean. In 1965 there was made public for the first time a world map drawn about 1440 — which had just come from a private collection and been added to the Yale University Library's holdings — showing, southwest of Greenland, a large island labeled Vinland and, in the corner, a Latin inscription to the effect that Leif Ericson and his men had discovered it and that Pope Paschal II had sent Bishop Eric Gnupson there. Thus, what Columbus did in 1492 was to rediscover America and provide the world with a clear and coherent verbal account of his experiences. The uniqueness of his achievement is thus to some extent literary.

His letter of 1493 is one of the landmarks of American literature. Formally, it is a letter, and the point of view is reportorial. It is not, however, a purely private missive; and the approach is not entirely objective. Printed in a number of

3

editions, it served as a public proclamation of the results of the
explorer's first voyage. Though the original manuscript is no
longer extant, it was presumably in Spanish. The versions
printed in 1493 are in Latin prose and in Italian verse (the latter being also a translation, even though Columbus himself
was Italian). The substance of the letter, however, is no
doubt there; and it is clearly a précis of the very full and vivid
journal which Columbus kept and which (since the original
manuscript of it is also no longer extant) must be largely reconstructed from the portions of it used in sixteenth-century
accounts of the voyages.

The journal of Columbus that emerges from these oblique
views of it opens with an explicit statement of the purpose of
the voyage:

> . . . acting on the information that I had given to your
> Highnesses touching the lands of India, and respecting
> a Prince who is called *Grand Can,* which means in our
> language King of Kings, how he and his ancestors had
> sent to Rome many times to ask for learned men of our
> holy faith to teach him, and how the Holy Father had
> never complied, insomuch that many people believing in
> idolatries were lost by receiving doctrine of perdition:
> *your Highnesses* . . . resolved to send me, Cristobal
> Colon, to the said parts of India to see the said princes,
> and the cities and lands, and their disposition, with a
> view that they might be converted to our holy faith;
> and ordered that I should not go by land to the east-
> ward, as had been customary, but that I should go by
> way of the west, whither up to this day, we do not
> know for certain that any one has gone. . . .

What Columbus said he was trying to do was effect an intellectual or spiritual contact between West and East.

Obviously, from many of the journal entries, he was a
man who made some of the same assumptions about Providence
as the Pilgrims and Puritans did later. Behind all of them there
was an intense religiosity which might be called, for short,
"Gothic Christianity." For most American writing during the

period between the Discovery and the Revolution, the highest common factor is an emphasis on religion.

From the Iberian peninsula and the British Isles (those extremities of Europe to which a dynamic expression of Christianity had moved by a series of stages westward), there came a task force which clashed with that other extreme wing of human civilization, Indian America — initially passive, fatalistic, matter-of-fact, Oriental. Thus figuratively was the globe encircled; and on American soil there was a meeting of East and West. Think for a moment of the traditional differences between those two halves of the globe as embodied in Gautama and Jesus. They relate to each other as the negative and positive poles in an electric circuit.

Collections of early accounts of travels (not merely to America but also to other parts of the globe) were assembled and printed in England by Richard Hakluyt in his *Divers Voyages* (1582) and by his successor Samuel Purchas in his *Pilgrimes* (1625). The "pilgrims" to whom Purchas referred were not a specific religious group. They were simply travelers.

In this sense Columbus was a pilgrim. A second example of one of these "pilgrims" is John Smith, who had fought the Turks in Hungary, been taken prisoner, escaped, and — still in his twenties — joined the group responsible for the first permanent English settlement in America at Jamestown, later becoming its "president." In 1608 his *A True Relation . . .* appeared in London. Its tempo is speedy: the four-month trip over is disposed of in the opening sentence. Yet Smith takes time to articulate a relationship between God's will and what happened: "God (being angrie with vs)," he writes, "plagued vs with such famin and sicknes, that the liuing were scarce able to bury the dead. . . ." Though usually associated with Virginia, he also explored and named New England, thus setting it off against New France to the north, Virginia and the Spanish colonies to the south, and Nova Albion at the same latitude on the Pacific. Smith was aware that he was writing in a "plain style," as he says in *A Description of New England* (1616): "I intreat your pardons, if I chance to bee too plaine, or tedious in relating my knowledge for plaine mens satisfaction." His description of "the Countrie of the *Massachusets*" as "the Paradise of all those parts" attracted the Puritans. Though not one himself, he concluded his description with a distinctly Biblical conception of colonization:

> But, to conclude, *Adam* and *Eue* did first beginne this innocent worke, To plant the earth to remaine to posteritie, but not without labour, trouble, and industrie. *Noe*, and his family, beganne againe the second plantation; and their seede as it still increased, hath still planted new Countries, and one countrie another: and so the world to that estate it is.

As with Columbus, one is struck by the prominence that John Smith, also not a member of the clergy, gave to religion.

Still a third "pilgrim" and also not a clergyman was William Bradford, who was repeatedly elected governor of the group that sailed to America in the *Mayflower* and landed near Plymouth Rock in 1620. Late in life, around mid-century, he wrote an account *Of Plymouth Plantation*, which is one of the finest of the Colonial chronicles. A figure of speech he used in this chronicle has given rise to the familiar name for this group of refugees from Jacobite England and Spain-threatened Leyden:

> So they lefte the goodly and pleasante citie, which had been ther resting place near 12 years; but they knew they were pilgrimes, and looked not much on those things, but lift up their eyes to the heavens, their dearest cuntrie, and quieted their spirits.

The group left just at the outbreak of the Thirty Years' War — the last and worst of the European religious conflicts (which cost Germany three-fifths of its population) and, at the same time, the first in which all Europe really took part.

On their arrival, in the midst of winter and surrounded by many dangers,

What could now sustaine them but the spirite of God
and his grace? May not and ought not the children of
these fathers rightly say: *Our faithers were Englishmen
which came over this great ocean, and were ready to
perish in this wilderness; but they cried unto the Lord,
and he heard their voyce, and looked on their adversitie,
etc. Let them therefore praise the Lord, because he is
good, and his mercies endure for ever.*

The eloquence here stems in part from Bradford's ability to
move so easily from writing in his own person to quoting the
Bible that one is scarcely conscious where he leaves off and
the Bible begins.

Though he was originally a Yorkshire farmer with no particular academic training, he had obviously read some other
books than the Bible: he quotes, for instance, from an account
of the great tribulations of the early Spanish settlers in
America. By no means was he an uneducated man: before the
end of his life he had even learned to read Hebrew. There is,
however, nothing pedantic about *Of Plymouth Plantation*:
it is as simple, direct, vivid, and transparent a piece of writing
as one could wish for. There is no attempt in it to achieve a
stained-glass-window gorgeousness. Bradford wrote in the
"plain style" — not because he would not have been able to
achieve an ornate style if he had wanted to, but because he
obviously did not want to. Toward the end of the account
he was much concerned with the inroads the devil had been
making in the Plymouth community: since the early harrowing but glorious days, Bradford felt, there had been a distinct
decline.

What did the American Pilgrims and Puritans write? Very
little of what looms so large in the twentieth century — so-
called entertainment. Practically no plays, novels, or short stories. But chronicles, official material, diaries, letters, sermons,
and poems. To use a later set of terms, we might say that they
inclined more to realism or naturalism than to classicism,
romanticism, or art for art's sake. Their writing for home
consumption tends to be plain, for they considered writing not

as an end but as a means; they distrusted rhetorical exhibition-
ism, and tried to hold to the actual text of the Bible as a guide
to possible further church reform. They tended to move a little more freely between prose and verse than Americans of
some subsequent periods have done, thinking of verse largely
as just a heightened form of eloquence, not as an autonomous
realm of thought or feeling. Bradford, for example, wrote a
great deal of verse which in subject matter is related to the
prose in *Of Plymouth Plantation*.

Somewhat as Bradford had done at Plymouth, John Winthrop, a lawyer who masterminded the Massachusetts Bay
settlement, kept a careful journal. A university graduate, he
was one of a dozen substantial citizens who in 1629 at Cambridge signed an agreement that within six months they would
emigrate to New England with their families, provided that "the
whole Government, together with the patent for the said Plantation, be first, by an order of Court, legally transferred and
established to remain with us and others which shall inhabit
upon the said Plantation." Normally, trading corporations had
been administered from the home country, and the original
draft of the Massachusetts patent had so provided — but, as
Winthrop later wrote, "with much difficulty we gott it ab-
scinded." At least, when the charter was obtained, there was
no specially prescribed place for the meetings of the company. This was the opening rift that, a century and a half later,
was to widen into the political independence of the United
States and, still later, the relative independence of the members
of the British Commonwealth of Nations.

Religious autonomy, however, Winthrop and his associates
did not want: they were not Separatists like the Pilgrims at
Plymouth. From aboard the *Arbella* as it was leaving Yar-
mouth in 1630 the group of leaders, with Winthrop as their
"Governor," issued a public letter "to the rest of their Brethren in and of the Church of England." During the voyage and
on to the end of his life he kept his journal — sober, detailed,
somewhat more laconic than Bradford's, less personal, more

self-conscious. As he said in a speech to his fellow passengers on the *Arbella*, " . . . wee must Consider that wee shall be as a Citty vpon a Hill, the eies of all people are vppon vs. . . ." The more personal side of Winthrop was reserved for his letters, of which a number between himself and his wife are preserved.

Repeatedly elected to office in the Bay settlement, Winthrop was wholly concerned with its success. Anti-Puritan forces in London tried to get the charter back. Winthrop astutely delayed and began preparing for military resistance. The Puritan revolution of 1642 in England — involving the beheading of the king and the establishment of the Commonwealth, the first European revolution in the modern sense of the word — seems to have been inspired in part by the success of the Puritans in America. Out of the first graduating class of twenty at Harvard, twelve — including George Downing, after whom Downing Street is named — went to England to participate in the stirring events there. One of Winthrop's own sons, Stephen, went over to serve as a colonel under Cromwell and as a member of Parliament.

In New England, meanwhile, a league was formed in 1643 for mutual protection, the United Colonies of New England, including Massachusetts, Plymouth, Connecticut, and New Haven, with Boston as the meeting place of the delegates and Winthrop as president. Late in Winthrop's journal there occurs the text of a speech he made in 1645: when in the town of Hingham factions blocked the naming of a captain of the local militia, Winthrop and his fellow magistrates settled the matter in rather summary fashion. Some of the enraged citizens charged him with having exceeded his prerogatives and brought him to trial, but he was acquitted. In summing up the matter before the General Court, he said — in effect — that there are two kinds of liberty: natural and civil or federal. The former will stand no authority; the latter is the proper end and object of authority. When a human being is placed in an office of authority, he then — insofar as he is exercising that office — is answerable to God. He is, of course, also a human being; but *with respect to the civil or federal liberty involved*, he is answerable to God alone:

> If you stand for your natural corrupt liberties, and will do what is good in your own eyes, you will not endure the least weight of authority, but will murmur, and oppose, and be always striving to shake off that yoke; but if you will be satisfied to enjoy such civil and lawful liberties, such as Christ allows you, then will you quietly and cheerfully submit unto that authority which is set over you, in all the administrations of it, for your own good. Wherein, if we fail at any time, we hope we shall be willing (by God's assistance) to hearken to good advice from any of you, or in any other way of God; so shall your liberties be preserved, in upholding the honor and power of authority amongst you.

The sermons of ordained Puritan ministers, often printed and circulated in pamphlet form or collected in volumes, constitute no inconsiderable part of the American literature of this period. In print, of course, they often appear more constricted and crabbed than they may have been under the conditions of actual delivery. John Cotton — a clergyman who worked hand in hand with Winthrop to make the Puritan theocracy solid and one of the patriarchs in the family of Boston clergymen which included Increase and Cotton Mather, and thus extended into the eighteenth century — had been famous early in his career, in England, for the impressive rhetoric he used in his sermons. But then, suddenly, he gave it up and began to talk from the pulpit in a down-to-earth way — which at first was not at all well received. When he came to America, he of course continued to preach in this plain style.

His efforts to speak plainly did not save him from getting embroiled in controversy. Historically Protestants had stood for faith rather than works, but under the practical exigencies of colonization there could be no neglect of work. John Cotton maintained that one first got the Spirit, and then both faith and works proceeded therefrom. An admirer of his in England,

Mrs. Anne Hutchinson, came over in 1634 with her husband and twelve children; and soon she began organizing, on her own, discussion groups in which she seems to have encouraged the idea that all one needed was to feel that one had the Spirit — that one could, in other words, discern one's spiritual state for oneself. Apparently she *thought* she was simply spelling out what Cotton had said; but before she finished, Cotton had to write half a dozen tracts to specify just what he had and had not meant to say, and Mrs. Hutchinson had to be banished from the Colony.

An example of the plain style in the early New England sermon — but with a little more fire to it than Cotton raised in his sermons — is the opening of Thomas Hooker's *A True Sight of Sin:*

> I answer, A true sight of sin hath two Conditions attending upon it; or it appears in two things: We must see sin, 1. Cleerly. 2. Convictingly, what it is in it self, and what it is to us, not in the appearance and paint of it, but in the power of it; not to fadam it in the notion and conceit only, but to see it with Application.
>
> We must see it cleerly in its own Nature, its Native color and proper hue: It's not every slight conceit, not every general and cursorie, confused thought or careless consideration that will serve the turn, or do the work here, we are all sinners; it is my infirmity, I cannot help it; my weakness, I cannot be rid of it; no man lives without faults and follies, the best have their failings, *In many things we offend all.*

Certainly he comes to the point here forcefully — a point which was to be reiterated in a later generation by Hawthorne through a fictional mode of presentation.

Conspicuously absent from the writing of the Puritans is anything like fiction presented frankly *as fiction.* Extended personal narrative, however, does appear, as in Mary Rowlandson's account of her captivity by the Indians, *The Soveraignty and Goodness of God* (1682):

> On the tenth of February 1675, Came the Indians with great numbers upon Lancaster: Their first coming was about Sunrising; hearing the noise of some Guns, we looked out; several Houses were burning, and the Smoke ascending to Heaven.

In detail she tells of twenty "removes" during her captivity and eventual release by ransom, remarks on several "special Providences," and sums up the meaning of the whole experience for her along the lines suggested by the title of the account. Thus it has at once some aspects of the memoir, the sermon, and the novel.

Though seventeenth-century writing in America was usually sober, clear, orderly, logical, and — in its way — earthy and elemental, it occasionally shows off rhetorically, particularly when addressed to a European audience. One of the more euphuistic stylists, Nathaniel Ward, had come to America in 1634 with a European background that included graduation from Cambridge, friendship with intellectuals in England and on the Continent, and excommunication by Archbishop Laud. Becoming minister at Ipswich (earlier called Aggawam), he wrote a book in which he assumed for literary purposes the character of a shoemaker, *The Simple Cobler of Agawam* (London, 1647), which begins: "Either I am in an apoplexy, or that man is in a lethargy, who doth not now sensibly feel God shaking the heavens over his head and the earth under his feet."

In other words, Civil War in England, Thirty Years' War on the Continent! In England the Puritans had had to compromise in order to seize and stay in power: they had, for example, begun to work with the Anabaptists and other religious groups, and had begun to try to pressure their American brethren into taking a more tolerant or liberal stand. But the Simple Cobler makes it clear that New and Old England now differ in this: New England is carrying on the old fight without compromise, and those who urge capitulation might as well stay in Europe. Some traits of the Simple Cobler seem in the line of descent from humor characters, and the figure seems almost to have taken on a life of its own: after Ward's death in 1652, when Lord Bellamont was being received as royal governor of Massachusetts in 1699, he was greeted with a pageant (one of the few recorded approaches of the Puritans to drama) in which a local schoolteacher and physician, Benjamin Thompson, dressed as the Simple Cobler of Agawam, stepped forth and read some witty verses of welcome that he had written.

Distinctly individual among the early New Englanders, also, stands Roger Williams, who arrived in Boston in 1631, was offered the position of minister there, but declined it because the congregation had not "separated" from the Church of England. For a while he was at Plymouth and Salem, but when he heard that the General Court of Massachusetts was about to deport him he fled south into the Indian region. What upset the Massachusetts authorities was his apparently anarchical belief that the land belonged to the Indians and therefore the English king had had no right to give the Bay Puritans title to it, and that the covenant of the church congregation in Boston was not validly based on the covenant between God and Abraham in the Book of Genesis. After the Puritans came to power in England in 1642, Williams went to London to secure from Parliament a charter for Rhode Island, in which there would be complete separation of church and state and no persecution for cause of conscience. On shipboard he put into final form *A Key into the Languages of America* (London, 1643) which is a sort of Narragansett dictionary, amply provided with meditations, bits of verse, and anecdotes. Arriving in London, he was in personal contact with Cromwell and Milton, and was instrumental in blocking a move by Parliament which almost set up in Great Britain a system of church and state modeled after that in Massachusetts. While he was in London he began a pamphlet skirmish with John Cotton, opening with a printed dialogue *The Bloudy Tenent of Persecution* (London, 1644).

Returning to Rhode Island, he was for a time "president" of that colony. In 1652 while he was in London on a second trip, he published a booklet which had developed from a letter to his wife on the occasion of her recovery from an illness, *Experiments of Spiritual Life and Health:*

> . . . O, that our heads were fountains and our eyes rivers of water, that we might weep with Germany, weep with Ireland, yea, weep day and night with England and Scotland (to speak nothing of other remote nations), in laying again and again to heart the strokes of God's most righteous judgments, in their most fearful slaughters and desolations. . . .
>
> But . . . as sure and wonderful will shortly be these two most wonderful and dreadful downfalls of those two so mighty monarchies (so great enemies to Christ Jesus) — the Turkish and the Popish — according to the prediction of the holy prophets! How fearful the effusion of the vials, in part fulfilled and yet to be poured forth in their season! And not a little wonderful is that mighty destruction of the nations, Gog and Magog, gathered as the sand of the sea against the camp of the saints of the holy city.

After the Restoration of 1660 England and America were still further estranged, and Williams' political activities were curtailed. But he continued to serve Rhode Island, particularly as a negotiator in King Philip's War of 1675 — a role which he was uniquely able to fulfill because he had lived among the Indians.

Perhaps it need hardly be pointed out that the early seventeenth century brought to New England a great many different individuals who happened to write. Distinctly not a Puritan was Thomas Morton, at Mt. Wollaston — or "Merry Mount" — near Plymouth. He and his men, according to Bradford, set up a maypole, drank and danced for days on end, consorted with Indian women, hung satirical verses on their pole, and engaged in even "worse practices" — raised, in other words, the very devil. Twice deported, Morton brought out at Amsterdam in 1637 his *New English Canaan*. In a style that exaggerated the manner of the medieval romance, he told, among other things, about his expulsion from the Colony. Nine Plymouth men, led by diminutive Miles Standish (referred to by Morton as "Captain Shrimp"), came out to get him (or, as Morton calls himself, "mine Host") thus:

> The nine worthies coming before the Denne of this supposed Monster, (this seven headed hydra, as they termed him,) and began, like Don Quixote against the Windmill, to beate a parly, and to offer quarter, if mine Host would yeald; for they resolved to send him for England. . . .

which they did, though he ultimately came back and lived out his days in the Maine woods.

The most extensive body of publication in Colonial America came from the Mathers — Richard, Increase, and Cotton. After difficulty with the ecclesiastical authorities in England, Richard came to Massachusetts in 1635, preached for many years in Dorchester, published a good deal of homiletic and expository material, helped prepare the *Bay Psalm Book*, and begat six sons, four of whom became preachers. The youngest, Increase, became minister of North Church in Boston, represented Massachusetts in London for a time, and was for sixteen years president of Harvard. In addition to scores of rather direct and terse sermons, he published *An Essay for the Recording of Illustrious Providences* (Boston, 1684), a classified compendium of weird incidents. Increase's son Cotton (the scion of two leading Boston ministerial families, as his mother was the only daughter of John Cotton) succeeded to the pulpit of "Old North" and more than doubled his father's impressive publication performance. The most substantial of Cotton Mather's works is his history of the church in New England from 1620 to 1698, *Magnalia Christi Americana* (London, 1702) — well over a thousand pages, beginning:

> I write the *Wonders* of the CHRISTIAN RELIGION, flying from the Depravations of *Europe*, to the *American Strand:* And, assisted by the Holy Author of that *Religion*, I do, with all Conscience of *Truth*, required therein by Him, who is the *Truth* it self, Report the *Wonderful Displays* of His Infinite

> Power, Wisdom, Goodness, and Faithfulness, wherewith
> His Divine Providence hath *Irradiated* an *Indian Wil-
> derness.*

The purpose of the *Magnalia* is to trace the manifestations of
Divine Providence in New England — particularly in the lives
of a host of notable individuals — from the first settlement to
the time of writing, in hopes thereby of encouraging piety.
From a purely historical and documentary point of view,
this work has great significance because it is based on many
sources of information no longer available. And from a literary
point of view it has a mighty impact, for Cotton had the will
and ability to articulate his unique insights into various episodes. What he was undertaking to write was, in his way, the
sort of thing that Vergil had done for Rome and that Whitman
was to do for "these States." There is about the *Magnalia*,
however, that crushing weight of erudition and industry that
is distinctly Puritan, together with the characteristic juxtaposition of the jubilant and the mournful note.

There are, however, shorter and simpler works by Cotton
Mather. His *Bonifacius* influenced Franklin, and his *Christian
Philosopher* anticipates much that was to be advocated still
later by the European Romanticists. He was an important Colonial writer — almost as important as Edwards and Franklin.

For a less formal glimpse of Puritan sensibility in the writings of a contemporary of Cotton Mather's there is the lively
private diary of the Boston businessman and later judge,
Samuel Sewall. In it he jotted down his thoughts and feelings,
summarized sermons he had heard, and recorded in detail the
incidents in his courtship, when a widower, of an eligible
widow. Once when she did not take off her glove, he told
her "twas great odds between handling a dead Goat, and a living
lady" and so, he noted, "Got it off." Sewall was one of the
judges in the witchcraft trials, but five years later publicly confessed that he had been in error. With his tract *The Selling of
Joseph* (1700) he became one of the first antislavery writers.
And in his *Phænomena* (Boston, 1697) he speculates elo-

quently on the continuing possibility of revelation in his immediate surroundings:

> As long as *Plum Island* shall faithfully keep the commanded Post; Notwithstanding all the hectoring Words, and hard Blows of the proud and boisterous Ocean; As long as any Salmon, or Sturgeon shall swim in the streams of *Merrimack;* or any Perch, or Pickeril, in *Crane-Pond;* As long as the Sea-Fowl shall know the Time of their coming, and not neglect seasonably to visit the Places of their Acquaintance: As long as any Cattel shall be fed with the Grass growing in the Medows, which do humbly bow down themselves before *Turkie-Hill;* As long as any Sheep shall walk upon *Old Town Hills,* and shall from thence pleasantly look down upon the River *Parker,* and the fruitfull *Marishes* lying beneath; As long as any free and harmless Doves shall find a White Oak, or other Tree within the Township, to perch, or feed, or build a careless Nest upon; and shall voluntarily present themselves to perform the office of Gleaners after Barley-Harvest; As long as Nature shall not grow Old and dote; but shall constantly remember to give the rows of Indian Corn their education, by Pairs: So long shall Christians be born there; and being first made meet, shall from thence be Translated, to be made partakers of the Inheritance of the Saints in Light.

Most of these old New Englanders could versify, moving as easily from prose to verse as they did from speech to writing to print. Ward has a number of pithy lines in his *Simple Cobler,* such as:

> When States dishelv'd are, and Lawes untwist,
> Wise men keep their tongues, fools speak what they list.

A friend of his, John Wilson — who came over in 1630 and was a pastor in Boston — was adept at the anagram. When a Puritan minister in Limerick, Claudius Gilbert, sent Wilson a copy of an anti-Quaker tract he had just published, Wilson promptly responded with some rhymes. He rearranged the letters of the author's name into *Tis Braul I Cudgel*, and used "brawl" and "cudgel" as his two main ideas. Some of the elegies written on this principle — for example, John Fiske's on John Cotton — are splendid. In this type of artful composition Wilson developed such skill that Cotton Mather likened it to God's in creating the world — though Nathaniel Ward seems to have thought less of it:

> We poor Agawams
> are so stiff in the hams
> that we cannot make Anagrams,
> But Mr John Wilson
> the great Epigrammatist
> Can let out an Anagram
> even as he list.

We have more visionary verse from Thomas Tillam, a Seventh Day Baptist who came over in 1638 but soon returned to England (whence, after the Restoration, he fled to Heidelberg). His poem *Uppon the first sight of New-England June 29 1638* stresses not the visual but the spiritual experience. The poet hails this "holy land" and hears a welcome from the Lamb of God:

> heare I'le bee with you, heare you shall Inioye
> my sabbaths, sacraments, my minestrye
> and ordinances in their puritye.

The town clerk at Woburn, Edward Johnson, similarly concludes a rather extensive history of New England from 1628 to 1652, part prose and part verse, usually referred to as the *Wonder-Working Providence of Sions Saviour in New England* (London, 1654):

> Thy workes are not in Israels Land confined,
> From East to West thy wondrous works are known
> To Nations all thou hast thy grace assigned,
> Thy spirits breathings through the World are blown.

But who were the major seventeenth-century writers of verse in Colonial America? Three stand out — all born in England and coming to America early, all somewhat conservative theologically, and all responsible for some long and quasi-dramatic works.

Anne Bradstreet (1612-1672) was the daughter of Winthrop's deputy on the voyage over in 1630, the wife of a prominent man of affairs in the Colony, and the mother of eight children — or, as she wrote,

> I had eight birds hatcht in one nest,
> Four Cocks there were, and Hens the rest.

— and, accordingly, the progenitor of many of the later New England "Brahmins." Just before the birth of one of her children, she wrote what she thought might be her farewell to her husband:

> And when thou feel'st no grief, as I no harms,
> Yet love thy dead, who long lay in thine arms.

When her house burned down, she consoled herself with the thought that her real home was in heaven:

> Thou hast an house on high erect,
> Fram'd by that mighty Architect,
> With glory richly furnished,
> Stands permanent though: this bee fled.
> It's purchaséd, and paid for too
> By him who hath enovgh to doe.

There are also poems about her father and mother, and love poems to her husband.

She was, however, more than just a seventeenth-century literary Grandma Moses. As her father had written a long poem *On the Four Parts of the World* (perhaps inspired by the long poems of the late sixteenth-century French courtier Guillaume Du Bartas), so she in turn wrote four of these "quaternions" — one on the four elements, one on the four humors, one on the four ages of man, and one on the four seasons of the year. In each quaternion, each of the four things — lightly personified and occasionally in the first person — says what it does. She also began a long poem on the four monarchies of the world — Assyrian, Persian, Greek, and Roman — but (because of the fire) did not quite finish the Roman. On the Civil War in England she wrote a *Dialogue between Old England and New*: the old mother confesses that she did wrong in persecuting the Puritans and not learning anything from what had happened in Germany, France, and Ireland; and the daughter promises moral, military, and financial aid, envisaging a new sack of Rome, and

> This done with brandish'd Swords to *Turky* goe,
> For then what is't, but English blades dare do,
> And lay her waste for so's the sacred Doom,
> And do to *Gog* as thou hast done to *Rome*.
> Oh *Abraham*'s seed lift up your heads on high,
> For sure the day of your Redemption's nigh,
> The Scales shall fall from your long blinded eyes,
> And him you shall adore who now despise,
> Then fulness of the Nations in shall flow,
> And Jew and Gentile to one worship go.

These poems were taken to London (unknown to her) by her brother-in-law and were brought out under the title *The Tenth Muse Lately sprung up in America* (1650). In the prefatory material of this volume there are some verses by Ward in which he says that Mercury and Minerva asked Apollo to judge between this and Du Bartas' book:

> They bid him Hemisphear his mouldy nose,
> With's crackt leering-glasses, for it would pose
> The best brains he had in's old pudding-pan,
> Sex weigh'd, which best, the Woman, or the Man?
> He peer'd, and por'd, and glar'd, and said for wore,
> I'me even as wise now, as I was before. . . .

Aside from merely ephemeral volumes, Anne Bradstreet's book of poems is one of the first by a woman to be published in English. In 1678 it went into a second edition (with additions); and some half-dozen times during the succeeding years her work has been reedited. Many of her poems — particularly those added in the second edition — anticipate attitudes that were to become widespread among poets writing in English a century later. In her *Contemplations*, for example, she reflects that if winter comes, spring cannot be far behind; and external nature, particularly the song of the nightingale, inspires her meditations:

> Under the cooling shadow of a stately Elm
> Close sate I by a goodly Rivers side,
> Where gliding streams the Rocks did overwhelm;
> A lonely place, with pleasures dignifi'd.
> I once that lov'd the shady woods so well,
> Now thought the rivers did the trees excel,
> And if the sun would ever shine, there would I dwell.

Michael Wigglesworth (1631-1705) was brought to America at an even tenderer age than was Anne Bradstreet. Graduating from Harvard, he became a tutor there and later pastor at Malden. His rather sizable works of edification in verse — which became tremendously popular in his day — were composed within self-imposed restrictions of careful regard for Scripture and avoidance of anything too obviously arty. In his *Day of Doom* (Cambridge, 1662) he describes the day of final judgment when Christ divides the elect from the non-elect. The reader can, of course, also take this analogically as referring to any great cataclysm, such as the Restoration or the atom bomb. The volume begins with a Preface "To the Christian Reader,"

> Readers, I am a fool,
> And have adventured
> To play the fool this once for Christ, . . .

then after a "Prayer unto Christ" the poem proper begins, quite innocently:

> Still was the night, Serene and Bright,
>   when all Men sleeping lay;

but then suddenly it is the end of everything. Christ is the judge. He allows many highly respected but nonelect churchmen to plead their case, but with inexorable logic he thunders back:

> How could you bear to see or hear
> of others freed at last,
> From Satan's pawes, whilst in his jawes
> your selves were held more fast?

As in Dante's poem, the ending undertakes to suggest the bliss enjoyed by the saved. Then there is a long "Postscript" in heroic couplets, in which Wigglesworth talks to the reader like a Dutch uncle; and finally there is a poem in quatrains headed *Vanity of Vanities: A Song of Emptiness to Fill up the Empty Pages Following*, in which the *Ecclesiastes* theme is developed according to the medieval *Ubi sunt* formula. The very last line of the work is in Latin: *Omnia praetereunt praeter amare Deum* — that is, "all is vanity but to love God." In addition to this somewhat bizarre work, Wigglesworth wrote *God's Controversy with New-England* (1662), *Meat out of the Eater* (1669), *Riddles Unriddled* (1689) — but perhaps one is enough. They are preachy — but the Puritans liked it that way.

Edward Taylor (1642-1729), having lost his teaching position in England as a result of the Restoration, came to America in 1668, graduated from Harvard, and for some fifty years was pastor of the frontier town of Westfield. In addition to begetting fourteen children and delivering thousands of sermons, he wrote — on his own — a great deal of devotional poetry, and at his death gave directions that the manuscript be destroyed. But it was not — though it was only in 1939 that part of it was published, and in 1960 virtually all of the rest. Thus within the past quarter-century, Taylor has emerged as perhaps the best of the seventeenth-century Puritan poets in America, working in a tradition that sometimes has been called metaphysical, baroque, or pietistic.

His inward and ecstatically mystical poetry is highly

wrought and very intense. The greater part of the manuscript of some four hundred pages is taken up with two series of poems, 217 in all, written in six-line sonnet-like stanzas. Taylor headed them: *Preparatory Meditations before my Approach to the Lords Supper. Chiefly upon the Doctrine preached upon the Day of administration.* Apparently, after he had made up his Communion Sunday sermon (of which we today have a series of fourteen), he composed a "preparatory meditation" to formulate for himself the poetic aspects of what he would endeavor to convey from the pulpit — beginning, usually, with a question or ejaculation, developing it, and ending with petition or praise. Thus there was normally a genetic relationship between the Scriptural text, the written sermon, the preparatory meditation, the sermon as delivered, and the ensuing Communion. To take an example, the third meditation in the second series is inspired by Romans 5:14 (" . . . who is the figure of Him that is to come"). The opening suggests a dark night of the writer's soul:

> Like to the Marigold, I blushing close
>   My golden blossoms when the sun goes down:
> Moist'ning my leaves with Dewy Sighs, half frose
> By the nocturnall Cold, that hoares my Crown. . . .

but as a vision of his Saviour dawns:

> When, Lord, mine Eye doth spie thy Grace to beame
>   Thy Mediatoriall glory in the shine. . . .

he is aware of his own unworthiness, and concludes:

> Is't possible such glory, Lord, ere should
>   Center its Love on me Sins Dunghill else?
> My Case up take? make it its own? Who would
>   Wash with his blood my blots out? Crown his shelfe
>   Or Dress his golden Cupboard with such ware?
>   This makes my pale facde Hope almost despare.
>
> Yet let my Titimouses Quill suck in
>   Thy Graces milk Pails some shall drop: or Cart
> A Bit or Splinter of some Ray, the wing

> Of Grace's sun sprindgd out, into my heart:
> To build there Wonders Chappell where thy Praise
> Shall be the Psalms sung forth in gracious layes.

This last stanza is rather closely packed: Yet let my tiny pen, he says in effect, receive a drop from the overflowing bucket of Thy Grace, or let me take into my heart a splinter from the beams that radiate from Thy Grace's sun and let me build in my heart a chapel of wonder, where psalms shall be sung in Thy praise. The metaphors here come thick and fast, and mix and fuse; the difference between the original and any attempt to paraphrase it makes obvious its truly poetic quality.

In addition to the Meditations, there is also in the manuscript a long quasi-dramatic work, "Gods Determinations touching his Elect," which is obviously poetry of a high order. Also Taylor wrote some ingenious and impressive funeral elegies, notably one on the death of Samuel Hooker (1697). Taylor's work exhibits features that are to be found in some of the later American poets, such as Emily Dickinson's clear imagery, Emerson's and Thoreau's nature-symbolism, and Whitman's use of "I" to represent mankind. Other aspects of this frontier clergyman's life and works transcend narrow historical and geographical limitations. A saintly person, he went far along the contemplative path toward mystical union with God, and the verbal precipitate of his experience deserves a place along with the accounts left us by other great European, African, and Asiatic mystics — though Taylor's differs from some of theirs in its effective combination of the contemplative and the active life.

Early writings from the rest of the colonies are more scattered and individualistic than those from New England. George Sandys, who came to Virginia in the early 1620's, translated Ovid's *Metamorphoses* and later wrote a five-act tragedy *Christ's Passion* (1640). Andrew White, a Jesuit, wrote a *Relation* of Maryland; and John Hammond gave an account of Virginia and Maryland in *Leah and Rachel* (1656). A cavalier with a somewhat flamboyant style, George Alsop came to Maryland in 1658, but after the Restoration returned to London, where he brought out *A Character of the Province of Mary-land* (1666). Of documentary interest are Daniel Denton's *A Brief Description of New York* (1670), John Lederer's *Discoveries . . . from Virginia . . . to Carolina* (1672), and Thomas Ash's *Carolina* (1682).

A lively satirical poem based upon his unfortunate experiences in Maryland is *The Sot-Weed Factor* (1708) by Ebenezer Cook, who had tried to establish himself there as a tobacco merchant but had been cheated by the natives. ("Sotweed" is tobacco.) Subsequently, in 1730, the account was continued in *Sot-weed Redivivus, by E. C.*

Like the North, the South had a taste for sermons and historical records. One of the outstanding Episcopal ministers in Virginia was James Blair, who, after taking his degree at Cambridge and serving in Edinburgh, came to Richmond in 1685. He was largely responsible for the establishment of William and Mary College in 1693, and headed it for the remaining fifty years of his life. Some 117 of his sermons, focusing on the Sermon on the Mount, were printed in four volumes in 1722 and reissued in 1740. Robert Beverley wrote a *History . . . of Virginia* (1705, 2nd ed. 1722), as did William Stith later — in 1747. Blair's sermons were translated and published in Denmark and a French version of Stith's history went through four printings.

In the South, too, ecclesiastical and civil controversies got into print. Around the 1730's there occurred throughout the Protestant world a sudden revival of religious activity in terms of a rather personal and emotional emphasis — a movement originally opposed to ecclesiastical and theological subtlety. In Germany it had manifested itself as "Pietism," around the university and an orphanage at Halle; with the Moravians it reached North Carolina and Pennsylvania; and as "Methodism" it was fostered by John and Charles Wesley, who came to Georgia in 1737. In America it is often called "The Great Awakening." Though then new, it has since become "old-time religion." In New England it first spread up the Connecticut Valley from the Dutch Reformed church in New Jersey; and

for about a decade it swept through the country — early out-
breaks at various places merging as in a forest fire. At its height
it involved several evangelists who traveled and preached ex-
temporaneously, cutting across sectarian and theological boundaries — the idea being not that the members of the congregation take notes as if they were in a college classroom, as
was often the case during a seventeenth-century sermon, but
rather that they listen and *feel*, and if the Spirit should move
someone, that he come forward at the appropriate time. One
of the sensational British evangelists who at first attached himself to the Wesleys in Georgia and was bent on establishing an
Orphan House in Bethesda, Georgia, was George Whitefield.
Among those who objected to him was Alexander Garden,
rector of St. Philip's in Charleston, who in 1740 issued six letters against Methodism, writing in one of them:

> As to the State of Religion in this Province, it is bad
> enough, God knows. Rome and the Devil have contrived
> to crucify her 'twixt two Thieves, Infidelity and En-
> thusiasm. The former, alas! too much still prevails; but
> as to the latter, thanks to God, it is greatly subsided, &
> even on the Point of vanishing away. We had here
> Trances, Visions, & Revelations, both 'mong Blacks &
> Whites, in abundance.

Garden haled Whitefield before the ecclesiastical court in
Charleston and urged his suspension, thus helping send him
to the North to upset things there, too.

Among the civil disputes that occasioned some writing in
the South there was "Bacon's Rebellion" in Virginia during
the 1670's: manuscript accounts, letters, and pamphlets about it
are contained in what are known as the Burwell Papers. In the
late 1730's there was another conflict of authority in Georgia:
the leading spirit in it, Patrick Tailfer, sarcastically dedicated
A True and Historical Narrative of the Colony of Georgia
(1740) to the governor, General Oglethorpe, as having "afforded us the opportunity of arriving at the integrity of the
primitive times by entailing a more than primitive poverty on
us."

Just as the Mather family was very Bostonian, so also was the Byrd family very Virginian. Though the original settlers in Virginia had each owned only 50 acres, some of the estates soon began to swell. Starting in the late seventeenth century with an inheritance of 1,800 acres, William Byrd I brought his estate — by astute dealings with other colonists, the Indians, and the Council (of which he was auditor) — up to 26,231 acres. At Westover, Virginia, he established the solid appurtenances of a Colonial magnate, and at his death in 1704 transmitted his estate intact to his son.

William Byrd II had been sent at the age of seven to relatives in England to be educated, had attended grammar school in Essex, become a member of the Middle Temple, and studied business practices in Holland. In 1696 he returned to his native land, became a member of the Assembly, and was often in England as an agent of the Colony in many delicate matters. As a Fellow of the Royal Society, in 1697 he presented a paper on the pigmentation of the skin of a partially white Negro. From 1709 on he kept a diary in shorthand, portions of which have been deciphered and published — a rather Pepysian account of experiences in England and in Virginia. As his father had done, so he too sent his children to England to be educated, and in the course of a very active life increased his estate to 179,440 acres.

Byrd's writings date largely from the second quarter of the eighteenth century and relate to his landholdings. With some other men he undertook to survey the boundary line between Virginia and the Carolinas, and wrote up the expedition as *History of the Dividing Line* (1728). After looking into possible mineral resources and visiting some 20,000 acres he had bought from North Carolina, he wrote *A Progress to the Mines* (1732) and *A Journey to the Land of Eden* (1733). Also among what are known as the "Westover Manuscripts" are many letters. William Byrd II's writing is clear, concise, and often humorous in a restrained, Addisonian way. He was a witty and versatile man, little given to nonsense. Frequently in his diary he notes that he rose early and read a chapter or so in Greek or Hebrew.

His heir, William Byrd III, kept things going at Westover and fought in the French and Indian War alongside Braddock and Washington. But his son fought on the Tory side in the Revolution and, after the failure of the British cause, took his own life.

A rather special branch of Colonial writing came from the Quakers. The founder of Pennsylvania, William Penn, was a writer of considerable wit and self-composure. Quaker writing tended to be plain and often took the form of journals. Outstanding personal records are those of Thomas Chalkley (1749), Daniel Stanton (1772), John Churchman (1779), and John Woolman (1774). The last named was truly a saintly person, who traveled about in utmost simplicity among the oppressed — the Indians, the slaves, the poor — and quietly protested against the injustices they suffered. His descriptions reveal a sympathy for natural things and a sense of wonder that one usually associates with the Romantics. We know that Charles Lamb, for one, was especially fond of Woolman's journal.

Also a truly saintly figure in eighteenth-century American literature — though with a different background — is Jonathan Edwards (1703-1758), representative of Puritanism at its best. Firmly and deliberately he restated essential insights of Christianity, particularly as they had been formulated by Calvin. At the same time, he was aware that Newton and Locke had placed much in a new light — as revolutionary in its time as the implications of Freud and Einstein have been in ours. Edwards' longer writings, on which his lasting significance must ultimately rest, are fragments of a great reformulation of fundamental Puritanism — his "uncompleted Summa."

Scion of a line of ministers, Edwards was born and bred in the Connecticut Valley — a part of New England extending inland from Long Island Sound toward what was then the frontier. He attended Yale College, and the crucial events of his career took place at Northampton and Stockbridge. His grandfather, Solomon Stoddard, had been a powerful figure in the churches of western Massachusetts, opening communion to all and thus virtually dispensing with public profession as a necessary prerequisite for church membership.

When Edwards succeeded to the Northampton pulpit in 1726, he was obviously expected to carry on what his grandfather had begun. Actually, what had occurred under Stoddard was a beginning of the Great Awakening, and what Edwards was to do in this movement was to give it a more theologically responsible formulation than it was to receive from the others whom it affected. One of his sermons preached at Enfield in 1741, "Sinners in the Hands of an Angry God," has often been reprinted — a most forceful sermon, particularly for a congregation living under constant threat of Indian attack:

> The bow of God's wrath is bent, and the arrow made ready on the string, and justice bends the arrow at your heart, and strains the bow, and it is nothing but the mere pleasure of God, and that of an angry God, without any promise or obligation at all, that keeps the arrow one moment from being made drunk with your blood.

The Revival, however, soon got out of hand. Spellbinders like Whitefield soon crowded in. For a certain kind of Puritanism, this proved to be not the Second Coming but the Day of Doom.

Edwards insisted that although religion was more than a purely intellectual matter, it was not to be confused with *mere* feeling run wild. Ultimately he came into conflict with his Northampton congregation, and had to reinstitute a public profession for membership in the church. After long and bitter controversy, he was in 1750 dismissed by his congregation. Stunned, he served for a while in an Indian mission in Stockbridge.

By a turn of events that might be considered a justification of his firmness at Northampton, he was asked to be president of an institution that had grown out of the Great Awakening and that is now Princeton. As he was beginning his duties there in 1758, an epidemic of smallpox broke out. In the mid-eighteenth century, inoculation (introduced into Boston by Cotton Mather) was neither so reliable nor so widely accepted as it is today. To show his belief in science and willingness to undergo himself what he recommended to others, Edwards had himself inoculated, and as a result of ensuing complications died.

His longer and late works include *Religious Affections* (1746), *Freedom of Will* (1754), *Original Sin* (1758), and *Two Dissertations* (1765): "The Nature of True Virtue" and "The End for which God Created the World." The first of these four books is in defense and criticism of the Great Awakening; the second — contrary to what its title might suggest — presents a closely reasoned deterministic view of man; and the rest deal with ethics and metaphysics. Throughout his mature work he places himself on common ground with present-day "realists" in philosophy, insisting that things really are for us as we perceive them. He takes, for example, the Biblical text, "One generation passeth away and another cometh, but the earth abideth forever" and remarks that there may seem to be nothing startling about this sentiment:

> But yet when, upon an occasion, I was more than ordinarily affected with the passing of one generation after another; how all those, who made such a noise and bluster now, and were so much concerned about their life, would be clean gone off from the face of the earth in sixty or seventy years time, and that the world would be left desolate with respect to them, and that another generation would come on, that would be very little concerned about them, and so one after another: it was particularly affecting to me to think that the earth still remained the same through all these changes upon the surface: the same spots of ground, the same mountains and valleys where those things were done, remaining just as they were, though the actors ceased, and the actors just gone. And then this text came into my mind.

To a thought resembling that of Famishing Coyote's and deepened by Scripture, the "plain style" in utmost purity has here been applied by Man Thinking.

Although Edwards was recognized abroad as a figure of more than American importance, his contemporary Benjamin Franklin (1706-1790) came to enjoy truly international fame. Both were born in the first years of the eighteenth century in New England, Edwards in Connecticut and Franklin in Massachusetts. Their paths, however, never crossed. One faced the frontier and became a more and more enlightened conservative; the other faced the homeland and became — first in terms of Philadelphia, then in terms of the Colonies as a whole, and finally in terms of that center of Enlightenment, France itself — a liberal.

Not the scion of a line of ministers, Franklin was the youngest son among the seventeen children of a candlemaker who had come to Boston from England. When twelve, Benjamin was apprenticed to his brother James, a printer, and developed his literary skill under actual conditions of typesetting and publishing — much as, in the next century and beyond the Mississippi, Samuel Clemens was to do. Before completing his apprenticeship, however, Franklin ran away to Philadelphia. Thus, in his *Autobiography*, he describes his arrival, weaving into his particularized and chatty account three of the themes that run through the whole narrative: his taking things as they come, his rise in social station, and his philanthropic impulses:

> Then I walked up the street, gazing about, till near the market-house I met a boy with bread. I had made many a meal on bread, and, inquiring where he got it, I went immediately to the baker's he directed me to, in Second Street. . . . He gave me, accordingly, three great puffy rolls. I was surprised at the quantity, but took it, and having no room in my pockets, walked off with a roll under each arm, and eating the other. Thus I went up Market Street as far as Fourth Street, passing by the door of Mr. Read, my future wife's father; when

she, standing at the door, saw me, and thought I made,
as I certainly did, a most awkward, ridiculous appearance. Then I turned and went down Chestnut Street and
part of Walnut Street, eating my roll all the way, and,
coming round, found myself again at Market Street
wharf, near the boat I came in, to which I went for a
draught of the river water; and, being filled with one of
my rolls, gave the other to a woman and her child that
came down the river in the boat with us, and were waiting to go farther.

In Philadelphia he continued to work as a printer. Then
for two years he was in London as a journeyman. While there
he wrote and published a "little metaphysical piece," *A Dis-
sertation on Liberty and Necessity, Pleasure and Pain,* in which
he maintained that there is no difference between vice and
virtue. The printing of this essay he later acknowledged as
among his *errata.* For, after further experience, he "began to
suspect that this doctrine, though it might be true, was not
very useful." To Franklin evil actions now appeared not "bad
because forbidden" but "forbidden because they are bad for
us." In other words, the whole "revealed" aspect of religion —
so important to the Puritans — had no particular meaning for
him. From a Protestant family background, he had moved in
his spiritual pilgrimage through a position technically known
as deism, to a basically theistic and humanitarian point of view
which he shared with other leading eighteenth-century figures
— with, for example, Voltaire, who had moved to this position from a Roman Catholic family background.

After returning to Philadelphia, Franklin published, among
other things, a newspaper, the *Pennsylvania Gazette;* a magazine, *General Magazine, and Historical Chronicle, for All the
British Plantations*; and an almanac, *Poor Richard.* The last,
which began in 1733 and ran till 1758, contains all sorts
of pithy sayings (many of them adapted from literary sources)
attributed to a fictitious character, Richard Saunders. One of
the best known of Franklin's writings of this period appeared
originally as a preface to the 1758 edition of the almanac and

is often called "The Way to Wealth": in a quasi-letter, Richard explains that he happened to stop at an auction where he heard a white-haired old man, Father Abraham, advising his fellows not to spend their money foolishly and constantly quoting to them *Poor Richard's Almanack*. "The old people heard it," the letter concludes, "approved the doctrine, and immediately practiced the contrary just as if it had been a common sermon." In a most engaging way this public letter brings together some of the best of the proverbs that had appeared in the almanac over a period of twenty-five years. From it many readers have jumped to the conclusion that Franklin was mainly concerned with advising people to save their money. This is, however, just a special aspect of his humor-character — called, ironically enough, *Poor* Richard — and here reflected through the imagined Father Abraham.

Rather early in his career, Franklin drew up for himself a program of self-improvement consisting of twelve virtues (to which he added a thirteenth, Humility, at the advice of a Quaker friend — though, Franklin later wrote, "I cannot boast of much success in acquiring the *reality* of this virtue, but I had a great deal with regard to the *appearance* of it"). Lightly disguised here under a veil of irony are the outlines of something well understood by the medieval schematizers of the virtues and vices; for, as he later concluded one section of the *Autobiography*:

> In reality, there is, perhaps, no one of our natural passions so hard to subdue as *pride*. Disguise it, struggle with it, beat it down, stifle it, mortify it as much as one pleases, it is still alive, and will every now and then peep out and show itself; you will see it, perhaps, often in this history; for, even if I could conceive that I had completely overcome it, I should probably be proud of my humility.

This also Edwards — and later Hawthorne — well understood.

Franklin had meanwhile organized a dozen fellow tradesmen into a sort of club, the Junto, through which he initiated

in Philadelphia various civic improvements, such as a sub-
scription library, a fire department, an academy, a hospital —
all of which are still active institutions today. So multifarious
were his public-service activities that by mid-century he had
retired from private business and devoted his full time to them.
He had become joint deputy postmaster for North America
and was actively working for a plan of union among the English colonies in defense against the French in Canada. He was
very much involved in experiments with electricity. In 1752
he flew his kite; and — fortunately having escaped electrocu-
tion, as some previous experimenters in Europe had not — he
not only established the relationship between static electricity
and the more dynamic sort that appears in the sky but also applied this knowledge in the lightning rod. His electrical experiments, published between 1750 and 1775, brought him international recognition; and when he was sent to London in
1757 to present the petition of Pennsylvania to the king that
their status be changed from that of a proprietary to a crown
colony, he went not just as an insignificant commoner but as
an internationally respected scientist — as well as sage and man
of letters.

The scope of his concern, having widened from Philadelphia to the North American colonies as a whole, now proceeded to embrace the British Empire itself; and he pleaded
earnestly that it be more broadly and liberally conceived.
While thus engaged in England, he happened to find a brief
period of leisure as house guest at the country home of the
Bishop of St. Asaph's, near Twyford. There he began writing
the document now known as his *Autobiography*. The form of
the first part is that of a letter addressed to his son, then governor of New Jersey. In a simple and informal manner, he related
his recollections of his family background and early experiences up to about 1730, when — working through the Junto —
he had embarked upon the program of civic improvement in
Philadelphia.

The date at which this first and most charming part of the
Autobiography was written, however, was 1771. Tension

between the American colonies and England was increasing. The beginning was, of course, laid aside under pressure of immediate events. Franklin returned to America in 1775 to serve in the Second Continental Congress. He helped draft the Declaration of Independence. The new Federacy promptly sent him to France, first as commissioner and then as minister, to arrange the delicate matter of aid from monarchical France to the struggling republic — a France which only a few decades before he had been trying to unite the English colonies against, and a highly sophisticated France which was on the verge of its own revolution. The truly difficult role which he was called upon to play was accomplished only by his remarkable tact and personal charm, and by the high international regard in which he was held.

During the 1780's some of his friends who had seen the first part of the *Autobiography* in manuscript wrote him asking that he continue it. One said the document was entertaining and useful (in the sense of giving young readers a model for emulation); another, that if he did not write the further account someone else would, that it would help attract good settlers to America, and that it would provide instruction in virtue itself. Apparently this last point proved the most persuasive to Franklin; for when (in 1784 at Passy) he did undertake a brief continuation, it was more in terms of the moral implications of his life. Then, back in America in 1788, he wrote a third section; and in 1789, almost on his deathbed, he wrote a fourth. These later portions were written without his having at hand copies of the earlier manuscripts; the formal idea of the letter to his son had been abandoned for a more impersonal type of writing; and considerable portions of the last two parts were quite obviously mere factual records. The work is, of course, a torso, and does not bring the account much past mid-century. The first two installments of it, however, constitute one of the earliest contributions of America to that body of writings which readers the world over would not willingly let die. The first part appeared in print the year after Franklin died — oddly enough, in a French translation brought out in

France on the eve of the French Revolution. This French version was promptly translated into English and printed in England. It was only during the next century that Franklin's complete and original text was published.

During the last decade of his life while he was envoy to the Court of France, Franklin wrote and published some charming essays. Many of them he referred to as "bagatelles" and printed on his private press at Passy. *The Whistle*, for example, is a sophisticated version of the same idea he had used in Father Abraham's advice at the auction — only here handled with the delicacy and economy of French eighteenth-century art, and addressed in a tone of gallantry to Madame Brillon. To her also — still in the same tone — he addressed a fantasy, *The Ephemera*, purporting to give the overheard conversation of two short-lived insects, concluding: "And what will become of all history in the eighteenth hour, when the world itself, even the whole Moulin Joly, shall come to its end and be buried in universal ruin?" The theme of the opening *Allegro* is still there in the *Scherzo*.

Not only were men in Europe aware of Franklin's work with electricity, they were also aware of his life as a whole. In the succeeding century, included in a series issued by the French Academy there is a volume on him in which he is characterized as "a good man, a master of wisdom adapted to every age, every condition, every society, and one of the founders of that American liberty which is not the privilege of a race, or of a given form of government, but pure and simple liberty." Sarmiento, who rose from poverty to leadership in South America, acknowledged but two books as "his own"; the Bible and Franklin's *Autobiography*. Obviously, Franklin's writings are of more than just local or documentary interest.

Thus the present chapter has brought us over halfway from the fifteenth to the twentieth century. The lightning of Christian Europe had flashed over the American earth and been conducted to the ground along the string of a kite. Religion — in its ecclesiastical and theological aspects — was henceforth to assume a comparatively limited role, crowded out by political, economic, scientific, technological, and aesthetic considerations. This is true not merely in America but in other parts of the world as well — East and West. Perhaps the phenomenon is a little more distinct in America because it was here that an acute confrontation of East and West took place — with results that were different from what either had been before. The figure who effects a liaison between the world of the pilgrims (that is, not solely Bradford's but also those that "toward Canterbury wolden ryde") and of the revolutionists (American and French) has just been considered, and has left us an incomparably frank and readable account of his early life.

From Pamphlets
2. to Fiction
Paine to Cooper

In ensuing decades the focus shifted from religious first to political and then to aesthetic and other concerns. As a result of the great fusion of Occident and Orient, American literature maintained a wide human relevance, the specific preoccupations of early writers being carried on into a more imaginative realm by Brown, Irving, and Cooper. The alignments continued, the Puritans tending to become Whigs and the Anglicans Tories — with monarchy, according to Paine, "the popery of government." From the pilgrims, in the larger sense, came the Founding Fathers. They favored the pamphlet, the state paper, the speech. Novels and plays they had little use for: Jefferson thought the novel a "great obstacle" to education, and Madison felt that "poetry, wit, and criticism, romances, plays, etc., deserve but a small portion of a man's time." Excellence in the political essay, however, was widely appreciated: shortly after the meeting of the First Continental Congress, William Pitt the elder told the House of Lords:

> For myself, I must declare and avow that in all my reading of history and observation — and it has been my favorite study — I have read Thucydides, and have studied and admired the master-states of the world — that for solidity of reasoning, force of sagacity, and wisdom of conclusion under such a complication of difficult circumstances, no nation or body of men can stand in preference to the General Congress at Philadelphia.

The political essay came to the fore after mid-century. James Otis, for example, insisted on representative taxation in 1762, and three years later was hinting that "Revolutions have been. They may be again." The Stamp Act of 1765 called forth four essays by John Adams and a series by John Dickinson, *Letters from a Farmer in Pennsylvania* (1767-1768), which appeared in some twenty newspaper, and several book, editions, including two in England and two in translation in France. "Who are free people?" he asked, and answered: "Not *those*, over whom government is reasonably and equitably exercised, but *those* who live under a government so *constitutionally checked* and *controuled*, that proper provision is made against its being otherwise exercised."

The mid-seventies elicited pamphlets on all sides. The pioneer out-and-out revolutionary pamphlet was Thomas Paine's *Common Sense* (1776). Born in England of Quaker ancestry, Paine spent his first thirty-seven years there, under not too happy circumstances. With a letter of recommendation from Franklin, he had come to Philadelphia in 1774 and obtained an editorial position. After attacking Negro slavery and other abuses, he came out carefully, deliberately, and objectively in 1776 for the political independence of the country, in a tract indicated as having been "written by an Englishman" whose identity was "wholly unnecessary to the public, as the object of attention is the *doctrine itself*, not the *man*." Though this pamphlet proceeds from the general to the specific, it closes with a plea for "*the rights of mankind and of the free and independent states of America*" — apparently not just the thirteen colonies.

While serving as aide-de-camp to General Greene in the ensuing conflict, Paine wrote a series of pamphlets known collectively as *The American Crisis*, beginning: "These are the times that try men's souls. The summer soldier and the sunshine patriot will, in this crisis, shrink from the service of their country, but he that stands it *now*, deserves the love and thanks of man and woman."

Paine figured in the devious matter of getting aid from

France as Secretary on Foreign Affairs in Congress, but he did not have quite the tact and discretion of Franklin. In the late 1780's he again went abroad, hoping to do for the French Revolution what he had done for the American; but his objections to the guillotining of Louis XVI landed him in jail, from which he was released as an American citizen through the intervention of the United States ambassador. The broadly human orientation of Paine's thought is suggested by the title of one of his works, the *Rights of Man*. "America," he wrote in another, *The Age of Reason*, "made a stand, not for herself only, but for the world, and looked beyond the advantages herself could receive."

Returning to the United States, he died in New York City in 1809, and was buried in New Rochelle. As in the case of Voltaire, there is some uncertainty as to just where his mortal remains now are: William Cobbett had them dug up to establish a shrine to his memory in England, but the shrine did not get built. As writer, Paine was to Franklin much as, in the next generation, Thoreau was to Emerson — more brilliant, more uncompromising, but not quite so richly endowed with common sense.

Among others, two Anglican clergymen espoused the Tory cause. Jonathan Boucher in Maryland preached *On Civil Liberty* in 1775 with a pair of loaded pistols lying on a cushion beside him (printed, after he later fled to England, in *A View of the Causes and Consequences of the American Revolution*, 1797): "It was the purpose of the Creator, that man should be social: but, without government, there can be no society; nor, without some relative inferiority and superiority, can there be any government. . . ." Samuel Seabury in New York issued the first of his pamphlets by a "Westchester farmer" in 1774, criticizing the embargo that had been voted by the First Continental Congress:

> . . . I am most nearly connected with you, being one of your number, and having no interest in the country but in common with you; and also because the interest of the farmers in general will be more sensibly affected

and more deeply injured by these agreements, than the interest of any other body of people on the continent. . . .

Alexander Hamilton, then only seventeen and an undergraduate at Columbia, answered Seabury — who before the end of 1775 was mobbed, imprisoned, and released, and after fleeing to the British lines, served as bishop of the American Episcopal church.

In connection with the ratification of the Constitution during the 1780's, there was a notable series of essays, *The Federalist,* by Hamilton, Madison, and Jay. Madison's fourteenth number, for example, closes thus:

> Hearken not to the unnatural voice which tells you that the people of America, knit together as they are by so many cords of affection, can no longer live together as members of the same family; can no longer be fellow-citizens of one great, respectable, and flourishing empire. Hearken not to the voice which petulantly tells you that the form of government recommended for your adoption is a novelty in the political world; that it has never yet had a place in the theories of the wildest projectors; that it rashly attempts what it is impossible to accomplish. No, my countrymen, shut your ears against this unhallowed language. Shut your ears against the poison which it conveys; the kindred blood which flows in the veins of American citizens, the mingled blood which they shed in defence of their sacred rights, consecrate their Union, and excite horror at the idea of their becoming aliens, rivals, enemies.

His rhetoric is more obvious than Paine's or Seabury's — is, as Jefferson characterized it, "pure, classical, and copious."

During the ensuing century the political tract declined in favor either of more sustained book-length publications or of periodical articles. Chronicles and memorials continued to be written: for example, David Ramsy — born in Pennsylvania, educated at Princeton, active as physician and congressman in South Carolina — wrote a *Life of Washington* in 1801.

As with every war, there were narratives of personal experience by participants in the conflict — particularly by those who had harrowing experiences of captivity and escape. The revolutionist Ethan Allen's war experiences were published in Philadelphia in 1779; the Tory James Moody's in London in 1782; the first-person narrative of John Slover, of Virginia, who had been kidnapped by the Indians when he was eight, had grown up among them, and had served in the Continental Army, saw print in 1783 through the efforts of Philip Freneau and H. H. Brackenridge. Some of these accounts were formulated in the tradition of the Puritan Indian-captivity narratives, the devilish Indians just being replaced by the devilish enemy, with stress on the role of Providence. Particularly from about 1820 to 1840, as the hardy veterans reached old age and as a wave of nationalism swept the country after the War of 1812, these Revolutionary War accounts became quite popular. One of the most interesting of them is the *Life and Remarkable Adventures of Israel R. Potter* (Providence, 1824), which Melville was to rework as a novel in 1855. These accounts of the impact of war on not specifically professional soldiers apparently served purposes of record, of morale building, and of urging veterans' claims.

Taken as a whole, the revolutionary generation — like the Puritans before them — were remarkably apt at versification. In 1765 an American in England had published anonymously a long poem *Opposition*, in the course of which — along with some personal abuse — he asked:

> Should not then Satire bite with all its rage,
> And just resentment glow through every page?

and prophesied that if oppression continued Americans might revolt within "five score years," but would not if accorded "the rights of subjects." Before, during, and after the Revolution there was much verse — topical words to be sung to familiar tunes, party songs, Army songs, ballads, hymns, even *vers de société*. One is struck by the gregariousness of these writers, who often worked together in literary clubs.

The colleges — particularly those in the middle colonies — fostered original work. At what is now the University of Pennsylvania, the provost, William Smith, edited during 1757-1758 *The American Magazine and Monthly Chronicle*, to which he contributed essays signed "The Hermit." One of his protégés, Thomas Godfrey (to whom he attributed "elevated and daring genius"), wrote the first full-length play in English by an American to be given a regular, known, professional stage performance, *The Prince of Parthia* (written in 1759, published posthumously in 1765, and performed in Philadelphia in 1767). Another of Smith's protégés, Francis Hopkinson, became a delegate to the Continental Congress and signer of the Declaration of Independence; later he wrote both words and music for a volume of songs published in 1788 and dedicated to Washington.

At what is now Princeton, the Tory-Whig dichotomy had given rise to two undergraduate literary societies, the Cliosophic and the American Whig. Leaders in the latter were James Madison, Philip Freneau, and Hugh Henry Brackenridge. The last two collaborated on a long blank-verse poem, *The Rising Glory of America*, for the Commencement exercises of 1771:

> 'Tis but the morning of the world with us
> And Science yet but sheds her orient rays.
> I see the age, the happy age roll on
> Bright with the splendours of her mid-day beams,
> I see a Homer and a Milton rise
> In all the pomp and majesty of song. . . .

In a way, Freneau can be credited with a "first" too — as the writer of a substantial body of distinctly American verse. Born in New York City in 1752 and developing sentiments not unlike Paine's, he wrote some anti-British verse a little before *Common Sense* appeared. Having served at sea during the ensuing war, he wrote a bitter poem *The British Prison-Ship*, presumably based on personal experience; and, for a while after the Revolution, he was commander of a ship to the West Indies. Three of his longer works in verse have particular interest: *Pictures of Columbus, The House of Night,* and *The Beauties of Santa Cruz.* At the urging of Jefferson and Madison, he served from 1791-1793 as editor of the *National Gazette* in Philadelphia and — according to Jefferson — "saved our Constitution." From 1797-1798 he edited a literary magazine, the *Time-Piece.* Though much of his writing is uneven and dated, at its best it is genuine poetry — such as this apostrophe to a distinctly American flower, *The Wild Honeysuckle* (1786), beginning

> Fair Flower, that dost so comely grow,
> Hid in this silent, dull retreat,
> Untouched thy honied blossoms blow,
> Unseen thy little branches greet:
> No roving foot shall crush thee here,
> No busy hand provoke a tear.
>
> By Nature's self in white arrayed,
> She bade thee shun the vulgar eye,
> And planted here the guardian shade,
> And sent soft waters murmuring by;
> Thus quietly thy summer goes,
> Thy days declining to repose.

Two British poets — Scott and Campbell — appropriated the highly characteristic last lines of two fine stanzas of Freneau's: one from his *To the Memory of the Brave Americans* (in honor of those who died at Eutaw Springs, South Carolina, in 1781):

> They saw their injured country's woe;
> The flaming town, the wasted field;
> They rushed to meet the insulting foe;
> They took the spear — but left the shield.

and the other from *The Indian Burying-Ground:*

> By midnight moons, o'er moistening dews,
> In habit for the chase arrayed,
> The hunter still the deer pursues,
> The hunter and the deer, a shade.

In a sense, Freneau might be considered really the first poet of the new country.

Brackenridge also did some pioneer work, but in prose. His *Modern Chivalry* was the first substantial fictional work published west of the Alleghenies, and one of the first American novels one can still read with much spontaneous enjoyment. There are, of course, some earlier ones: William Hill Brown's *The Power of Sympathy* (1789), about a young man who discovers that his sweetheart is his half-sister and, with a copy of *Werther* beside him, shoots himself; and Susanna Rowson's *Charlotte Temple* (1791), about an English girl who runs away to New York and is abandoned there to die in childbirth (the latter, reprinted over a hundred times, being the *Ur*-grandmother of some later naturalism and its vulgarization, the "true" story). But as one might attribute some primacy to Freneau as poet, so might one also to Brackenridge as novelist.

Born in Scotland of poor farm parents, Brackenridge was brought to America at the age of five. Having completed his education at Princeton, he and Freneau taught school in Maryland, where he wrote some blank-verse plays on recent events for the pupils to act, *The Battle of Bunkers Hill* and *The Death of General Montgomery*. In 1778 as a chaplain in Washington's Army he delivered *Six Political Discourses Founded on the Scriptures*. During 1779 in Philadelphia he edited the *United States Magazine*, in which some of Freneau's poems and some of his own prose appeared:

> The honest husbandman who reads this publication will rapidly improve in every kind of knowledge. He will be shortly capable to arbitrate the differences that may arise among his neighbours. He will be qualified to be a Magistrate. He will appear a proper person to be appointed Sheriff in his county. He will be equal to the task of legislation. He will be capable of any office to which the gale of popularity amongst his countrymen may raise him.

Settled in western Pennsylvania as a lawyer by 1786, he established the *Pittsburgh Gazette* there and became a justice of the state supreme court.

Modern Chivalry was intended, Brackenridge wryly states, to "fix the English language" and give a model of style, leaving out of consideration entirely the matter of sense, as it is absurd "to expect good language, and good sense at the same time." The leading characters — deriving apparently from Don Quixote and Sancho Panza — are a man of goodwill, Captain Farrago, and his ignorant Irish servant, Teague O'Regan. As the pair travel around frontier Pennsylvania, Teague is always trying to do something he does not know how to do — run for office, join the American Philosophical Society, help in drawing up Indian treaties, be an actor, teach Greek, and so on — and the Captain has to get him out of the resulting difficulties. At one point Teague ("as they would neither let him go to Congress, nor be a philosopher, he must do something"), slips into the bedroom of a chambermaid at an inn; and she — in the dark — cries out in fright. All the guests come running, and in the resulting confusion Teague accuses a clergyman of being the one who has misbehaved. The Captain points out that no harm has been done, and they all go back to their rooms. But some time later, gossip about the incident makes trouble for the clergyman with his consistory, and he appeals to the Captain for help. The Captain, accordingly, persuades Teague to acknowledge his part in the affair: "these people, you may be assured, have a considerable influence in the other world. This clergyman can speak a good word for you when you come there, and let you into half the benefit of all the prayers he has said on earth." Teague agrees but thinks the priest ought to pay a little "smart money," for it is "a thankless matter to do these things for nothing." Of course, it is possible to read *Modern Chivalry* — which, like Freneau's poetry, is uneven — as a series of tracts. But at times it has an additional dimension of imaginatively created experience that merits its being considered literature.

As at Philadelphia and Princeton, seeds were sown at New Haven that were to blossom in the activities of a group of Yale graduates known as the Hartford or Connecticut Wits. In a sense they may be called the first American school of poetry.

A clever member of this group was John Trumbull, who for the Yale Commencement of 1770 — at which he received his M.A. — published his vision of a day when American poets would

> with lofty Milton vie,
> Or wake from nature's themes the moral song,
> And shine with Pope, with Thomson, and with Young.
> This land her Steele and Addison shall view,
> The former glories equal'd by the new;
> Some future Shakespeare charm the rising age,
> And hold in magic chains the list'ning stage;
> Another Watts shall string the heav'nly lyre,
> And other muses other bards inspire.

Just before the Revolution broke out, he began his professional legal training by serving in the office of John Adams in Boston. One of Trumbull's poems, *The Progress of Dulness*, satirizes three types of respectable mediocrity: the yokel sent to college (presumably Yale), Tom Brainless; the would-be man-of-the-world, Dick Harebrain; and the empty-headed Harriet Simper. After having chased Dick, Harriet in desperation marries Tom, who has now become a well-settled parson; and she is heartily received by the "tag-rag gentry," who

> Greet her at church with rev'rence due,
> And next the pulpit fix her pew.

Another of Trumbull's poems, *M'Fingal* (begun in 1775 and destined to be reprinted scores of times on both sides of the Atlantic) burlesques General Gage's proclamation of martial law in Boston: the Tory blusterer M'Fingal tells the town meeting that

> The power, display'd in Gage's banners,
> Shall cut their fertile lands to manors;
> And o'er our happy conquer'd ground,
> Dispense estates and titles round.
> Behold! the world shall stare at new setts
> Of home-made Earls in Massachusetts. . . .

but the Whig champion, Honorius, answers him and the meeting breaks up in disorder. Later, in 1782, Trumbull issued a continuation of the poem, in which M'Fingal is tarred and feathered and hoisted up on the Liberty Pole. Still later, Trumbull became a judge in the higher courts, and spent the last six years of his life in the frontier town of Detroit.

A somewhat more sober member of the Connecticut Wits was Timothy Dwight, grandson of Jonathan Edwards, who later became president of Yale College. His *The Conquest of Canaan* (1785), based on the Book of Joshua but also related to the settlement of America and the Revolution, is an eleven-book epic in heroic couplets. Like much of the furniture, portraiture, and architecture of the early federal period, it has qualities of solid craftsmanship — as in the rising visual images (ground, sheep, trees, cliffs, peak, sun, heaven) and then the suddenly encompassing olfactory image:

> In living green, the lawns at distance lay,
> Where snowy flocks mov'd round in vernal play;
> High tower'd the nodding groves; the cliffs sublime
> Left the low world, and dar'd th' assaults of time;
> And the sun trembled round a thousand spires;
> All heaven was mild; and borne from subject vales,
> A cloud of fragrance cheer'd th' inchanting gales.

Dwight also wrote a verse satire *The Triumph of Infidelity* (1788), ironically dedicated to Voltaire, and a long quiet narrative poem *Greenfield Hill* (1794) on the section of Connecticut where he spent several years as minister. As president of Yale from 1795 on, he strengthened the faculty, started a medical school, and lectured the seniors on rhetoric, philosophy, and religion. Among his posthumous publications were *Theol-*

ogy (five volumes, 1818-1819) and *Travels* (four volumes, 1821-1822).

The most visionary of the Connecticut Wits was Joel Barlow, who came from a less educated background than Trumbull and Dwight and whose undergraduate career at Yale was interrupted by the war. After serving as an Army chaplain, he became an editor, lawyer, and land speculator in Hartford. His prophecies of the future glory of America appeared in *The Prospect of Peace* (1778) and *A Poem* (1781). About this time he began an American epic with Columbus as hero, and in 1787 issued *The Vision of Columbus*, in nine books, dedicated to Louis XVI (who subscribed for twenty-five copies). Barlow went to France in 1788 as a real-estate agent and later plunged into the French Revolution, writing in its defense and in 1792, as an honorary citizen of France, undertaking to organize Savoy and spread pro-French influence in the Piedmont. In a French inn, coming across something he had often eaten as a farm boy in America, he wrote one of his most often reprinted poems *The Hasty Pudding* (1796), about how Connecticut people prepare and eat cornmeal mush. In Paris in 1797 he further developed and revised his Columbus poem as the *Columbiad*, published in an edition of 1807 with illustrations by the American artist and engineer Robert Fulton, who was also with Barlow in France during and after the Revolution there. Whereas *The Vision of Columbus* as revised and reprinted in Paris in 1793 had concluded with a "View of a general council of all nations assembled to establish the political harmony of mankind," the *Columbiad* goes on to describe this United Nations type of assembly in action, legislating and discarding symbols of oppression:

> Each envoy unloads his wearied hand
> Of some old idol from his native land;
> One flings a pagod on the mingled heap,
> One lays a crescent, one a cross to sleep;
> Swords, sceptres, mitres, crowns and globes and stars,
> Codes of false fame and stimulants to wars
> Sink in the settling mass. . . .

This vision inspired Constantin Volney's antimonarchical work which Jefferson and Barlow translated as *The Ruins* and which influenced Shelley's *Queen Mab*. As the French Revolution passed into its imperialistic phase, Barlow returned to Washington, whence he undertook a mission for the State Department to make contact with Napoleon on his retreat from Moscow. Near Vilna, in subzero weather, Barlow contracted pneumonia and died in the Polish village where he lies buried. *Advice to a Raven in Russia* was one of his last poems: "Black fool, why winter here?" he asks the bird that would feed on the frozen remnants of Napoleon's work:

> . . . from their visual sockets as they lie,
> With beak and claws you cannot pluck an eye.
> The frozen orb, preserving still its form,
> Defies your talons as it braves the storm,
> But stands and stares to God, as if to know
> In what curst hands he leaves his world below.

Associated with Barlow abroad was David Humphreys, one of General Washington's colonels, who wrote sonnets, elegies on notable men and events in the war, and propaganda verse, including *An Address to the Armies* (1780), which was also published and read publicly in London and was brought out in Paris with parallel French text. After diplomatic service abroad, he returned to Connecticut and set up a woolen mill in Humphreysville. His belief in the moral value of industry is evidenced by *A Poem on Industry*, first published in 1792 and revised in 1802. He translated a play from the French under the title *The Widow of Malabar*, produced in Philadelphia in 1790, and wrote an original play about an admirable American named Newman, *The Yankey in England*, presented by a group of his factory hands.

These Connecticut Wits attracted other members to their group. Lemuel Hopkins, a physician in Hartford with an honorary Master's degree from Yale, collaborated with Barlow, Trumbull, and Humphreys in a long burlesque epic that appeared in installments, *The Anarchiad* (1786-1787). Others joined the group: Dwight's younger brothers Theodore and

Nathaniel; two other physicians, Elihu H. Smith and Mason F. Cogswell; and Richard Alsop, who with Theodore Dwight started a series in prose and verse, *The Echo* (1791-1805). Verse from their pens ranges from attacks on medical quackery to political abuse. Occasionally it evinces homely touches, as in some lines supposedly written by the newsboy of the *Connecticut Courant* to his customers but actually written by one of the *Anarchiad* group in ironical disparagement of what they themselves had been writing:

> . . . for all these Jokes so tickle us,
> It made them Folks important instead of being ridiculous,
> And when you keep pelting at 'em, and trying to be so witty,
> Their Friends will stick to 'em like sheep-ticks and vote for
>   'em out of pity.

Not of the Connecticut group but originally from Boston and Harvard was an incisive critic of current American literature, Joseph Dennie, lawyer and editor of a paper, *The Farmer's Museum*, in Walpole, New Hampshire. Associated with him was another young lawyer, Royall Tyler, later chief justice of Vermont, who wrote *The Contrast*, a lively comedy introducing some consciously American characters, and a novel *The Algerine Captive*, published at Walpole. Another contributor to *The Farmer's Museum* was Thomas Greene Fessenden of Dartmouth, who wrote some Yankee local-color poems *The Country Lovers* and *The Rustick Revel*. A little later, in 1801, Dennie edited a Philadelphia magazine *The Port Folio*, writing over the signature "Oliver Oldschool" and bringing out new work by American and British writers.

During this early national period, descriptive and factual material about the Middle and Far West was published: Lewis and Clark's journals, for example, in 1814, somewhat as accounts of explorations had figured in the publications of earlier centuries. Some of these accounts had literary influence: the Philadelphia Quaker botanist William Bartram's *Travels* (1791) — embodying observations made as far afield as Florida and the Mississippi — furnished images to the British and French

Romantics. Over seventy books by French travelers to America — notably Crèvecoeur, St. Mèry, and Volney — appeared
during this time; and soon there were even more by Englishmen. Also, as in earlier periods, there were accounts of religious
activities in the new region — the journals, for instance, of
Cartwright, Dow, and Asbury.

Three writers, however, stand out as authors of prose
works of genuine literary significance — Charles Brockden
Brown, Washington Irving, and James Fenimore Cooper.
Charles Brockden Brown (1771-1810), a precocious child of
Quaker parents in Philadelphia, attended the Friends' Latin
School and studied law, but instead of practicing undertook as
soon as he had come of age to live by his pen — thus taking his
place as the first important American author to approach writing as a serious, professional, full-time activity. Early he projected epics about Columbus, Pizarro, and Cortez. Active in the
Belles Lettres Club, he contributed essays and poems to magazines and, under the influence of Godwin's *Caleb Williams*,
began in 1795 "a Philadelphia novel." His first work to be sepa-
rately published was a dialogue *Alcuin* (1798), in which an intellectual widow Mrs. Carter urges educational and political
equality for women and a young teacher Alcuin outlines a
utopian state of society in which this would be possible.

The first and most successful of Brown's novels is *Wieland*
(1798), about a studious young man, with a wife and four
children, living on the banks of the Schuylkill near Philadelphia. In his childhood Theodore Wieland and his sister Clara
had been orphaned by the deaths of their religious fanatic father and their mother, and had been brought up with an in-
adequately religious education by a maiden aunt. Early in the
novel the narrator Clara says that it "will exemplify the force
of early impressions, and show the unmeasurable evils that flow
from an erroneous or imperfect discipline." The overly im-
pressionable Wielands and their overly rationalistic brother-in-
law Henry Pleyel are victimized by a mysterious character
Carwin, who makes them think they are hearing voices —
driving Theodore to murder his wife and children, Henry to

suspect Clara of an affair with Carwin, and Clara herself to be driven temporarily insane after an encounter with Theodore, who has tried to kill her too. Hectic and headlong, the novel poses the question of whether human actions are completely understandable on the basis of sense impressions, or whether, as Clara concludes, "Ideas exist in our minds that can be accounted for by no established laws."

In an unfinished sequel, *Memoirs of Carwin the Biloquist*, it is explained that, when Carwin was younger, his mind had been perverted by an older man Ludlowe, who thought the world could be reformed by an elite group of the "enlightened and disinterested" but who later turned to persecuting Carwin.

As a boy Cooper read *Wieland* and never forgot it. Keats wrote a friend that it was "very powerful — something like Godwin. Between Schiller and Godwin. A strange American scion of the German trunk. Powerful genius — accomplish'd horror." Hawthorne gave Brown a place of honor in his literary hall of fame. According to Thomas Love Peacock, the half-dozen works most influential upon Shelley were Goethe's *Faust*, Schiller's *Robbers*, and four of Brown's novels. In French and German translations, too, they were read on the Continent. In one of Franz Schubert's last letters the composer urges a friend to procure for him some more of Brown's novels.

Ormond (1799) features the fine and intelligent Constantia Dudley (whence Shelley's *To Constantia Singing*), who displays unusual fortitude and exemplifies some of the ideas suggested in *Alcuin*. She is, however, "unacquainted with religion" and "formed her estimates of good and evil on nothing but terrestrial and visible consequences." Unfortunately, she attracts the attentions of unscrupulous Ormond, who thinks one can do nothing but evil until there is a change "in the principles of the social machine." Actually, he just wants to get her in his power — if necessary in the worst manner. Her father urges Constantia to be cautious and Ormond — professing to be acting in her best interests — proceeds to have him murdered. When Ormond finally tries to rape her, she kills him.

Arthur Mervyn (1800), in addition to touching on various aspects of documentary interest (such as a description of the yellow fever epidemic that raged in Philadelphia in 1793), focuses on a country boy who comes to the pestilential city. He is initiated into its corrupt ways, gets into scrapes but always manages to land on his feet, and ends up headed for a happy married life with a wealthy Jewess some years his senior, whom he refers to as "dear mamma."

Edgar Huntly (1799) moves on into the wilderness, where there is tension between frontiersmen and Indians (as later in Cooper) and excursions into insanity on the part of the main character (as in Poe). A friend of Huntly's, who has tried to contaminate him with his own irreligion, is murdered; and Huntly, brooding on the event, follows an insane man whom he suspects of being the murderer until he temporarily loses his own sanity. Toward the end of the book he recovers and exclaims: "What light has burst upon my ignorance of myself and of mankind! How sudden and enormous the transition from uncertainty to knowledge!"

Jane Talbot (1801) features a young widow who is, as she confides to the reader, "very far from being a wise girl." She is courted by Henry Colden, who in his youth was infected by free thought through reading Godwin but has now recovered a more healthy frame of mind. Jane's adopted mother — doubting that he really has — opposes the match, and Jane tells Henry that he is "not passionate enough." He goes off on a cruise, is put off on a Pacific island during a mutiny, finds his way to Japan, and via Batavia and Hamburg reaches home again. With the integrating experience of world travel and with the maturity that has come from the passage of time, he marries Jane, thus involving both head and heart in the joining of hands.

After having pioneered in the psychological novel, the modern picaresque, the frontier novel, and the mature romance — all within but half a dozen years — Brown moved on to other kinds of writing. He published some shorter fiction, a political pamphlet urging that the United States seize the Loui-

siana Territory from the French, and a number of other articles on political matters of the day. Much of his efforts in the
last years of his brief life went into the editing of magazines
and into the raising of his family — for he, like Wieland, had
a wife and four children.

The other two major American writers of the early nineteenth century, Irving and Cooper, lived comparatively longer
— both were born shortly after the Revolution, in the 1780's,
and both were still alive in the 1850's. They came of reasonably
well-to-do Federalist family background, were associated with
New York, early attained international fame, and for extensive periods lived abroad. Thus some of the best-known pieces
of fiction about America came to be written in Europe. There
were, of course, many differences between Irving and Cooper:
Irving's best-known writing, especially in shorter forms, is atmospheric and evocative while Cooper's is extensive and forthright; the bachelor Irving was comparatively modest and re-
tiring while Cooper, the father of five daughters and two sons,
was always involved in one controversy or another. Irving reminds one of Lamb; Cooper, of Balzac, Dumas, or Scott. But
both Irving and Cooper belong to world literature: readers in
many lands — and multitudes who get their literary experience
largely at second hand — know Rip Van Winkle and Leatherstocking as they do Robinson Crusoe or Don Quixote. Irving
helped open up short fiction as a form of conscious art and pioneered in the imaginative treatment of history; Cooper inau-
gurated the panoramic cycle of the frontier and the novel of
the sea — the latter to be developed further by Melville and
Conrad. Both dealt with a wide range of subject matter: Irving from Columbus to Washington and beyond, from the
Moorish background of Columbus' Spain to life on the prairies in the new West and the exploration of the Northwest;
and Cooper from the clash between European and Indian
America to the complexities of the Old World in Venice in
one direction and to voyaging in the Pacific in the other.

Washington Irving (1783-1859) — at the age of six patted
on the head by the First President, after whom he had been

named — was the youngest of eleven children in a New York City merchant family. He studied law early and — along with other members of the Calliopean Literary Society — wrote some essays for the *Morning Chronicle* over the signature "Jonathan Oldstyle, Gent." (as Dennie in Philadelphia used the pseudonym "Oliver Oldschool"). Partly for reasons of health, Irving was sent at the age of twenty-one to Europe for two years. Returning in 1806, he passed the bar examinations the next year and entered the Wall Street law office of an elder brother. About this time he and a group of friends issued a series of twenty essays, the *Salmagundi* papers, characterized by a rather sophomoric display of high spirits. Also involved in this enterprise were three of his brothers, James K. Paulding (who was later to write many essays, short stories, a long poem, and five novels, the most notable of which is *The Dutchman's Fireside*, 1831), and Henry Brevoort (who was to write an account of his fur-trading experiences in *Travels and Adventures in Canada*).

In 1809, with the initial collaboration of one of his brothers, Washington Irving brought out a *History of New York*, purporting to have been written by a pompous Dutch historian Diedrich Knickerbocker. Though containing a certain amount of historical information, in the opening books it burlesques the opinionated manner of the classical Greek historians — the revolutionary generation's favorite study — and in the later books pokes fun at recent and current personalities and events in American history, with Wouter van Twiller a caricature of Adams, Wilhelmus Kieft of Jefferson, and Peter Stuyvesant of Madison. Quite apart from the topical references, however, the humor here — as in *Candide* or *Gulliver's Travels* — still comes through. A Dutch ship, for example, has been modeled after the "fair form" of a Dutch woman:

> Accordingly, it had one hundred feet in the beam, one hundred feet in the keel, and one hundred feet from the bottom of the stern-post to the tafferel. Like the beauteous model, who was declared to be the greatest belle in Amsterdam, it was full in the bows, with a pair

of enormous cat-heads, a copper bottom, and withal a
most prodigious poop!

Of all the Dutch governors, Stuyvesant was the last, best, and
most bullheaded, for

a ruler who follows his own will pleases himself; while
he who seeks to satisfy the wishes and whims of others
runs great risk of pleasing nobody. There is nothing too
like putting down one's foot resolutely, when in doubt,
and letting things take their course. The clock that
stands still points right twice in the four-and-twenty
hours: while others may keep going continually and be
continually going wrong.

When the Knickerbocker History became known in England,
it delighted many of the leading writers there: Scott wrote a
letter to Irving hailing him as already a master.

Briefly in 1811 Irving lobbied in Washington for his brothers' hardware importing business, during the War of 1812 was a
staff colonel, and in 1813-1814 edited the *Analectic Magazine*.
By 1815, however, he was off to Europe again, where he wrote
"Rip Van Winkle" and "The Legend of Sleepy Hollow," ostensibly by "the late Diedrich Knickerbocker," but actually
in a much more atmospheric and nostalgic manner than that
displayed in the burlesque *History of New York*. Irving's new
pseudonym was Geoffrey Crayon, and the public image created over this signature was that of an attractive, sensitive, re-
tiring observer, who preferred to use words as if he were
sketching in pastels.

What happens in these stories is much less important than
the way they are written. From the very opening of "Rip Van
Winkle," for example, one is led into a magic world induced by
the writer's silken style:

Whoever has made a voyage up the Hudson must
remember the Kaatskill mountains. They are a dismembered branch of the great Appalachian family, and are
seen away to the west of the river, swelling up to a

noble height, and lording it over the surrounding country. Every change of season, every change of weather, indeed, every hour of the day, produces some change in the magical hues and shapes of these mountains, and they are regarded by all the good wives, far and near, as perfect barometers. When the weather is fair and settled, they are clothed in blue and purple, and print their bold outlines on the clear evening sky; but, sometimes, when the rest of the landscape is cloudless, they will gather a hood of gray vapors about their summits, which, in the last rays of the setting sun, will glow and light up like a crown of glory.

The plot was derived from German folk legend, as recounted in Otmar's *Volkssagen*; but the central motif of a person's witnessing the activities of supernatural creatures and returning to his former surroundings an old man is worldwide. The story, however (as Irving told Brevoort in a letter of 1824), is "merely a frame on which to stretch my materials." Ostensibly Knickerbocker has hidden himself by presenting folk material; but actually, when the story reaches its climax, one realizes that Irving, through the symbolical figure of Rip Van Winkle, is expressing his own feelings of alienation from the surrounding world.

Three of "Geoffrey Crayon"'s collections appeared by the early 1820's: *The Sketch Book*, *Bracebridge Hall*, and *Tales of a Traveller*. The last Irving thought his best: entirely fictional, it reveals in its initial section, "Strange Stories by a Nervous Gentleman," a fresh conception of narrative in the ghost stories "The Bold Dragon" and "Adventure of the German Student." In the latter, dream precedes event and leads on to insanity, with no blurring of the sequence by attempted rationalization. Influential critics of the day found this volume childish, indelicate, or offensive; and Irving, who did not like to give offense, resumed his concern with imaginatively tinged history.

In 1826 he went to Spain, intending to translate de Navarette's collection of documents on fifteenth-century explorers and their background. Instead of merely translating it, however, he developed this and other material into *The Life and Voyages of Columbus* (1828), *The Conquest of Granada* (1829), *Voyages of the Companions of Columbus* (1831), and *The Alhambra* (1832). Thus full artistic treatment was given Columbus and the Spanish-Moorish background to his voyages. Knowing that the young Boston historian William Hickling Prescott was already working in the same field, Irving in 1838 generously turned over to him the "New World" part of the project he had originally envisaged. Through Irving's four volumes and Prescott's *Conquest of Mexico* (1843) and *Conquest of Peru* (1847) there came into existence a rich fulfillment — though in prose — of some of the same urge that had impelled earlier writers like Barlow, Freneau, and Brown to undertake long poems on Columbus.

In London from 1829 to 1832, Irving assumed virtual charge of the legation. Returning to the United States, he visited the Middle West and South, and wrote *A Tour on the Prairies* (1835). Then, working in John Jacob Astor's library in New York, he wrote *Astoria* (1836) and *The Adventures of Captain Bonneville, U.S.A.* (1837). Meanwhile he had bought a cottage, "Sunnyside," on the Hudson. While minister at the Court of Spain from 1842 to 1845 he wrote some hundred thousand words of official correspondence still in the State Department archives. His final volume of sketches was *Wolfert's Roost* (1855) and his final historical project was a five-volume *Life of George Washington* (1855-1859).

Irving's efforts as a writer were directed toward achieving a lasting — and not merely an immediate — effect:

> I wish in everything I do, to write in such a manner that my productions may have something more than the mere interest of narrative to recommend them, which is very evanescent; something, if I dare use the phrase, of classic merit, i.e. depending upon style, etc., which gives a production some chance for duration beyond the mere whim and fashion of the day.

He had high regard for the shorter forms of writing:

> It is comparatively easy to swell a story to any size
> when you have once the scheme and the characters in
> your mind; the mere interest of the story, too, carries
> the reader on through pages and pages of careless writ-
> ing, and the author may often be dull for half a volume
> at a time, if he has some striking scene at the end of it;
> but in these shorter writings, every page must have
> merit. . . . I believe the works that I have written will
> be oftener re-read than any novel of the size that I
> could have written.

But his historical work also opened up important fields to be
developed further as the century advanced, notably by the
Boston historians. The art in his late monumental work on the
life of Washington is skillfully concealed: the manner is unobtrusive, the proportions spaciously calculated. Irving's style
had a normal course of development — more boisterous in his
early, rich in his mature, and spare in his late, writing. With
him style took on unprecedented importance, subtlety, and in-
timacy. Anyone who would translate Irving into another language faces quite a task: Irving himself said in one of his letters that style could not be translated.

He was one of the very first of our classic authors to arouse
a substantial and warm personal response from individuals on
both sides of the Atlantic. Byron, after reading "The Broken
Heart" in *The Sketch Book*, wrote: "That is one of the finest
things ever written on earth. Irving is a genius; and he has
something better than genius, — a heart. He never wrote that
without weeping; nor can I hear it without tears." Dickens
wrote Irving in 1841:

> There is no living writer, and there are very few among
> the dead, whose approbation I should feel so proud to
> earn. And with everything you have written upon my
> shelves, and in my thoughts, and in my heart of hearts,
> I may honestly and truly say so.

Carlyle, on hearing of Irving's death, wrote: "It was a dream of mine that we two should be friends!" Before the end of Irving's life he had received an honorary doctorate from Oxford, a gold medal from the Royal Society of Literature, and membership in various European and American learned societies. There were also many evidences of widespread popular affection for this very modest man: at his funeral there was a fantastically large crowd (the weight of which is said to have depressed the church floor), and all sorts of places and things have been named after him: hotels, steamboats, wagons, and — though he was not much of a smoker — cigars. If, as Howells said, Mark Twain was the Lincoln of our literature, Irving — though a bachelor — was the literary Father of His Country.

With James Fenimore Cooper (1789-1851), however, the pioneering was not so much in literary style and artistic finish as in thought and feeling conveyed through the subject matter of forest, sea, and human society. He tended to make his writing not an end in itself, but a means to an end — moral, political, social, religious. His writing was no more writing for writing's sake than that of Paine or Columbus.

Like Irving he was a little brother in a big family — twelfth child of thirteen. Born in Burlington, New Jersey, of Quaker ancestry, he was taken at the age of one to Cooperstown, New York, near Otsego Lake, the region he was later to make the setting of most of the Leatherstocking series. For two years he went to Yale, for three he was in the Navy, and in 1811 married — his wife having inherited land in Westchester County. They settled down there to the semirural activities of a family soon to include seven children. During the first half of Cooper's life there was very little to correspond to Irving's gradual, dilettante approach to authorship.

The fact that Cooper had been a "little" brother, however, played its part in his beginning to write. When the death of five of his brothers left their families in some financial stringency, he wished to help. Whim also played a part: he was reading a novel (presumably one of Jane Austen's) to his wife and declared in disgust that he could do better. Challenged, he wrote his first book, *Precaution* (1820) — along with Hawthorne's it is one of the poorer first novels in literary history.

Before it had come off the press, Cooper had started another, *The Spy* (1821), dashing off sixty pages in the first few days and — before he got to it in sequence — letting the publisher print the last chapter. Like an unlicked bear cub this book has a great deal of vitality and was an immediate success. Set in the "neutral ground" of Westchester County during the Revolution, it deals forthrightly with the moral ambiguities that result from an attempt to avoid taking sides once war has broken out. George Washington appears in disguise as Mr. Harper; and in vainly attempting to reward Harvey Birch, the spy who has aided him at the cost of general rejection, Washington articulates a theme that was to run through all of Cooper's writing: "That Providence destines this country to some great and glorious fate I must believe, while I witness the patriotism that pervades the bosoms of her lowest citizens."

After the publication of *The Spy* Cooper moved to New York City to find a school for his daughters and to be closer to his publisher. There he founded a club, "The Lunch" or "The Bread and Cheese," which included the poet and journalist William Cullen Bryant, Cooper's publisher Charles Wiley, the painter and inventor S. F. B. Morse, the poet Fitz-Greene Halleck, and — as honorary member — Washington Irving. "Mr. Cooper engrossed the whole conversation," Bryant wrote his wife soon after one of the meetings, "and seemed a little giddy with the great success his works have met with."

The upstate New York area he had known in his childhood was the scene of his third novel, *The Pioneers* (1823), the first to be written in his Leatherstocking series. He was to work over this Otsego Lake region in his fiction more than once and to make it his own, much as Hardy was to do with Wessex or Faulkner with Yoknapatawpha County. Subtitled "A Descriptive Tale," *The Pioneers* contains local scenes which have been termed by D. H. Lawrence "marvellously beauti-

ful"; Balzac has spoken of Cooper's "painting of the phenom-
ena of nature" as "the last word of our art." This novel, too,
marks the first appearance of the old hunter Natty Bumppo —
called by the villagers Leatherstocking and known also as
Deerslayer, Hawkeye, Pathfinder, and *la longue Carabine* —
a basically untutored frontier scout, purified and ennobled by
his long contact with nature. Cooper was later to write four
other novels dealing with Leatherstocking's earlier and later career (*The Last of the Mohicans*, 1826; *The Prairie*, 1827; *The
Pathfinder*, 1840; and *The Deerslayer*, 1841) — the complexity
of the issues increasing as Cooper pondered on the conflict between Indian and European America, between man and nature.
"Better than anyone in 'Scott's lot,'" declared Thackeray,
Leatherstocking "ranks with our Uncle Toby, Sir Roger de
Coverley, Falstaff — heroic figures, all."

In *The Pilot* (1824), Cooper struck out in another direction
— the novel of the sea. According to his preface, he wrote it
with Scott's *Pirate* in mind to show how someone who had
really been in the Navy would write a sea story. John Paul
Jones plays a role in this novel as Washington did in *The Spy*
(and as Scott often works a well-known historical figure into
the action of his novels); and Long Tom Coffin — like Harvey
Birch — is an unforgettable character. But most important in
this novel — as Conrad pointed out in acknowledging his debt
to Cooper (who, he said, "wrote as well as any novelist of his
time") — is the way the sea itself is more than mere background. Cooper deals with man *in nature*, with man sometimes
as part of, or sometimes at odds with, nature. Plot and setting are
interacting aspects of his novels. This is an important step in
the direction of naturalism. And it runs through all of Cooper's
work, from *The Spy* on: the "neutral ground" establishes the
human problem of neutrality; the area in which the pioneers
have settled dooms Leatherstocking; the shoals through which
John Paul Jones must pilot the ships are related to the ambiguities of loyalty among the characters in the novel. Half-
heartedly used, this relationship might be called the "pathetic

fallacy"; but with Cooper's gusto and intense feeling for the dense reality of nature it is artistically fruitful.

In 1826 Cooper and his family sailed to Europe, partly to secure copyright advantages that could be gained only by European residence and partly for the education of the children. Since the time of William Penn — that is, for six generations — the Coopers had been in America. The novelist's seven-year stay in Europe, from which he returned to America in 1833, proved somehow traumatic in his relationship with his American public. While in Europe he wrote, at Lafayette's request, a volume on *Notions of the Americans* (1828) in answer to some condescending books about America by European travelers. In 1830 he was in Paris during the July Revolution. In 1832 he issued a pamphlet *Letter to Gen. Lafayette* in which he maintained that a republic like the United States was not more expensive in its operations than a monarchy. The struggle of the Poles for freedom elicited Cooper's active support. Forthrightly dealing in three of his novels with Europe he wrote about the evils of the aristocratic system in Italy (Venice), Germany (Limburg), and Switzerland (Berne): *The Bravo*, 1831 (best of the three); *The Heidenmauer*, 1832; and *The Headsman*, 1833 — against the injustices perpetrated by a politically, socially, or ethically closed party or class. In all of this writing, Cooper's attitude toward democracy is consistent enough, but it resulted in his getting entangled in controversy, in which he was not the most tactful person in the world. Besides, he was undertaking a very delicate task — that of viewing critically European ideals and standards through fiction — and he found that those who felt affronted were quick to defend themselves in subtle and savage ways. Soon after mid-century Hawthorne and Howells were to try this task again, but more circumspectly. Only with Henry James toward the end of the century, however, was this task to be carried out with anything like successful precision. In the 1830's Cooper had rushed into the European controversy in the same way he had undertaken to outdo Jane Austen — without much precaution.

After Cooper's return to America, he wrote *A Letter to His Countrymen* (1834), in which he declared he would write no more novels. He continued, however, to write nonfiction — notably his political essay *The American Democrat* (1838) and *The History of the Navy of the United States of America* (1839) — the first full history of the Navy, a volume still useful today. Ultimately, in the 1840's, he returned to writing fiction — and, in fact, wrote some of his most interesting work during the last decade of his life.

The later novels include the Littlepage trilogy: *Satanstoe* (1845), told by young Cornelius Littlepage in the eighteenth century and showing the system of ownership of large tracts of land in Westchester County and above Albany; *The Chainbearer* (1845), told by Cornelius' son Mordaunt just after the American Revolution; and *The Redskins* (1846), told by Mordaunt's grandson, a generation later — the scene being at first abroad, in Paris, and then back home. The series shows the developing resentment against the property rights of a typical older family in New York State, and was written by Cooper in immediate response to the antirent rioting that had broken out in the 1840's — though it also has broader implications in view of the many attacks on private property in both America and Europe and the ethical symbolism of much in the trilogy: in the middle volume, for instance, the title character is a poor surveyor (definer of boundaries or limits) bearing the chains (accepted responsibilities) he uses in his occupation; these chains are also often borne by his niece, whom the Littlepage heir marries. But on the surface the trilogy is a panorama of American life in New York State, extending over a century and tracing the history of a family — a kind of novel which Cooper was the first to develop in American fiction.

In the novels of Cooper's last years there is an increasingly religious tone. *The Crater* (1847), for example, is a utopian novel, set in the South Seas — the first utopian novel in American literature. *Jack Tier* (1848), in a contemporary setting, is a grim account of action at sea in a greedy, unprincipled world — from which the first mate emerges through a shipwreck experience. *The Oak Openings* (1848), the last of Cooper's Indian novels, focuses on a conflict between Parson Amen (a type of the crucified Christ) and Scalping Pete (an Indian, converted by witnessing the parson's martyrdom). The tendency to present Christian situations or values in fictional guise is one with which most readers are familiar through the later novels of Dostoievsky, as is also the attempt to suggest true religiosity through characters who would usually be considered feebleminded or psychologically abnormal — an attempt which Cooper made many times but, of course, never succeeded in carrying through on the scale of *The Idiot*. Cooper's *Sea Lions* (1849) and *The Ways of the Hour* (1850) are also novels with strong underlying ideas and original conceptions. There was no flagging of energy in his writing, and there was no overt religious about-face in his life — though he did become more active within the Protestant Episcopal church as he grew older. In fact, religion provides a highest common factor for all he wrote during his thirty years of active composition.

He himself modestly stated in 1850:

> If any thing from the pen of the writer . . . is at all to outlive himself, it is, unquestionably, the series of "The Leather-Stocking Tales." To say this, is not to predict a very lasting reputation for the series itself, but simply to express the belief it will outlast any, or all, of the works from the same hand.

The five Leatherstocking novels, having been written at different times in his vigorous career, reflect different areas of his concern and different degrees of complexity — the first to be written being in some ways the simplest, the last (but first in terms of subject matter) the richest in meaning. With the passage of time, of course, the immediate occasions that elicited the works of Cooper have been generally forgotten; but the Leatherstocking series — particularly the novel devoted to the earliest stage in the action — constitutes a durable and widely available symbolic formulation of the complex issues involved in the clash between East and West on New World soil.

The Work of Art,
3. Closed and Open
Poe to Whitman

Within but a decade the prophecies began to be fulfilled. Many Americans — Poe, Bryant, Emerson, Thoreau, Hawthorne, Longfellow, Lowell, Mrs. Stowe, Melville, Whitman — had written some of their best work by the 1840's and 1850's: *Tales of the Grotesque and Arabesque* (1840), *Essays, First Series* (1841), *The Scarlet Letter* (1850), *Walden* (1851), *Moby Dick* (1851), *Leaves of Grass* (1855). Between 1830 and 1860, if ever, rose our Wattses, Addisons, Homers. The quarter-century before the Civil War was the period of American literary classics — a "flowering" or "golden day" or "renaissance." It was a distinct era in world literature, like that of Periclean Athens, Augustan Rome, Elizabethan England, or Louis XIV's Versailles. Though without patron and spread over Boston and New York, it fostered the mutual stimulation of creative personalities who held certain facts to be self-evident.

As we look back on it today, we can see it as a host of writers mainly concentrated along the northeastern seaboard devoting themselves to perfecting the work of art — the sheer structure of words we call literature. At first they worked in terms of smaller units — the phrase, the sentence, the work to be read "at a single sitting." Like anyone doing something he has never done before, they held on to what was right there before them. Soon, however, they undertook larger, more venturesome enterprises, and along with the short story, and

69

short lyric there arose the free verse epic and the symbolic novel.

The United States was then enjoying three-quarters of a century of comparative peace between the Revolution and the Civil War — as contrasted with the relatively shorter periods between the Civil War and World War I or between World Wars I and II. Actually, the Revolution had also been an early stage in a "world war" (though that phrase did not come into fashion till our century, which likes to reserve it for its own wars). The revolutionary impulse, after appearing in England in 1642, had gained strength in America and had been retransmitted to Europe in apparently virulent form. The French Revolution then carried it to extremes and it ended up, oddly enough, with Napoleon, who precipitated what was virtually a world war. Though thwarted in France, the revolutionary impulse recrossed the Atlantic along the sea-lanes opened up by Columbus to Latin America while European imperialism forged ahead in Asia; but the United States was able to stay out of the worldwide phase of the early nineteenth-century conflict — except for brief involvement in what is usually referred to as the War of 1812 — because she had already fought in the preliminary bout.

The most widely influential author of this period was Edgar Allan Poe (1809-1849), born after but dying before Irving and Cooper. Born in Boston, he was early orphaned and taken into the household of a wealthy Richmond merchant, John Allan (whence the middle name). Between the ages of six and eleven Poe was with the Allans in England. At eighteen he went briefly to the University of Virginia but, as a result of strained relations with Allan, returned to his native city and enlisted in the Army after he had issued his first volume, *Tamerlane and Other Poems* (1827), as simply "By a Bostonian." During a temporary reconciliation with Allan, following a peacetime enlistment, he was sent to West Point, but remained there only a short time and was soon on his own as writer and magazine editor in Richmond, Philadelphia, and New York. An incomplete novel of his, *The Narrative of A. Gordon Pym*

(1838), was published, the account ending as the ship with the Nantucket stowaway heads toward the Antarctic pole and something mysterious and white looms ahead. Poe's offer to continue the novel to its conclusion was declined by the publisher. Some twenty-five of his sketches and short stories, however, appeared in a collective volume *Tales of the Grotesque and Arabesque* (1840).

Shortly after Poe undertook his first editorial position, with the Richmond *Southern Literary Messenger* in 1835, he married; but in 1847 the death of his wife from tuberculosis, in New York, was one of his many traumatic experiences. During the last few years of his life he was trying frantically to get backing for a magazine that would correspond in America to one of the established European literary journals. He also wished to remarry. In 1849 — ill in Baltimore — he was found unconscious on the street and was taken to a hospital, where he died without having given a clear account of what had happened. The man whom he had earlier appointed his literary executor had been harboring a grudge against him, and after Poe's death did much to disparage him in the eyes of his countrymen.

In Europe, however, Poe's influence was great. In fact it was even enhanced by his neglect in the United States. Europe, in the throes of reaction against the earlier political and social successes of democracy, felt that the case of Edgar Allan Poe showed how the world's model large-scale democracy treated its man of genius. Baudelaire translated Poe's brilliant final extensive cosmological "prose poem" *Eureka* (1847) and many other Poe works; Dostoievsky published part of *Eureka* in Russian in his magazine *Vremia*. The French Parnassian and Symbolist groups developed their programs directly from Poe. His artistically constructed psychological and detective fiction influenced Dostoievsky (whose characters often show a sheer willfulness reminiscent of Poe's "Imp of the Perverse"); A. Conan Doyle (whose Sherlock Holmes is the middleman between Poe's M. Dupin and scores of later detectives); and Jules Verne and H. G. Wells (with their early "science fiction"). The split personality presented in Poe's "William Wilson" reappears in Stevenson's "Dr. Jekyll and Mr. Hyde" and "Markheim." The streamlined manner of many of Poe's short stories is a forerunner of the "Hemingway style"; and Poe's insistence on the autonomy of art helped formulate Pre-Raphaelite, Art Nouveau, and other "Decadent" as well as subsequent movements in France and England. The great Danish literary historian of the nineteenth century, Georg Brandes, in assessing the foreign writers who had done most to mold French literature, placed Poe first — even before Tolstoi, Dostoievsky, Heine, or Shelley. In view of the widespread influence of French literature during the late nineteenth and early twentieth century, Poe's writing had a different sort of world influence from Franklin's or Irving's or Cooper's, involving theory and method as well as subject matter, altering men's conceptions of the very nature and function of literature. What Poe intended is easier to understand in him than it is in some of those who — directly or indirectly, knowingly or unknowingly — followed in his footsteps.

The existence of deprecatory remarks about Poe's writings (such as are to be found about all authors, even the greatest) does not alter the fact that those works have elicited high praise and are basic to what is usually referred to as modernism in the arts of the world. The composers Debussy and Ravel and the illustrator Aubrey Beardsley said they were trying to do in their media what Poe had done in words. The Goncourt brothers in their journal for 1856 maintained that Poe's was "the literature of the 20th century." Mallarmé wrote a distinguished sonnet in his honor in 1875. Valéry characterized Poe's contribution to literary method in both prose and poetry as unrivaled. Beginning with E. D. Forgues' penetrating analysis of Poe's work in 1846, by the end of the century some fifty French critical studies of Poe had appeared. As early as 1858 in Spain Alarcón wrote an enthusiastic essay; in Spanish America the Nicaraguan poet Darío reverenced Poe as *"il divino Edgardo."* In Russia Poe influenced Chekhov, Andreyev, and the poet Balmont (who undertook to translate Poe's works in

1906). British poets — Tennyson, Lang, Swinburne, Rossetti — also recognized him early, and Yeats declared him "always and for all lands a great lyric poet."

Poe's *Eureka* presents a world view as thoroughgoing as that of any of the eighteenth-century philosophers and distinctly mid-nineteenth century in its purpose of bringing together insights afforded by the sciences and the arts. The natural universe (Poe believed, on the basis of several kinds of evidence he considered objective) is contracting, and is headed toward extinction — or, what amounts to the same thing, identity with God. Nevertheless, Poe rejected sharply any tendencies to equate the existing world of nature with the divine: to do so would be sheer anthropomorphism and pantheism, which he abhorred. So far as he was concerned, nature as it appears to the five senses is simply a mask for death and corruption. For him, the existing natural order and the supernatural order are quite distinct from each other. In this respect, his Anglican religious beliefs coincided with normal older Christian attitudes toward the "pomps and vanities of this wicked world."

From such beliefs Poe derived his aesthetic position. In nature *as conceived by God* there is perfect adaptation of means to ends — or what Poe calls, in *Eureka*, mutuality or reciprocity of adaptation:

> The pleasure which we derive from any display of human ingenuity is in the ratio of *the approach* to this species of reciprocity. In the construction of *plot*, for example, in fictitious literature, we should aim at so arranging the incidents that we shall not be able to determine, of any one of them, whether it depends from any one other or upholds it. In this sense, of course, *perfection* of *plot* is really, or practically, unattainable — but only because it is a finite intelligence that constructs. The plots of God are perfect. The Universe is a plot of God.

What Poe here envisions is writing that derives its meaning from its relationship to details not in the outside world but within itself. He here approaches a conception of the work of art as self-contained.

In his review (1842) of Hawthorne's *Twice-Told Tales*, Poe presents his idea of a short story more concretely. The wise literary artist, he says, does not start out with incidents and then fashion his thoughts to accommodate them, but he begins by conceiving "a certain unique or single *effect* to be wrought out" and then invents "such incidents . . . as may best aid him in establishing this preconceived effect." In other words, the cause should derive from the effect. In this regard, Poe makes no essential distinction between the poem and the story — or, for that matter, between verbal and other arts. Unity in the work of art is fundamental. In *The Poetic Principle* (1850) he rejects the claim of the epic or the novel to be considered a true work of art, the aim of which should be elevation of the soul,

> no mere appreciation of the Beauty before us — but a wild effort to reach the Beauty above. Inspired by an ecstatic prescience of the glories beyond the grave, we struggle by multiform combinations among the things and thoughts of Time to attain a portion of that Loveliness whose very elements, perhaps, appertain to eternity alone . . . those divine and rapturous joys, of which *through* the poem or *through* the music, we attain to but brief and indeterminate glimpses.

The work of art, as he thus conceives of it, exists not for the sake of conveying information, urging the claims of truth or duty, or arousing passion. Its purpose is simply not of *this* world. In rejecting the didactic poem, Poe speaks for the "poem *per se*," the "poem and nothing more," the "poem written solely for the poem's sake."

Pushing Poe's position a bit further, one may say that he came close to enunciating a doctrine of "art for art's sake." But actually he did believe in more than that — in the supernatural. The difference between Poe and the advocates of art for art's sake is like that between any leader and his followers. What the master says offhandedly is picked up and exaggerated, and the harder the would-be disciples try the more they go astray.

Comparatively early, Poe was concerned with what poetry might be — not what it happened to have been in the eyes of men, but what it *might be* as sensed in the realm of spirit, by a more-than-human being or angel, as he says in "Israfel" (1831):

> If I could dwell
> Where Israfel
>   Hath dwelt, and he where I,
> He might not sing so wildly well
>   A mortal melody,
> While a bolder note than this might swell
> From my lyre within the sky.

Poe felt that his this-worldly limitations prevented his poetry's being what it should be: it *ought* to be a revelation of a realm of eternal beauty *other than* this world; actually it had to be mere indications of stray glimpses and flashes of this realm that had come to him in moments of heightened awareness. Apparently Poe thought of the present here-and-now world as no more all-sufficient than have most serious thinkers within the Hebraeo-Christian-Muslim tradition, which is basically supernaturalistic (as distinct from the basically nature-bound ancient Greek, Hindu, and Marxist traditions).

The poems in which Poe exemplifies his program are too long to include here, and cannot very well be dismembered or quoted from, so intense is his emphasis on the *interrelation* of the parts. He has himself analyzed one of the best known of his poems, *The Raven*, in his essay *The Philosophy of Composition*: after summarizing it as straight narrative up to the last two stanzas, he says that he then

> added the two concluding stanzas of the poem — their suggestiveness being thus made to pervade all the narrative which has preceded them. The under-current of meaning is rendered first apparent in the lines —
> "Take thy beak from out *my heart*, and take
>   thy form from off my door!"
> Quoth the Raven "Nevermore!"

It will be observed the words, "from out my heart," in-
volve the first metaphorical expression in the poem.
They, with the answer, "Nevermore," dispose the mind
to seek a moral in all that has been previously narrated.
The reader begins now to regard the Raven as emblem-
atical — but it is not until the very last line of the very
last stanza, that the intention of making him emblemati-
cal of *Mournful and Never-ending Remembrance* is
permitted distinctly to be seen:

> And the Raven, never flitting, still is sitting, still is
>   sitting
> On the pallid bust of Pallas, just above my chamber
>   door;
> And the eyes have all the seeming of a demon's that
>   is dreaming
> And the lamplight o'er him streaming throws his
>   shadow on the floor;
> And my soul *from out that shadow* that lies floating
>   on the floor
> Shall be lifted — nevermore.

"Mournful and never-ending remembrance" was precisely the
initial emphasis in the opening lines.

   Ulalume, a shorter and more concentrated poem, achieves
even more strikingly this circularity of structure. Here the narrator, attracted by the crescent moon at the end of an avenue
of cypress trees, is suddenly stopped by an inscription on the
tomb of his loved one along the way. Did he start to stray down
the pathway because the tomb was there, or was the tomb
there because he started to stray down the pathway? It is
easy to attribute specific or symbolical meanings to Poe's poems from his own experience — such as his endeavors to remarry after his wife's death — or from the reader's own experience or imagination. But what is revolutionary about Poe's
writing was the firmness of imagined structure underneath.
The work of art had here become a *something in itself*, not just
a mirror-image of something *outside it* in the everyday world
of external nature.

   His short stories have the same quality as his poems. In

The Pit and the Pendulum, for example, the narrator in the opening sentence says, "When they at length unbound me," and in the closing sentence the French are — by implication — unbinding him. This circular form is not only there in the over-all structure but also in episodes within the story. During most of the first half-dozen paragraphs the narrator thinks he has been confined alive to his tomb; toward the end, the walls begin to push him into the pit, which would, again, be his tomb. But from both possibilities he is unexpectedly saved. The whole story follows a pattern of apparently inevitable disaster and unexpected rescue. Salvation, Poe believed, was not to come through the normal operations of external nature — a belief quite different from that of his fellow Bostonian Emerson and most of the other Romantics.

The Tell-Tale Heart is even more of a gem than *The Pit and the Pendulum* — shorter, more concentrated. Does the narrator's hypersensitivity cause his insanity, or his insanity cause his hypersensitivity? Actually, both cause and effect exist here in perfectly circular relationship, as the crime engenders its own psychological punishment, and the punishment may have engendered — or in the story may be engendering — the crime. This relationship between crime and punishment was to be later explored on a more extensive scale by Dostoievsky.

Poe's criticism is of a piece with his short stories and poems. "Every work of art," he wrote, "should contain within itself all that is required for its own comprehension." This is an assumption still made by many — from the common reader to the "New Critics." Referred to in his day as "the man with the tomahawk," Poe was painfully wrong in some of his judgments, but painfully right in others. As a magazine editor he was effectual, raising the circulation in each instance about eight times above what it had been before he took over. More important, however, is the influence of his general critical essays, which have been highly praised by the great British historian of criticism, George Saintsbury, and by the influential American critic Edmund Wilson.

Had Poe's work not possessed a firm substructure of thought and a radically aesthetic element, manifested in both his poetry and prose, he would have been simply another one of "the Romantics," who during the first half of the nineteenth century were to be found everywhere. True, there are some superficially Romantic aspects to his work. But there was something more, and precisely what that "something more" was amounts to a truly new contribution from America to world literature.

A writer born earlier and living longer than Poe was William Cullen Bryant (1794-1878), born in Cummington, Massachusetts, attending Williams College for a year, then reading law and being admitted to the bar. Eventually, however, he turned to journalism in New York City, becoming editor-in-chief and part owner of the *Evening Post* and by the end of his life building up a million-dollar personal estate. Best known are his early poems written when he was still in his twenties. Though not specifically Christian, his serene contemplation of death, *Thanatopsis*, is stylistically related to the old Puritan "plain style" sermon:

> To him who in the love of Nature holds
> Communion with her visible forms, she speaks
> A various language. . . .

When such a person becomes terrified at the thought of death, he should go out under the open sky and listen to the still voice that, in that nonverbal language, delivers a message to him, which can be verbalized and translated or applied thus: death is universal and dignified; so, when you die, go

> Like one who wraps the drapery of his couch
> About him, and lies down to pleasant dreams.

To a Waterfowl and *The Yellow Violet* formulate experiences in nature and ensuing trains of feeling and thought: in the latter poem, the flower which has caught the poet's eye in April is overlooked later, in May:

So they, who climb to wealth, forget
 The friends in darker fortunes tried.
I copied them — but I regret
 That I should ape the ways of pride.

A more mature poem of his is *To the Fringed Gentian* (1829), in which the late-blooming blue flower, like the *blaue Blume* of the German Romantics, conveys a message of hope:

Blue — blue — as if the sky let fall
A flower from its cerulean wall.

Most of Bryant's writing was frankly intended as public (and even, increasingly, propagandistic) utterance, reflecting his belief in progress and sympathy with libertarian movements around the world — as summed up in such poems as *The Antiquity of Freedom* (1842) and specifically applied in *O Mother of a Mighty Race* (1846), *Our Country's Call* (1861), *The Death of Lincoln* (1865), and *The Death of Slavery* (1866). As journalist, also, he wrote not only editorials on current matters but also tales, travel books (based on his journeys to the prairies, Europe, and the Near East), and essays on the life and works of individual authors (including Cooper, Irving, and Verplanck) as well as on literature, particularly poetry. He translated poems from foreign languages (notably Spanish, and also Portuguese and German) and in the early 1870's published versions of the *Iliad* and the *Odyssey*. Fine and solid as Bryant's achievement was, however, its importance today is generally considered more national than international.

Contemporary with Poe and Bryant were a number of writers whose importance was local. "The Literati," Poe called them, and was inclined to rate next in importance after Bryant Fitz-Greene Halleck, John Jacob Astor's secretary, who is sometimes represented in anthologies by *Marco Bozzaris* (1823), a poem inspired by the Greek resistance to the Turks; and Nathaniel Parker Willis, who wrote some *New Yorker*ish sketches *Pencillings by the Way* (1835), some plays set in medieval Italy, *Bianca Visconti* (1837) and *Tortesa the Usurer* (1839), and a psychological novel *Paul Fane* (1857). Besides many others in New York City, there were individuals and groups in other cities, often centering around magazines.

In Charleston, William Gilmore Simms (1806-1870) did for South Carolina what Cooper had done for New York, and from 1849-1857 was active on the *Southern Quarterly Review*. He was the first full-time, professional author of the Deep South and articulated the Confederate position in the Civil War. Particularly in view of the importance of the southern tradition in serious American writing today, we should get an idea of Simms's assumptions and achievement. The best known of his over thirty published fictional works is *The Yemassee* (1835) — not, he pointed out in his preface, a novel but a romance. The distinction between these genres was clear in the nineteenth century, before a popular tendency to refer to all extended works of fiction as "novels" blurred it: a novel (like Jane Austen's) was "the felicitous narrative of common and daily occurring events," a romance (like Scott's) was a "poem in every sense of the word . . . the substitute which the people of today offer for the ancient epic" — suggesting a continuity between the idea of a "great American epic" and a "great American novel." Based on an attempt by the Yemassee Indians under their stoical chief Sanutee to exterminate the British colonists in South Carolina in 1715, *The Yemassee* shows the Southerners overcoming an obstacle to the development of their way of life, just as they had overcome the wilderness itself and were to overcome the constraint laid on them by the mother country (in *The Partisan*, 1835; *Woodcraft*, 1854; *The Forayers*, 1855; and *Eutaw*, 1856). The Indians, of course, embodied an ancient past but, being irresponsible, were doomed to expulsion. Similarly, the Revolution represented heroic resistance to England by the Southerners. The Civil War, when it came, also represented a foreign attempt to deter the Southerners from creating a stable and structured society which would permit each member of it to know his rightful place and thus in the eyes of the world would be a unique fulfillment of specifically human potentialities. If some Southerners had been irresponsible (Simms implies in *The Partisan*), they had been so only in prerevolutionary days. As early as 1841 Simms in his *Confession* urged that Mexico, Cuba, and the West Indies be annexed, to provide "the natural balance, which, in a few years, the southern states of the Union will inevitably need."

In Richmond there was the *Southern Literary Messenger*, with which John Pendelton Kennedy of Maryland was associated. In 1832 Kennedy published his *Swallow Barn*, a series of Irvingesque sketches evoking old Virginia plantation life, and in 1835 — the same year as *The Yemassee* — his *Horse Shoe Robinson*, a novel also set in the era of the Revolution in the Carolinas but with somewhat different implications, since Kennedy was of the Upper South and during the Civil War sided with the Union.

In Philadelphia a physician, Robert Montgomery Bird, brought out several novels during the 1830's, notably one which in his lifetime went through over thirty editions (including German, Polish, and Dutch) and was widely played in at least four dramatic versions: *Nick of the Woods; or The Jibbenainosay* (1837). This novel of frontier Kentucky is notable for Nathan Slaughter, an ostensibly peaceful Quaker who goes around surreptitiously killing Indians and carving crosses on them (because they massacred his family), and young Ralph Stackpole, an irrepressible, voluble compulsive horse thief. One of the best of Bird's novels, *Sheppard Lee* (1836), is about a young man who as a temporarily disembodied spirit inhabits, in succession, the bodies of a rich man, a man-about-town, a miser, a slave, and a decadent Southerner. Bird also wrote plays performed by Edwin Forrest: among others, a heroic tragedy set in ancient Rome, *The Gladiator* (1831), about a slave uprising led by Spartacus (a play which has had over a thousand performances on both sides of the Atlantic), and a domestic tragedy, *The Broker of Bogotá* (1834), as well as some comedies.

In Boston there appeared in 1803 the *Monthly Anthology*, edited by William Tudor (a Yankee ice exporter who is said to have been responsible for the custom of putting ice in drinks). Among the contributors to this Boston magazine was the pastor of the First Church there, William Emerson. In time the *Monthly Anthology* turned into the *North American Review*, with a rotating editorship that included many on the faculty of Harvard, where the growing influence of German scholarship early gave the magazine a geographically extensive audience. At one time, for example, a dozen copies a month were being sold in Calcutta; at another, Louis XVIII banned it in France because he was afraid of its political influence.

Although William Emerson died when his four sons were quite young, the second one — Ralph Waldo Emerson (1803-1882) — was able to attend Boston Latin School and Harvard College and Divinity School. In 1829 he became pastor of the Second Church in Boston. Married in the same year, he seemed on the point of uneventfully carrying on his ancestral career. Within less than three years, however, his wife died and he encountered difficulties in his pastorate. Before resigning he preached a farewell sermon, *The Lord's Supper* (1832), in which he said that church history showed no uniformity in the way the Lord's Supper had been understood or celebrated, that the Scriptural authority for its perpetual observance rested on only one Gospel (where, he felt, much was to be taken only figuratively), and that the rite was an Eastern custom "foreign and unsuited" to the West and to him personally. He added: "I am about to resign into your hands that office which you have confided to me. It has many duties for which I am feebly qualified. It has some which it will always be my delight to discharge according to my ability, wherever I exist." As his forefathers had left the Roman church for a succession of churches, each further reformed than the last, so Emerson kept right on going — though this did not end his spiritual pilgrimage or his essentially priestlike role. Unlike Jonathan Edwards (a man of similar background, character, and early career), Emerson when he reached an impasse with his congregation on the administration of the Lord's Supper turned over the office and embarked for Europe. The mood in which he sailed east was quite different from that of the pilgrims two centuries before when they had sailed west. In his shipboard

diary he on one occasion listed all his inadequacies and concluded: "What under the sun canst thou do then, pale face?
Truly not much, but I can hope." Ostensibly he had gone to
Europe for his health, to observe some of the achievements of
"social man," and to meet such individuals as Wordsworth,
Coleridge, Landor, and Carlyle (with only the last of whom
he was not somewhat disappointed). Within two years after
his return in 1833 he settled in Concord, remarried, and during
the rest of his long life wrote and lectured.

In contrast to a Poe work, an Emerson essay is usually an
ascending spiral of increasing amplitude and abstraction. Basically the form is oratorical, for many of the essays are reworked
lectures — often ending with a peroration. In his first important published work, *Nature* (1836), he says that the historical approach, then so much in the ascendancy, involves a
secondhand relationship with nature and God. Why not a first-
hand one? The word "nature" he acknowledges he is using
here in two ways — for the objective (as opposed to the subjective) aspects of reality and for essences unchanged by man
(as opposed to "art") — because "in inquiries so general as our
present one," he says, "the inaccuracy is not material." We
might observe, however, that he uses the word "nature" in
a much more comprehensive sense than Poe does. In brief,
Emerson asks, "Why nature?" and answers — in sections of increasing abstraction — that it has commodity uses, is beautiful,
serves as the basis of language, and carries with it certain dis-
ciplinary values. Has it absolute existence? Though common
sense suggests that it has, further consideration finds it depend-
ent on ideas. Idealism, though not fully explaining matter, may
be taken as a "useful introductory hypothesis."

> As a plant upon the earth, so a man rests upon the bosom
> of God; he is nourished by unfailing fountains, and
> draws at his need inexhaustible power. Who can set
> bounds to the possibilities of man? Once inhale the
> upper air, being admitted to behold the absolute natures
> of justice and truth, and we learn that man has access
> to the entire mind of the Creator, is himself the creator
> in the finite.

The practical application, as given in the last paragraph of *Nature*, is "Build therefore your own world."

Radiating from his Concord base, Emerson found lecture audiences more receptive to his ideas than his Boston church congregation had been. In 1837, for example, he was asked to give the address at the public announcement of new members of Phi Beta Kappa at Harvard — a festive occasion, preceded by an academic procession and a brass band. His oration, *The American Scholar*, first presents the subject in the abstract: the scholar is simply Man Thinking, just as the planter is Man Food-Gathering, and has learned from nature, the past, and action (books, as such, occupying here a secondary role in his training). His duty is to trust himself and to encourage others to do likewise. The increased interest in common things and in the individual is a heartening "sign of the times." True, there is much academic time-serving, but,

> if the single man plant himself indomitably on his instincts, and there abide, the huge world will come round to him. Patience — patience; with the shades of all the good and great for company; and for solace the perspective of your own infinite life; and for work the study and the communication of principles, the making those instincts prevalent, the conversion of the world. . . . A nation of men will for the first time exist, because each believes himself inspired by the Divine Soul which also inspires all men.

With this secular evocation of the old plain style sermon, Emerson was digging at roots of Christian emotion and vision deep in the New England soul. Oliver Wendell Holmes called this oration "our Intellectual Declaration of Independence." Its implications are at once religious, political, and intellectual. It is a coherent formulation of an ideal for American scholarship different from the German one then being domesticated at Harvard.

Emerson was surrounded in Concord by an active and varied group of individuals. The Social Circle, made up of some twenty-five townsmen, met at the Emerson home each week. Another group which met at one another's houses and in which Emerson sometimes participated later came to be known as the "Transcendental Club," which included another ex-minister, George Ripley, editor of a fourteen-volume *Specimens of Foreign Standard Literature* and "archon" of the Brook Farm experiment; John Sullivan Dwight, for some thirty years editor of the Boston *Journal of Music*; Elizabeth Peabody, later editor of a short-lived magazine, *Aesthetic Papers*; Margaret Fuller, author of *Woman in the Nineteenth Century* and later foreign correspondent for the New York *Tribune* covering the revolution of 1848-1849 in Italy; Bronson Alcott, education reformer, father of the novelist Louisa May Alcott, and later leader of the highly idealistic Fruitlands experiment at Harvard, Massachusetts; Jones Very, whose poems and essays purported to have been dictated by the Holy Ghost; Orestes Brownson, later to turn to Roman Catholicism and to try to reform it along lines set forth in his *Convert* — a very interesting effort, known in Roman Catholic circles as "Americanism," which was sternly rejected by the Vatican in the late nineteenth century but has come to be more sympathetically received now in the late sixties; James Freeman Clarke, author of *Self-Culture* and *Ten Great Religions*; and Theodore Parker, prominent Unitarian minister. George Ripley's experiment in communal living, Brook Farm, in West Roxbury (now part of Greater Boston), had a peripheral relation to this "Transcendental" group and enrolled during the seven years of its operation some 140 members, including farmers, Harvard students, an English nobleman, a Spaniard, two Filipinos, the son of a Louisiana planter, and Hawthorne. During its first three years it issued a periodical *The Phalanx*; then it published a weekly, *The Harbinger*, with a circulation of about a thousand.

In his personal relationships with many individuals Emerson was unusually generous. He made it financially possible for Bronson Alcott to visit Alcott House, a school established near London along lines set forth by Alcott in his published writings. He edited Jones Very's sonnets and secured their publication. He helped Thoreau get settled near Walden Pond and the Hawthornes in the Old Manse. He saw to it that Carlyle's *Sartor Resartus*, which had received only periodical publication in England, was brought out in Boston — its first appearance as a book anywhere.

Meanwhile Emerson was lecturing and reworking his lectures into books. In the late 1830's he gave addresses at graduations and meetings of college literary societies and library associations. By the 1840's he was giving sequences of ten or a dozen lectures in Boston. In 1847, at the insistence of an admirer in Edinburgh, he went to Britain, where he lectured in some twenty-five towns, mainly to members of Mechanics' Institutes. By the 1850's he was lecturing widely in the Middle West. Out of all this activity came his principal books: *Essays, First Series* (1841), *Essays, Second Series* (1844), *Representative Men* (1850), *English Traits* (1856), and *The Conduct of Life* (1860).

In his chapter on "Literature" in *English Traits* (based on his trips to England), Emerson criticizes British writing of the day for being utilitarian and insular — as, in other words, pursuing aims that are more documentary than literary. In Hallam's and in Mackintosh's recent literary histories, he writes,

> one still finds the same type of English genius. It is wise and rich, but it lives on its capital. It is retrospective. How can it discern and hail the new forms that are looming up on the horizon, new and gigantic thoughts which cannot dress themselves out of any old wardrobe of the past?

Dickens, he says, "writes London tracts," and Macaulay teaches that the merit of modern philosophy "is to avoid ideas and avoid morals." To Emerson the purpose of literature is no more *of this world* than it is to Poe — though Emerson would grant it a more overtly didactic aim.

Like many other American authors, Emerson was somewhat rhapsodic in his approach to writing. "I am," he said, "in all my theory, ethics, and politics a poet." Among his *Poems* (1847), he uses devices that Whitman later exploited — lines of differing length, lists of names and things, inset songs (in, for example, "Hamatreya"). In "Bacchus," he calls for a wine that will inspire him to write down original and archetypal ideas

> . . . with the pen
> Which on the first day drew,
> Upon the tablets blue,
> The dancing Pleiads and eternal men.

Of his earlier poems, perhaps the best known is the *Concord Hymn*, beginning "By the rude bridge that arched the flood"; of his later, *Brahma* (reflecting his interest in the *Vedas*), beginning

> If the red slayer think he slays,
> Or if the slain think he is slain,
> They know not well the subtle ways
> I keep, and pass, and turn again.

Emerson's Orientalism was prompted, to some extent, by his belief that Asia was spiritually more vigorous than Europe:

> By the law of contraries, I look for an irresistible
> taste for Orientalism in Britain. For a self-conceited
> modish life, made up of trifles, clinging to a corporeal
> civilization, hating ideas, there is no remedy like the
> Oriental largeness. That astonishes and disconcerts Eng-
> lish decorum. For once, there is thunder it never heard,
> light it never saw, and power which trifles with time
> and space.

(It is interesting that this desire for a purging Himalayan storm to break over a decadent London was to reappear, during the next century, toward the end of T. S. Eliot's *The Waste Land*.) Coleridge, whom Emerson regarded as one of the best minds in England, "seems to mark the closing of an era." Of the intellectual class in both Old and New England — which Emerson belonged to — he wrote, "It is the surest sign of national decay, when the Brahmins can no longer read or understand the Brahminical philosophy."

In his *Essays, Second Series* there appeared an extended discussion of "The Poet." The poet is a man among men, Man

Saying (rather than primarily Man Knowing or Man Doing). He "stands among partial men for the complete man, and apprises us not of his wealth, but of the common wealth." The true poet will be known because "he announces that which no man foretold." Not artifice, but nature determines the poet, "For it is not meters, but a meter-making argument that makes a poem, — a thought so passionate and alive that like the spirit of a plant or an animal it has an architecture of its own, and adorns nature with a new thing." "Verse form" is quite unimportant in this conception — an assumption that Emerson and others had long been making. Even in *Nature*, he had closed with a long quotation from "a certain poet" (presumably Alcott), which is no more and no less poetry than the rest of the essay.

Emerson's essays had intense and widespread effect. Two years after *Nature* appeared it fell into the hands of the Polish refugee poet and professor in Paris, Mickiewicz, who lent it to the historian Edgar Quinet, and together they and some of their colleagues at the Sorbonne were inspired by it to attack Jesuitism there in the 1840's. Mickiewicz also called it to the attention of the famous bluestocking mistress of Franz Liszt, the Countess d'Agoult, who in 1846 published the first French monograph on Emerson, in which she said that *Nature* was "not yet art" but had for the first time reconciled individualism and pantheism, "from whence may be born an original art." According to Matthew Arnold, Emerson's essays were the most important prose work of the century. Froude said they broke for him the fetters of the church. Tyndall said that whatever he had done the world owed to Emerson. While Nietzsche was in exile at Pforta in 1874, he came across Emerson's essays and found in them a prefiguration of his ideas of the *Übermensch*. Tolstoi in his *Message to the American People* (1901) asked them why they paid so little attention to the voices of Emerson and his associates. Intellectual leaders in India were aware of Emerson's writings. The development of Emerson's ideas abroad — as of Poe's — was to reinfluence

twentieth-century American writers, unaware of the interven-
ing circuit and inevitable distortion.

In considering Emerson's international breakthrough alongside Poe's, however, we must also take into account the work
of a younger man early associated with him, Henry David
Thoreau (1817-1862). Born in Concord, Thoreau attended
Harvard College and briefly taught school, but found his teaching experience unsatisfying: he would not whip the pupils reg-
ularly enough for the school committee; then he and his
brother John conducted their own school for a few years, but
John's death made continuation of it emotionally impossible
for Henry; finally Emerson got him a job as tutor on Staten
Island, but Thoreau grew homesick for Concord. Emerson's
gift for steady lecturing he did not have. What he really wanted
to do was write — something truly original and natural, something definitely his own. In the late 1830's and 1840's he was
often at the Emersons' house and — in the Emersons' absence
on lecture trips — looked after the place and attended to the
Transcendentalists' magazine, the *Dial.* Some of his verse and
essays appeared there and elsewhere. He had come to know
oriental literature at Harvard, and Emerson had directed him
to the *Bhagavad Gita.*

After returning from Staten Island convinced that teaching and New York were not for him, he had been encouraged
to build a cabin in Emerson's woodlot on nearby Walden Pond
and — on July 4, 1845 — had begun a stay of two years and
two months there. During that time he observed, thought, kept
an extensive journal, worked over material that he was later
to publish in the two books he was to live to see in print, and
occasionally made longer trips than just into town. On at least
one occasion he sheltered a runaway slave who was on his way
to Canada.

Like many other Concord intellectuals, Thoreau was
deeply opposed to slavery. During his second summer at
Walden, the United States annexed a former part of free Mexico
as the slave state Texas. Both Emerson and Thoreau were

deeply shocked by the resulting Mexican War, which — at least in principle — increased the extent of slavery on the face of the earth. At Walden Thoreau had already irritated some of those in authority. Consequently, when he refused to pay his poll tax as a gesture of protest, he was told that he would have to go to jail. He proceeded to do so. Tradition has it that Emerson came to his cell and asked, "Henry, what are you doing in jail?" and Thoreau answered, "Waldo, what are you doing out of jail?" Against Thoreau's wishes, his poll tax was paid and he was released next day. But he subsequently lectured on the principle involved in his refusal, and reworked his lecture as an essay *Civil Disobedience*.

When Gandhi was studying law in London, he came across this essay and — he wrote in his *Autobiography* — adopted the title as the slogan for the passive-resistance movement that ultimately won for India its independence from Britain. Gandhi's interest in Thoreau's writings was long and intense: he translated and published in his *Indian Opinion* in South Africa a portion of *Civil Disobedience*, read Henry Salt's early biography of Thoreau, and studied Thoreau's other works. Subsequently, Nehru sponsored translations of some of them into the principal languages of India. Of course, there are deeply ingrained Indian thought processes also involved in this influence; but this relationship between Thoreau's essay and Indian freedom has a certain symbolical neatness: Emerson and Thoreau, fascinated by the sacred writings of India, had contributed something to the transmutation of ancient potentialities into present action — had helped the Brahmins understand the Brahminical philosophy.

The first book that Thoreau published was *A Week on the Concord and Merrimack Rivers* (1849), based on a camping trip he and John had taken in 1839. The book is arranged according to the days of the week, and moves with the easy flow of a river between observation and reflection, between prose and verse. Thus the form of the book follows actual relationships in the natural world — temporal and geographical. First there had been the experience (heightened by John's subsequent death), and the experience had almost embodied it-self in the words of the book. It is an idyll. But it proved not particularly impressive to its few American readers. Two un-enthusiastic reviews appeared: the title had led James Russell Lowell to expect something more jolly, and in its ideas George Ripley smelled pantheism. About the only heartening re-sponse came from Europe: Anthony Froude, Fellow of Exeter College, Oxford, author of the *Nemesis of Faith*, wrote Tho-reau: "When I think of what you are — of what you have done as well as what you have written, I have the right to tell you that there is no man living upon this earth at present whose friendship or whose notice I value more than yours."

The other book that Thoreau published was *Walden: or Life in the Woods* (1854). In it he included his jail experience and the observations and reflections of his two years and two months beside Walden Pond — the most truly fresh and beau-tiful book of America's flowering-time. As Dante at the start of the *Divine Comedy* recounts his getting lost, so Thoreau in writing of his "life in the woods" uses a kind of double-talk: one needs to reflect on each sentence, each phrase, even each word, and bring to the reading some contribution of one's own in the way of thought, feeling, and experience. When Tho-reau says "woods" he means also woodenness, "pebbles" stoni-ness, "stars" ideals. "Time," he wrote,

> is but the stream I go a-fishing in. I drink at it; but while
> I drink I see the sandy bottom and detect how shallow it
> it. Its thin current slides away, but eternity remains. I
> would drink deeper; fish in the sky, whose bottom is
> pebbly with stars. . . .

Though taking *Walden* in small doses, one should not over-look the fact that the whole book follows the seasons in a year — summer, autumn, winter, spring — and ends on a vision-ary, springtime note: "Only that day dawns to which we are awake. There is more day to dawn. The sun is but a morning star."

After returning to Concord from Walden, Thoreau served

as a surveyor, conducted his family's pencil and graphite business after his father's death, helped fugitive slaves on their way to freedom, spoke publicly in defense of the antislavery martyr John Brown, and contributed occasional essays to magazines. As time went on, the temperamental differences between him and Emerson sharpened. Thoreau, the year before his death, made a trip to Minnesota, partly for reasons of health (for he and other members of his family had tuberculosis) and partly because of his interest in the Indians, about whom he would have written his third book had he lived longer. Though subsequent volumes compiled from his journals, magazine articles, and other papers were issued, they do not have the artistic perfection of the two that he could see through the press.

As with Paine and Poe, he was not allowed to rest in peace. For the *North American Review* in 1865, on the occasion of the issue of an edition of Thoreau's works, Lowell wrote a long and sophisticated attack. Abroad, *Walden* eventually came to appeal to a number of different groups and individuals in different lands — the Fabian Socialists, for example, in England and Tolstoi in Russia. Ultimately, it stands as literature, as an artistic work of unique originality and purity. Hearing it read to him as a boy, Yeats dreamed of his lake isle of Innisfree. W. H. Hudson spoke of it as "the one golden book in any century of best books." Marcel Proust hailed Thoreau as a brother. If the Countess d'Agoult was right in speaking of *Nature* as "not yet art" but the possible source of "an original art," certainly between Emerson and Thoreau some giant steps toward that art were taken.

In characterizing Emerson's and Thoreau's international breakthrough, one might place it at the opposite pole from Poe's — emphasizing nature rather than art, predicated on an expanding rather than a contracting universe, and developing by synthesis rather than by analysis. Each operated on somewhat different individuals and at different levels around the earth. To Poe, Emerson and his circle seemed hopelessly vague; to Emerson, Poe was the "jingle man." In any cultural epoch, there are often outstanding personalities who never really make contact with each other — such as, in the previous century, Edwards and Franklin. The failure of Poe and Emerson to appreciate each other, however, was not just accidental or personal: their differences were ideological. The deep and fundamental opposition here involved is not mutually exclusive but complementary — like that between the positive and negative poles in an electric circuit, without which there is no current.

Transmitted to Europe, this electric tension manifested itself in Dostoievsky's attack on the Nietzschean *Übermensch*, from *Crime and Punishment* to *The Brothers Karamazov*. Among mid-nineteenth-century Americans intensely aware of the two poles — nature and art — one of the most notable was Hawthorne. In trying to bridge them, he was not nearly so successful as his great Russian contemporaries — partly because he was so close to the tensions, worked mostly in smaller forms, and was incapacitated by ill-health in his fifties. Who knows whether — had he lived another quarter-century, as did Dostoievsky and Tolstoi — he might have surmounted the impasse he reached in his writing?

Born in Salem of an old New England family, Nathaniel Hawthorne (1804-1864) was orphaned by the death of his ship captain father in Surinam, Dutch Guiana. From 1821-1825 Hawthorne attended Bowdoin College in the same class as Longfellow and a future president of the United States, Franklin Pierce. After graduation Hawthorne returned to Salem and wrote with a singleness of purpose no less than Thoreau's was to be — but fiction rather than essays. After a premature first novel, *Fanshawe* (1828), by mid-century he published mainly short tales in scattered periodicals and gift books and brought out three volumes selected from them: *Twice-Told Tales* (first series, 1837; second series, 1842) and *Mosses from an Old Manse* (1846). In these collections appear such fine stories as "Rappaccini's Daughter," set in Italy; "The Birthmark," in which a man, trying to remove the last vestiges of a blemish in his wife, kills her; "The Minister's

Black Veil," in which a minister wears a veil to exemplify the secrecy of the inmost human soul; "Young Goodman Brown," about a witches' sabbath; and "Ethan Brand," in which a man who has gone out seeking the Unpardonable Sin and has made a girl "the subject of a psychological experiment" finds that Sin in his own heart, and when he throws himself into a kiln all his bones are turned to lime but his heart remains uncalcined. *Twice-Told Tales* elicited a thoughtful review from Poe, who hailed Hawthorne as one of our "few men of indisputable genius" and discussed the tale and short story in a way that has given this review a classic position in the theory of American short fiction, and was well received in England, where by 1851 five editions had been printed. *Mosses from an Old Manse* became the subject of a penetrating essay by Melville, "Hawthorne and His Mosses."

The title of this third collection is an allusion to the house where Hawthorne and his growing family were living at the time. Back in the late 1830's and engaged to be married, he had worked in the Boston Custom House and in 1841 had lived at Brook Farm, but neither of these had proved a satisfactory solution to the financial responsibilities of marriage. Emerson came to the rescue with a house in Concord that had belonged to his step-grandfather, the Reverend Ezra Ripley — the house, in fact, where *Nature* had been written.

Returning to Salem in 1846 as customs inspector, Hawthorne began his best-known novel, *The Scarlet Letter* (1850) — an immediate success in America and in England (where, by the following year, three editions had appeared). A short and saturnine work set in seventeenth-century Puritan Boston, it takes its title from the scarlet "A" which Hester Prynne has been obliged by the community to wear because she has borne an illegitimate child, Pearl. Actually, the father is the minister of the community, Arthur Dimmesdale. Hester's husband, Roger Chillingworth, tortures Dimmesdale mentally out of a cold wish to experiment with another human being. The story traces the differing effects of guilt — to some extent recognized in Hester, compounded in Chillingworth, and hidden in Dimmesdale but ultimately confessed in a gesture so shattering to him that it causes his death. An important motif throughout the novel is the shifting force of the letter "A." Though the old Puritans may have been a little clumsy about some things, Hawthorne implies, they were not far wrong about the sinfulness of man. The validity of an older religious point of view — as in Dostoievsky — is thus reasserted.

After losing his customhouse job in 1849 when the political administration changed, Hawthorne moved to Lenox, Massachusetts, where he was soon to enjoy the companionship of Melville, and in a burst of activity wrote *The House of the Seven Gables* (1851), a novel about a curse uttered against a Puritan, Judge Pyncheon, and now working itself out in the children's children unto the third and the fourth generation. The interpenetration of past and present is here explored — the cumulative effects of greed and increasing sterility, from which the younger characters are finally able to break away. It is a pioneering venture in the type of novel depicting the decline of a once proud house, such as was to be carried on in the twentieth century by notable writers in the South.

Hawthorne, having moved to West Newton, wrote *The Blithedale Romance* (1852), a novel in the contemporary setting of Brook Farm. The narrator is a young poet, Miles Coverdale, who through his alienation from life around him plays an ambiguous role in the action. Through his consciousness a situation is presented in which an ostensibly unselfish but monstrously self-centered man, Hollingsworth, attracts the affections of two contrasting half-sisters — one a colorful, sophisticated, powerful, self-assertive woman, Zenobia (who commits suicide when she is rejected in favor of her half-sister); the other a self-effacing girl, Priscilla (who by the end of the novel has even engaged the affections of the seemingly uninvolved and rather cynical narrator).

In the early 1850's Hawthorne also wrote some other volumes, such as *A Wonder Book* (1851) for children and a campaign biography of Pierce (1852). By the end of the 1850's a good deal of his work had also been published abroad — in French, German, Spanish, Russian. In 1853 he was appointed consul at Liverpool; and, although he began several novels abroad, he brought to completion only *The Marble Faun* (1860), set in Rome. The title here refers to a statue by Praxiteles which Count Donatello resembles. At the beginning of the novel he is a simple child of nature. But he loves Miriam, a woman with a past, who prompts him to murder her pursuer. The guilt thus shared transforms both Donatello and Miriam into fully human beings (whence the title of the book as it was published in England, *Transformation*). Mere witnessing of the murder has at first stunned the virginal New England girl in the novel, Hilda. But eventually both she and Kenyon (the character who is the observer and stand-in for the author) also assimilate the experience — though Kenyon is puzzled by the nature of sin, for it

> educated Donatello, and elevated him. Is sin, then, — which we deem such a dreadful blackness in the universe, — is it, like sorrow, merely an element of human education, through which we struggle to a higher and purer state than we could otherwise have attained? Did Adam fall, that we might rise to a far loftier paradise than his?

The merit of Hawthorne's work was recognized both at home and abroad. He was the only American author to be given a volume in the British "English Men of Letters Series" — a notable monograph, appearing in 1879, by Henry James.

The principal stress in all of Hawthorne is on the importance of recognizing that the essentially human condition will inevitably fall short of the perfect or the ideal or the abstract — the claims of which had been so eloquently urged by Poe and Emerson. Hawthorne questioned whether anyone has the right to meddle in the life of another. This is an essential human problem — felt in the relation between successive generations, in any attempts at reform, and in time of war — the Civil War, for instance. It is also the problem of the writer as he deals with his raw material of experience and imagination — of life — and fashions it into a work of art. Cooper had been scarcely aware of this as a problem; Poe was all for art; Hawthorne was aware of the claims both of art and life. Though he never lived to resolve the conflict, the narratives he left are unforgettable. Each one incises a sharp image on the memory of the reader. Thoreau once said his aim in writing a sentence was to make it like a diamond which the reader would swallow without digesting. To some extent this ideal of hard, sharp statement underlies all four great American writers of the second quarter of the nineteenth century — Poe, Emerson, Thoreau, and Hawthorne. They are, accordingly, at their best in short forms. With them it is a matter of quality rather than quantity. But what they wrote at their best is what literature is — not just American literature, but literature.

A number of writers born about the same time as these four have also been of national and international importance, such as Longfellow, Holmes, Lowell, Whittier, Mrs. Stowe, Melville, and Whitman. Longer-lived than Poe, Thoreau, or Hawthorne, they were still writing after the Civil War. Some of them notably helped to keep the country together during that conflict and to formulate the meaning of the nation that emerged from it. Some of their work figures in a body of imaginative experience shared by almost everyone educated in American schools. Thus these authors are important individually, regionally, and nationally. But also, from an international and more general point of view, some of them expanded the forms, subject matter, and audience available for literature.

As Emerson, Thoreau, and Hawthorne were associated with the country village of Concord, so Longfellow, Holmes, and Lowell were associated with the university town of Cambridge, where they were on the Harvard faculty. They tended, accordingly, to be more academic and eclectic.

As the oldest and most gracious member of the group, Henry Wadsworth Longfellow (1807-1882) in Cambridge might be compared to Emerson in Concord. Born in Portland, Maine, and graduated from Bowdoin College, Longfellow after three years in Europe returned to teach modern languages at his alma mater for five years, during which he married. On a second visit to Europe his wife died; and when he returned to take up his duties as professor of modern languages at Harvard in 1836, he had so far published only some textbooks, scattered magazine poems and sketches, and an Irving-esque volume of travel essays, *Outre-Mer*.

Soon, however, in 1839, he brought out a volume of poems and a prose romance that were at the time quite new and sensational. In the former, *Voices of the Night*, "The Prelude" promises not pretty nature poems but

> All forms of sorrow and delight
> All solemn Voices of the Night
> That can soothe thee, or affright.

One nocturnal voice, in "Hymn to the Night," welcomes the dark, irrational side of life, and enunciates a death-wish in a prayer for

> The welcome, the thrice-prayed for, the most fair,
>   The best-loved Night!

Another, in "A Psalm of Life," declares that

> Life is real! Life is earnest!
> And the grave is not its goal.

Still another, in "The Reaper and the Flowers," contemplates death as soothing and lovely. These "voices of the night" are, in other words, moods. In the latter volume, *Hyperion*, Longfellow presents an impetuous personal narrative, mainly about his current courtship of a wealthy Boston girl (who finally married him). What Longfellow was doing in these two volumes was conveying in English the spirit of a current type of German Romantic writing, particularly that of Novalis and Jean Paul, and was enlarging the possible base for literary achievement in America by establishing an area of freer, more immediate and varied, more personal statement than had prevailed hitherto.

Two years before his second marriage, he had brought out another very popular volume of verse, *Ballads and Other Poems*, notable for some of its narratives like "The Skeleton in Armor" and "The Wreck of the Hesperus." He also wrote some poems on slavery, which not only suggest his political sentiments but also show the extent to which he conceived of poetry as willed composition rather than as a spontaneous overflow of powerful feeling based on experience. In "The Slave's Dream," for example, the dying Negro recalls his former days of freedom and glory as an African king:

> And then at furious speed he rode
>   Along the Niger's bank;
> His bridle-reins were golden chains,
>   And, with a martial clank,
> At each leap he could feel his scabbard of steel
>   Smiting his stallion's flank.

More familiar from the period of Longfellow's professorship is *Evangeline* (1847), a long narrative poem, based on the exile of the French Acadians from Canada: Evangeline searched for her betrothed from Philadelphia to the bayous of Louisiana, only to find him at last on his deathbed. This poem became popular immediately, not only in the original but also in numerous translations, especially the French. It is emotionally moving, particularly for those who may have come to poetry with more experience of nature than art. Longfellow disregarded some of the limitations that Wordsworth had placed on poetry half a century before: a kind of poetic diction reappears, though on another basis than that objected to by Wordsworth. Slight deviations from prose idiom (such as "the son of Basil the Blacksmith" instead of "Basil the Blacksmith's son") and a prevailingly dactyllic verse pattern give it a ceremonious air, like the speech of a cultivated foreigner.

Longfellow's *The Spanish Student* (1843) is a verse play about the successful efforts of a Spanish dancer, Preciosa, to elude a lecherous nobleman. Longfellow's final work of prose fiction, *Kavanagh* (1849), deals incidentally with the plight of young Churchill, who tries to combine teaching with creative writing, and Hathaway, who has projected a new magazine *The Niagara* and wants "a national literature altogether shaggy and unshorn, that will shake the earth, like a herd of buffaloes thundering over the prairies!" But Mr. Churchill urges the superior claims of universality:

> As the blood of all nations is mingling with our own, so will their thoughts and feelings finally mingle in our literature. We shall draw from the Germans, tenderness; from the Spanish, passion; from the French, vivacity, to mingle more and more with our English solid sense.

In addition to the major works of the forties, shorter poems appeared in *The Belfry of Bruges* (1845), including the sonnet "Mezzo Camin":

> Half my life is gone, and I have let
>   The years slip from me. . . .
>   And hear above me on the autumnal blast
>   The cataract of Death far thundering from the heights.

In 1854 he resigned his professorship but continued to live in Cambridge, writing *Hiawatha* (1855), a reworking of American Indian legends in the verse pattern of the *Kalevala*, and *The Courtship of Miles Standish* (1858), in the same pattern as *Evangeline* but with the action and clash of contrasting characters better distributed throughout.

During the year 1861 (with the outbreak of the Civil War, in which his son was wounded) the poet lost his second wife in a tragic accident, a fire in his home. Needless to say, this experience left him scarred — physically in a way that was hidden by the full white beard which he thereafter wore, and emotionally as evidenced by the fact that he could bring himself to confront the experience directly in his writing only many years later, toward the end of his own life, in the fine sonnet "The Cross of Snow."

His *Tales of a Wayside Inn*, in imitation of the *Canter-*

bury Tales, began to appear in 1863, and his translation of the
Divine Comedy appeared in 1867. The work that he himself
regarded most highly is his verse drama *Christus: A Mystery*,
begun in the 1840's but ultimately brought out, complete, in
1872. Here Longfellow undertook to deal with various aspects of Christianity in Biblical, medieval, and modern times.
In fact, his translation of the *Divine Comedy* may have been
in part undertaken as preparation for it. *Christus* — like the
Divine Comedy — consists of three large sections: *I. The Divine Tragedy*, largely based on the four Gospels and concluding with the Apostles' Creed, symbolizing hope; *II. The
Golden Legend*, largely based on Hartmann von Aue's
twelfth-century romance *Der arme Heinrich*, about a prince
whose illness can be cured only by the willing blood sacrifice
of a virgin, symbolizing faith; and *III. New England Trage-
dies*, based on Cotton Mather's *Magnalia* and other Puritan
records, about Quaker and Salem witchcraft persecution, symbolizing love.

In his later years Longfellow was deeply venerated. When
he got on the horsecar in Cambridge, everyone rose as one
man in respect. His seventy-fifth birthday was celebrated in
every schoolhouse in the United States. Hundreds of editions
of his works had been issued or were soon to be issued
in America and Europe. Just ten days before he died, he wrote
the final lines of his last poem, *The Bells of San Blas*:

> Out of the shadows of night
> The world rolls into light;
> It is daybreak everywhere.

Longfellow's work has had a surprisingly wide and deep
effect. Phrases from his poems are part of the American ver-
nacular — "the spreading chestnut tree," "the forest primeval,"
"speak for yourself, John." In England he was, and still is, regarded highly: given honorary degrees by both Oxford and
Cambridge, he is the only non-British poet to be buried in the
Poets' Corner of Westminster Abbey; and the cover illus-
tration on the *Penguin Literature of the United States* (1954) is

the bust of Longfellow. In Scandinavia, in Spain, in Latin America, he was and is widely read. Baudelaire acknowledged having borrowed from him twice in *Les Fleurs du Mal* and that "Le Calumet de Paix" was derived from him. Bunin translated *Hiawatha*. Even today in Russia the three nineteenth-century American "greats" are Cooper, Longfellow, and Twain. Red China brought out Longfellow's poems in 1957. Like Poe, Emerson, and Thoreau he achieved a place in world literature — or, as he called it, "universality" — though on a somewhat more consciously traditional basis.

Another Harvard professor of literary renown was Oliver Wendell Holmes (1809-1894), born in Cambridge, educated at Harvard and in Paris, and eventually to become professor of anatomy at Harvard Medical School (1847-1882). Among his best-known poems are *Old Ironsides*, against a proposal to scrap the frigate *Constitution*; *The Deacon's Masterpiece, or the Wonderful One-Hoss Shay*, about a buggy so perfect in all its parts that when it wore out it collapsed all at once (usually taken to be a satire on Calvinism in New England); and *The Chambered Nautilus*, with its last stanza beginning "Build thee more stately mansions, O my soul." Among his prose writings there are three volumes of amusing imaginary boarding-house conversations, the first, *The Autocrat of the Breakfast-Table*, for the most part written for the initial issues of his colleague Lowell's *Atlantic Monthly* in 1857. In addition to prose writing in the technical field of his profession, Holmes also wrote three volumes of what he called "medicated fiction": *Elsie Venner* (1860), about a snake girl; *The Guardian Angel* (1867); and *A Mortal Antipathy* (1885). In each, many matters are touched on that were later to be dealt with by Freud and others; but the underlying question raised in the fictional situation presented is this: if a person is born physically abnormal, how can he be considered as exercising free will?

A third Harvard professor was James Russell Lowell (1819-1891), also born in Cambridge and educated at Harvard. In 1848 he brought out three volumes, principally in verse: the witty *Fable for Critics*, which extensively formulated the public image of many of the writers of his day; the medievalistic *Vision of Sir Launfal,* about a knight who planned to go in search of the Holy Grail but, as the result of a dream, decided to stay in his castle and devote himself to good works; and the first series of *Biglow Papers,* a set of poetic essays in New England dialect against the Mexican War (later, during the Civil War, Lowell issued a second series).

Shortly after mid-century, however, Lowell experienced a number of family tribulations; and as he found his way back to writing, he pursued reflective and scholarly aims. Of course, on occasion he still wrote poems, the greatest of which was his *Ode Recited at the Harvard Commemoration* (1865), in memory of some hundred student casualties in the Civil War. In 1855 he had succeeded Longfellow as professor of French and Spanish at Harvard, and continued actively teaching for over twenty years. He was editor of the *Atlantic Monthly* when it was founded in 1857, and — a little later — was an editor of the *North American Review.*

In 1877 he was appointed minister to Spain, and in 1880 to England. Many of the speeches delivered during his ambassadorship are superb — for example, the one on "Democracy" given at Birmingham in 1884, ending: "Our healing is not in the storm or in the whirlwind, it is not in monarchies, or aristocracies, or democracies, but will be revealed by the still small voice that speaks to the conscience and the heart, prompting us to a wider and wiser humanity." Stylistically, Lowell expressed himself with great elegance and distinction. In defending the study of classical languages in college, for example, he wrote: "Oblivion looks in the face of the Grecian Muse only to forget her errand." His essays on literary subjects give him a place alongside the leading critics of the late nineteenth century, as well as among the masters of English prose. Lectures and periodical articles, reworked as essays, were brought together in such volumes as *Among My Books* (first series, 1870; second series, 1876) and *My Study Windows* (1871). These and other of his activities brought him international recognition — degrees, presidency of the Modern Language Association, suggestions that he undertake positions of academic honor abroad. The last years of his life, however, were spent in the family home in Cambridge.

Other Harvardians of what Holmes called "Brahmin" stock were the lawyer Richard Henry Dana, Jr., best known for his *Two Years Before the Mast* (1840), and Charles Eliot Norton, professor of the history of art at Harvard (whom Ruskin referred to as "my first tutor"). Particularly in later life these former Harvard students met once a month at the Parker House in Boston as the Saturday Club and began to take on some of the airs of the old Hartford Wits of the century before.

A New England writer peripheral to the Boston group, having been born (of Quaker background) at Haverhill, Massachusetts, and becoming a laborer, teacher, and journalist in Boston, Hartford, and Philadelphia, was John Greenleaf Whittier (1807-1892). As early as 1831 he published a volume of poems on incidents from Colonial days, *Legends of New England*. Soon, however, he had been caught up in the abolition movement and — as a member of the Massachusetts Legislature and the editor (1847-1860) of an influential magazine, the *National Era* — was very active in the cause of freeing the slaves. Some of his verse is occasional and propagandistic: *Massachusetts to Virginia* (1843) protests against the return of fugitive slaves to the South, and *Ichabod* refers to Webster after his *Compromise* speech of 1850 as if he were already dead. Other poems of Whittier's were set to music and are sung in church: the current Episcopal hymnal includes seven of his texts, notably *Dear Lord and Father of Mankind*. After the Civil War he retired to Amesbury, Massachusetts, writing poetry that recalled an earlier America, notably *Snow-Bound* (1865) and *The Pennsylvania Pilgrim* (1872). To the end of his rather long bachelor life, Whittier maintained Quaker customs; and his late verse is marked by great serenity. Though there is much in his work of both historical and literary inter-

est, his importance — like Bryant's — is today generally regarded as more local and national than international.

Harriet Beecher Stowe (1811-1896), however, elicited
international as well as national response with her *Uncle Tom's
Cabin* and demonstrated that there was still some vitality in
the old Puritan tradition. Born at Litchfield, Connecticut, she
was the daughter of the vigorous minister Lyman Beecher and
the sister of four nationally known clergymen. In 1832 her father went to Cincinnati to establish Lane Seminary. There she
married a teacher, Calvin E. Stowe (himself a figure of some
importance in the history of American education). Though
they had half a dozen children, she managed to write some
stories for religious magazines. A collection of her sketches,
dealing with descendants of the *Mayflower* Pilgrims, was published in 1843. After she and her husband had returned to New
England (he to teach at Bowdoin), she wrote the novel for
which she became famous, *Uncle Tom's Cabin* (1852), as
well as another antislavery novel, *Dred* (1856). Later in her
career she returned to writing work evocative of the American
past (*The Minister's Wooing*, 1859; *The Pearl of Orr's Island*,
1862; *Oldtown Folks*, 1869), which contributed substantially
to the development of post-Civil War local-color writing.

Unless Mrs. Stowe had written *Uncle Tom's Cabin*, Sumner said, Lincoln would not have been elected; and Lincoln
himself told her that she had "made the book that made this
great war." But actually what it "made" was a particular view
or interpretation of one cause of the Civil War. Perhaps more
than any other one thing, *Uncle Tom's Cabin* brought to a
focus much that had been rather diffused, somewhat as had
Paine's *Common Sense* three-quarters of a century before —
appealing, however, not so much to common sense as common
sensibility. Today many people still think that the Civil War
was fought to free the slaves. But, as Lincoln wrote to Greeley
in 1862,

> My paramount object in this struggle is to save the
> Union, and is not either to save or destroy slavery. If

I could save the Union without freeing any slaves, I would do it; and if I could save it by freeing all the slaves, I would do it; and if I could save it by freeing some and leaving others alone, I would also do that. What I do about slavery, and the colored race, I do because I believe it helps to save the Union; and what I forbear, I forbear because I do not believe it would help to save the Union.

Viewed objectively, the Civil War in the United States was a war to establish a unitary national state — the same development (but with some features reversed) that was taking place in Germany and Japan. By mid-nineteenth century a great power simply could no longer operate as an assembly of sovereign states with the paramount authority left indefinite. In the "United States," the difficulty led to a conflict between the forces represented by the first half and the last half of its name. But what emphasized the Negro and human rights aspect was such imaginative writing as *Uncle Tom's Cabin.*

There are, however, larger dimensions to this novel. Today in Germany one still sees it on display in bookstores; and West Berliners still call one of their streets *Onkel Toms Hütte,* despite all their renaming of streets to honor the hero of the hour. Tolstoi, in *What Is Art?* (1898), declared that *Uncle Tom's Cabin,* with its contribution to a better relationship among men, was what literature *should* be — instead of most of what had come to be admired in his own day. How this book was read in Russia of the 1850's can be sensed from Baron Wrangel's reminiscence of hearing, as a boy of ten with his sisters, *Uncle Tom's Cabin*:

> My sisters could not get over the horrors of slavery and wept at the sad fate of poor Uncle Tom.
> "I cannot conceive," said one of them, "how such atrocities can be tolerated. Slavery is horrible."
> "But," said Bunny, in her shrill little voice, "we have slaves too."

In Britain the novel was soon issued by over forty different publishers in more than a million and a half copies; and it became a document in the struggle of English labor for the Reform Act of 1867. Three Paris newspapers ran French translations of it at the same time. Versions have been published in at least thirty-seven languages — including three in Welsh (Uncle Tom apparently helping to focus the feelings of the coal miners).

The response was not just from the oppressed. George Sand, Alfred de Musset, Heine, Turgenev, Macaulay took the book quite seriously. Somewhat Dickensian, it also has scenes of Cooper-like amplitude. Moreover, it appealed to many kinds of people, on many different levels, being widely played on the stage and furnishing motifs for popular songs, business enterprises, and even knickknacks — much as *Werther* had done three-quarters of a century before. *Uncle Tom's Cabin* came out of a period when human rights for all men were being reenvisioned and proclaimed by a scion of American Puritanism, working in a mode — fiction — which one would not perhaps have expected from the tradition in which her mind had been formed.

All over the United States at this time there was much literary activity. In New England "Boston historians" such as Prescott, Motley, and Parkman were working in a twilight zone between literature and history opened up by Irving. New York attracted many New Englanders. When Brook Farm disbanded, the "archon" went to work on the New York *Tribune*, as did also one of the members, George William Curtis, who during the early 1850's wrote some books on his travels in the Near East, and eventually settled down in the "Easy Chair" of *Harper's Magazine* (founded in New York in 1850). Richard Henry Stoddard and Thomas Bailey Aldrich gravitated to New York, where a multiplicity of literary groupings and levels prevailed, without the Harvardian orientation of intellectual Boston. More characteristic of New York than it would have been of Boston is the fact that the two major writers to emerge there at mid-century — Melville and Whitman — never attended college and never met each other.

In Philadelphia, which had been the leading city in Franklin's day, many of the older magazines were still being edited and published. As in Boston, a great deal of learned work was being done — Allibone's *Dictionary of . . . American Authors*, Furness' Variorum Shakespeare, Lea's *History of the Inquisition*. Bayard Taylor, indefatigable world traveler, lecturer, and versifier, known today mainly for his translation of *Faust*, went with Perry on the expedition that "opened up" Japan in 1853 and wrote about the events — after Hawthorne in Liverpool had been urged to come along but, unfortunately, had declined the invitation. Taylor's friend George Henry Boker wrote eleven verse plays, notably one that was pirated and produced for a hundred nights in London, *Calaynos* (1851), and another that is a highly romantic poetic drama, *Francesca da Rimini* (1855). Charles Godfrey Leland did a good deal of translating, wrote *Hans Breitmann's Ballads* in mixed German-English, and published a number of books on the gypsies. By the last quarter of the century Stoddard, Taylor, Boker, Aldrich, and Stedman — all close friends and all committed to defending what they considered idealism against the inroads of realism — had come to exercise a conservative role in American letters, like that of the Saturday Club and the Hartford Wits.

In the North, by this time, free Negroes were writing and publishing pamphlets, autobiographical accounts of escape from slavery, documents issued in connection with the activities of Negro churches and fraternal orders, and songs for abolition meetings. There were Negro magazines and newspapers, the first of which, *Rights for All*, had been started in 1827 by two Negroes — Samuel Cornish, a Presbyterian minister, and John B. Russwurm, a graduate of Bowdoin College. Outstanding early works by Negroes in this pre-Civil War period are Frederick Douglass' autobiography (1845) and William Wells Brown's novel *Clotel* (1853).

In the South the literary situation was more scattered and diversified. One center was Charleston, with *Russell's Magazine* (1857-1860), edited by the poet Paul Hamilton Hayne

and his friend Henry Timrod, whose *Cotton Boll* describes a
scene in which

> The endless field is white;
> And the whole landscape glows,
> For many a shining league away,
> With such accumulated light
> As Polar lands would flash beneath a tropic day!

Other writers elsewhere in the South wrote historical romances
in the tradition of Scott and Cooper. Of the thirty-one books
written by John Esten Cooke, outstanding are *The Virginia
Comedians* (1854), about prerevolutionary Williamsburg, and
Surry of Eagle's Nest (1866), about the Civil War. His older
brother Philip Pendleton Cooke also wrote prose romances and
poetry.

Still other Southerners were exploring new and heady ideas
— such as the application of Darwinian concepts to political
theory and the possibility of expansion into lands to their south
and west and gaining access to the Pacific. Others were writing in German and French: Karl Anton Postl ("Charles Seals-
field"), who landed in New Orleans as a German immigrant
in 1823 and wrote many works of fiction, some of which
influenced Longfellow and Simms and are widely read in Germany today, particularly *Das Cajütenbuch* (1841); Friedrich
Gerstäcker, who wrote some 150 volumes in German, notably
Nach Amerika! (1855); a group of free Negroes in New Orleans
who collaborated on *L'Album Littéraire* (1843); and François-
Dominique Rouquette, a Louisiana Creole educated in Paris
but living long among the Indians, *Fleurs d'Amérique* (1857).
Another strand in the variegated literary fabric of the pre-
Civil War South was that of humor, random pieces often ap-
pearing first in newspapers and later being republished in book
form: Augustus B. Longstreet's *Georgia Sketches* (1835),
William T. Thompson's *Major Jones's Courtship* (1843), and
Joseph G. Baldwin's *Flush Times of Alabama and Mississippi*
(1853).

In the Middle and Far West, the vogue of humor spread rapidly, often supplied by newspapermen who had originally come from the eastern seaboard, such as Charles Farrar Browne, city editor of the Cleveland *Plain Dealer*, with his "Artemus Ward" sketches (popular in England as well as the United States), and David Ross Locke, editor of the Toledo *Blade*, with his "Petroleum V. Nasby" letters (particularly appreciated by Lincoln). In the period after the Civil War, this kind of writing was to be brought to the peak of its perfection by Mark Twain.

In considering the two major New York authors Melville and Whitman, one must realize that their active careers extended well beyond the Civil War: both were born in 1819, embarked around mid-century on the work for which they are most widely acclaimed today, and died in the early 1890's. Melville gave epic scope to fiction in *Moby Dick*, and Whitman to poetry in *Leaves of Grass*: what usually had been confined to relatively closed forms they opened out to the full. But there is a difference between the sense in which these two achievements figure in world literature. The interest in Melville is largely a twentieth-century phenomenon: the first full-length biography and collected edition of his works did not appear till the 1920's and serious study, criticism, or translation till the 1930's. The interest in Whitman, however, has been continuous since *Leaves of Grass* in its first version appeared. In this respect, the difference is like that between the verse of Edward Taylor and that of Anne Bradstreet, or like that between Egyptian and Hebrew literature. Also the implications of Melville's writing relate more obviously to that of Poe and Hawthorne, Whitman's to that of Emerson and Thoreau.

Herman Melville (1819-1891) was born in New York City into a patrician family which experienced financial reverses about the time he was coming into his teens. As a result, he worked at various jobs — clerking, farming, teaching — in and near Albany and Pittsfield. At twenty he shipped on a packet boat for Liverpool and at twenty-two on a whaler for the South Seas. After a year and a half on board, he and a fellow sailor jumped ship in the Marquesas and lived for about a month among the reputedly cannibal islanders. From there he managed to get to Tahiti on a mutiny-ridden Australian whaler, and eventually to Honolulu, where he signed on as a common seaman with the frigate *United States,* which arrived in Boston in 1844.

He began to write his books on the basis of experiences during these four years spent mostly in the Pacific. His first volume was brought out in England as the *Narrative of a Four Months' Residence Among the Natives of a Valley of the Marquesas Islands* and in the United States as *Typee: a Peep at Polynesian Life* (1846) — a fairly straight account of adventure in a region where, as he said, "I have no doubt that we were the first white men who ever penetrated thus far back into their territories." Thus a mid-nineteenth-century Captain John Smith issued something between a report and a picaresque. These features were maintained in Melville's succeeding volume *Omoo* (1847), which took the account on to Tahiti. Minor differences between Smith's and Melville's accounts arise from Smith's advocacy of colonization and conversion of the natives, as against Melville's opinion that the Europeans, particularly the missionaries, had corrupted them.

In 1847, Melville married Elizabeth Shaw, daughter of the chief justice of Massachusetts. His manner of writing became more allegorical. In *Mardi* (1849) the narrator and his companion desert a whaler to explore a chain of Pacific islands and encounter a group of natives bent on sacrificing a lovely white girl Yillah (absolute truth). She disappears; and he — accompanied by his friends (King Media, mind; Mohi, history; Babbalanja, philosophy; and Yoomy, poetry) — is pursued by three murderous sons of the priest; he searches for her all over the South Pacific (the islands standing for various countries of the world — Dominora for England, Vivenza for the United States, etc.). Ultimately the friends retire to a Christian "snug harbor" on the island of Serenia; but the narrator — Taji, or the human soul — continues his search beyond the termination of his earthly life. Some allegorical elements also appear in *Redburn* (1849), based on Melville's first service at sea and tracing a young idealist's disillusionment, and in *White-Jacket* (1850), based on his return from Honolulu to Boston in an American warship, here called the *Neversink*, ". . . a fast-sailing, never-sinking, world-frigate, of which God was the shipwright; and she is but one craft in a Milky-Way fleet, of which God is the Lord High Admiral."

In 1850 Melville moved with his growing family from New York City to a farm near Pittsfield, not far from the Hawthornes at Lenox, Massachusetts. The two men were then at the peak of their achievement as writers, Hawthorne being fifteen years the elder: *The Scarlet Letter* and *White-Jacket*, 1850; *The House of the Seven Gables* and *Moby Dick* (dedicated to Hawthorne), 1851; and *The Blithedale Romance* and *Pierre*, 1852.

The work in which Melville boldly forged ahead from writing allegorically tinged reports to fashioning a prose work of truly epic character is *Moby Dick*. Much that had gone before found here its fulfillment. Cooper in his novels of the sea had foundered on the rocks of symbolism. In Poe's novel the ship bearing the hero had headed for the South Pole when something big and white loomed up, but the publisher declined to bring out any more of the story. The New Englanders had concentrated on perfection of detail, on a scale adequate for the Atlantic community but not for the Pacific — or the whole — world. Behind Melville, without his realizing it, was the urge to make contact with the Great Khan.

About *Moby Dick* there is a kind of inscrutability and universality in the possible interpretation of the symbols that is comparable to that of the most powerful writing of both West and East — Shakespearean, Homeric, Biblical, Far Eastern. What is symbolized by this White Whale, which has so aroused Captain Ahab that he assembled a crew from the four corners of the earth, infected them with his monomania, and led them to their destruction — all save the narrator, who tells the reader to call him Ishmael? What is it that Melville is here implying? The formulation of all the possible interpretations — such as

the self-destructive nature of personal vengeance, the exces-
sive demands of Puritanism, the dangers of perfectionism —
would be endless. Ahab — like Taji and like many of Hawthorne's characters — simply will not accept human limitations,
and pays the penalty. There is about Ahab a fearful fasci-
nation. But the point is that any interpretation necessarily
presents a partial view of anything, which is not itself really
an interpretation of something else, but the thing itself. What
this book *is*, in itself, is a work of literature, of great density
and palpability. It has about it at once a tangible solidity and
vast openness that mark it as one of the great works of art in
the history of man. It is to the sea as a Sung landscape is to the
land.

The next book that Melville wrote, *Pierre* (1852), might
be compared with Hawthorne's *Blithedale Romance* — both
books set in the immediate surroundings, each with a would-
be writer as an important character, who for a time comes in
contact with a reform enterprise (Brook Farm and its offspring
in New York City), each book sharply critical of what was pass-
ing for idealism and insistent upon the interpenetration and
ambiguity of good and evil. Hawthorne, however, with his
normally pearly gray and often iridescent style, manages to
carry off gracefully some things that Melville, with his rougher
approach, almost seems to be burlesquing: the difference between them is like that between Irving and Cooper, or between Emerson and Thoreau. At the beginning of *Pierre*, the
title character, only son of a wealthy widow and engaged to a
lovely and faithful girl, encounters another girl who claims
to be his illegitimate half-sister. In what at first seems to him
a noble gesture, he abandons the former, is disinherited, and
goes off to New York with the latter. But soon he has both
women living with him under one roof, and his attempt to
support them by writing is unsuccessful. Gradually he comes
to realize that perhaps his half-sister is not what she claims to
be, and that his motives in making the noble gesture may have
been — unknown to him at the time — mixed. Morally, psychologically, and artistically the work — as Arnold Bennett

declared in 1928 — "essays feats which the most advanced
novelists of today imagine to be quite new."

More successful is the Melville novelette *Benito Cereno*,
included in *The Piazza Tales* (1856). Less so are *Israel Potter*
(1855) and *The Confidence Man* (1857), increasingly disillusioned, increasingly nihilistic. Except for verse, Melville did
not publish much after 1857. A number of external reasons
contributed: in 1857 his publishers were hard hit in the first
of the severe international depressions that emanated from the
United States; in 1857, also, Melville went on what would have
been called in medieval times a pilgrimage to the Holy Land
(on the basis of which he wrote a long poem *Clarel*, 1876).
After all this — and the Civil War too (the subject of some of
his best short poems in *Battle-Pieces*, 1866) — he was never
quite the same again. In 1863 he brought his family back to
New York City and worked as a customs inspector till 1885.
During the last half of his life he can hardly be considered as
having been maladjusted, and there is nothing particularly
mysterious in a war's quieting a man down.

Like Hawthorne, Melville left at his death much writing
in various states of completion. Quite late he had written a
short novel, *Billy Budd*, which was published in 1924 and
has subsequently been widely read, as well as seen and heard
in dramatic and operatic versions. Based upon a historical situation around 1797 when — as an aftermath of the French Revolution — the British Navy was edgy about possible mutiny, the
action deals with a "handsome sailor" who has been unjustly
accused and, through a chain of circumstances, is condemned
to be executed. The captain is aware of Billy's innocence, but
believes that — all things considered — the letter of the law
must take its course. Billy is hanged, but his last words are a
blessing upon the captain. In the dawning light, Billy's soul is
thought by some to have ascended to heaven, an echo of the
event is preserved in the sailors' songs, and the official account
is oddly involuted in its expression (seeming to support the
captain, but allowing also of an opposite interpretation). Like
Cooper, Melville in his later years formulated in the not spe-

cifically religious mode of fiction whatever insights into life
he had gained.

The vogue for *Billy Budd* is part of the post-World War
I Melville revival. Throughout the nineteenth century Melville had had a limited following, more intense in Europe than
in the United States: Stevenson first learned of the South Seas
from *Omoo*, and various individual British writers felt a relationship between Melville's and Whitman's work. The first
collected edition of Melville's works — in sixteen volumes
— came out in England in 1922-1924. As with any author suddenly revived, however, there is always the danger of his being
invested by his revivers with qualities which they are seeking
rather than those which are necessarily there — in this instance, a kind of metaphysical sophistication which actually is
less impressive than are his sheer literary qualities of action,
drama, characterization, and verve. Though he may come to be
regarded as the author of but a single book of lasting literary
value, that one book obviously belongs not alone to American
but to world literature.

Whitman was also the author of one supreme work,
Leaves of Grass; but it was the work of a lifetime: the first edition appeared in 1855 and the tenth in 1892, the year of his
death. Continually revised and expanded, it was the literary
precipitate of a whole life, as were the *Divine Comedy* and
Faust. Like many earlier writers, Whitman did not feel any
great challenge in the possibility of writing in parvenu fictional
forms, of enlarging — as Melville in his early career had done
— their artistic and symbolic potential. Whitman concentrated
on that more elemental type of literature, poetry — the
medium used by most of the great writers of the world. Interestingly enough, both he and Melville transferred their main
efforts from prose to poetry at about the same time. Though
there is, of course, no evidence of direct influence, the general
purpose behind the shift may have been similar. Working the
rest of his life largely in poetry with the singleness of purpose
of a Thoreau or a Hawthorne, Whitman invested it with a freedom that permitted of as natural a movement to and from it as

there had long been between spoken and written prose — a
freedom that had existed in the seventeenth century and that
he reinstated in what has come to be called "free verse." He
wrote with an integrity and amplitude that made his work a
realization — as Thoreau's had also been — of the possibility
noted by the Countess d'Agoult that out of Emerson's reconciliation of individualism and pantheism there might be born
"an original art."

Born in a part of Long Island that has since become suburban to New York City, Walt Whitman (1819-1892) was one
of a large family, which was neither socially nor intellectually prepossessing — his father a farmer and carpenter, his
mother with certain Dutch and Quaker elements in her background. When Walt was five, the family moved for a while to
Brooklyn, where he attended elementary school but quit at
the age of ten. Rather early — like Franklin, like Twain — he
began to work in printing offices and became a typesetter,
reporter, and editor. Meanwhile he had on occasion taught
school and worked at his father's trade. By the 1840's he was
editing newspapers — notably the Brooklyn *Daily Eagle* —
and contributing to New York periodicals.

During his thirties he published mainly prose — editorials
advocating the territorial expansion of the United States into
Latin America (but opposed to the spread of slavery into new
territory) and favoring free trade and immigration. A novel of
his, *Franklin Evans* (1842), advocated temperance.

Early in 1848, with one of his brothers, he went to New
Orleans and worked for a few months on a newspaper there,
the *Crescent*. In it he brought out one of his early pieces of
newspaper verse, "Sailing the Mississippi at Midnight." This
New Orleans visit has intrigued many admirers of Whitman
because many years later he informed the British critic J. A.
Symonds, who had written asking him about his sex life:
"Though unmarried I have had six children — two are dead
— one living Southern grandchild fine boy, writes to me occasionally. . . ." No evidence has been discovered that this
statement was anything but what Huck Finn was later to call "a

stretcher." By June of 1848 he was back in Brooklyn, editing the *Freeman*, running a printing office and bookstore, making speeches, carpentering.

One of his poems published in a New York newspaper,
"Blood-Money," is obviously based on Matthew 26-27:

Of the olden time, when it came to pass
That the beautiful god, Jesus, should finish his work on earth
Then went Judas, and sold the divine youth,
And took pay for his body. . . .

It is usually taken to refer also to Webster's "Compromise"
speech (as too does Whittier's *Ichabod*). Though Whitman —
like Melville — was not a strong adherent of institutionalized
religion, he was concerned with religion on a personal and inward basis, as his Quaker ancestors had also been. A special aspect of "Blood-Money" is its relaxation of emphasis on rhyme
and meter. After all, much of the really great poetry of the
world is without rhyme or meter — the Bible, for instance, or
the works of Homer as Whitman knew them in prose translation. Thus he came to write what has since been called "free
verse," and pioneered in exploiting it to the full. His verse,
different as it is from Longfellow's, yet has some features in
common with it, notably a departure from prevailing traditions
and the restoration of certain more remote ones which had
apparently lapsed for centuries.

Of course, Whitman wrote not only free but also rhymed
and metered verse. At the very heart of *Leaves of Grass*, for
instance, the section devoted to *Memories of President Lincoln*
includes both the rhymed "O Captain! My Captain!" and
"When Lilacs Last in the Dooryard Bloom'd" in free verse. At
all periods in his career he used, on occasion, rhyme, meter, and
tropes. He also wrote a vast amount of prose, some of which
he ultimately turned into verse. The first edition of *Leaves of
Grass* (1855) has a prose preface, much of which became a
poem entitled "Poem of Many in One" in the second edition
and "By Blue Ontario's Shore" in later editions — part of it, as
a matter of fact, in rhyme.

This original prose preface is interesting in both form
and content. Every so often using three dots to indicate either
potential line divisions or pauses, he begins with a rather strong
statement of the way he thinks America looks upon the past:

> America does not repel the past or what it has pro-
> duced under its forms or amid other politics or the idea
> of castes or the old religions. . . . accepts the lesson
> with calmness . . . is not so impatient as has been sup-
> posed that the slough still sticks to opinions and manners
> and literature while the life which served its require-
> ments has passed into the new life of the new forms . . .
> perceives that the corpse is slowly borne from the eating
> and sleeping rooms of the house . . . perceives that it
> waits a little while in the door . . . that it was fittest
> for its days . . . that its action has descended to the
> stalwart and wellshaped heir who approaches . . . and
> that he shall be fittest for his days.

No doubt Whitman in time came to recognize that this 1855
preface was a little extreme — the idea, for instance, that the
President's taking his hat off to the people and not they to him
was "unrhymed poetry," or,

> As if it were necessary to trot back generation after
> generation to the eastern records! As if the beauty and
> sacredness of the demonstrable must fall behind that of
> the mythical! As if men do not make their mark out of
> any times! As if the opening of the western continent by
> discovery and what has transpired since in North and
> South America were less than the small theatre of the
> antique or the aimless sleepwalking of the middle ages!

His poems on Lincoln's assassination, his "Passage to India,"
and his own deeper involvement in celebrating the myths of
democracy and science (brought together within that of religion) were to show him that much of the 1855 preface had
only the sensational value of a headline and — when its purposes had been served — needed to be put to other uses or
thrown away, like an old newspaper.

Throughout his career there was much of the journalist

in Whitman — each day rather a thing in itself, and each edition to be approached afresh once the previous one had been issued. The best in *Leaves of Grass* is fundamentally topical, inspired by events of the day — "Come Up from the Fields Father," "Crossing Brooklyn Ferry," and many others. Viewed perhaps from a longer-range perspective, his contribution to the permanent literature of mankind may well prove to have been a distillation of journalism into poetry — somewhat as, say, Shakespeare's was of the merely theatrical. Now in the late twentieth century, when the newspaper has begun to yield the center of the stage to other mass media, Whitman's role in world literature may be a little easier to visualize than it once was.

In the 1855 preface Whitman quite clearly says how he then expected *Leaves of Grass* to be of use to his reader:

> This is what you shall do: Love the earth and sun and the animals, despise riches, give alms to every one that asks, stand up for the stupid and crazy, devote your income and labor to others, hate tyrants, argue not concerning God, have patience and indulgence toward the people, take off your hat to nothing known or unknown or to any man or number of men, go freely with powerful uneducated persons and with the young and with the mothers of families, read these leaves in the open air every season of every year of your life, re-examine all you have been told at school or church or in any book, dismiss whatever insults your own soul, and your very flesh shall be a great poem and have the richest fluency not only in its words but in the silent lines of its lips and face and between the lashes of your eyes and in every motion and joint of your body. . . . .

When he says that you should read the book throughout the year, perhaps he thought of it as a sort of almanac — like his earlier fellow printer's in Philadelphia — and he then develops a prophetic expansiveness like Brackenridge's in telling you what will happen if you read on. A little farther along in the same preface Whitman says:

Without effort and without exposing in the least how it is done the greatest poet brings the spirit of any or all events and passions and scenes and persons some more and some less to bear on your individual character as you hear or read.

The main part of the first edition of *Leaves of Grass* is a long poem subsequently divided into fifty-two sections (one for each week in the year?), without title in the first edition but in the second called "Poem of Walt Whitman, an American" and in later editions "Song of Myself." It begins:

I celebrate myself, and sing myself,
And what I assume you shall assume,
For every atom belonging to me as good belongs to you.

The use here of "good" instead of "well" is rather poetic license — a slight departure from normal prose usage (as often occurs in Longfellow). It might be taken as part of an incipient effort to reestablish a kind of poetic diction — though, of course, not on a Graeco-Roman basis. Ostensibly quite personal, "Song of Myself" follows rather freely a sequence from the here-and-now to more ultimate matters of life, death, eternity, God — whom the poet addresses without undue ceremony:

Listener up there! what have you to confide to me?
Look in my face while I snuff the sidle of evening,
(Talk honestly, no one else hears you, and I stay only a minute
    longer.)

Do I contradict myself?
Very well then I contradict myself,
(I am large, I contain multitudes.)
I concentrate toward them that are nigh, I wait on the door-
    slab.

Whitman's use of parentheses here establishes a second level of statement, like the aside in Shakespeare.

In the ensuing and concluding section of "Song of Myself," Whitman alludes to death: at sunset one's shadow lengthens and merges with all the earth's shadows; if you want to find him, look for him under the leaves of grass:

The spotted hawk swoops by and accuses me, he complains of
    my gab and my loitering.

I too am not a bit tamed, I too am untranslatable,
I sound my barbaric yawp over the roofs of the world.

The last scud of day holds back for me,
It flings my likeness after the rest and true as any on the
    shadow'd wilds,
It coaxes me to the vapor and the dusk.

I depart as air, I shake my white locks at the runaway sun,
I effuse my flesh in eddies, and drift it in lacy jags.

I bequeath myself to the dirt to grow from the grass I love,
If you want me again look for me under your boot-soles.

You will hardly know who I am or what I mean,
But I shall be good health to you nevertheless,
And filter and fibre your blood.

Failing to fetch me at first keep encouraged,
Missing me one place search another,
I stop somewhere waiting for you.

This is magnificent "modern" poetry. But is it to be taken all too solemnly — this "I" popping up under the soles of our shoes? There is a freshness to Whitman in the original *Leaves of Grass* which is likely to be forgotten by those who have experienced the full impact of some of his later writings or the encomia of some of his devotees.

Having sold only a few copies of his book (some of the type for which he had set up himself), he received from Emerson a heartening acknowledgment of a complimentary copy — "the most extraordinary piece of wit and wisdom that America has yet contributed," wrote Emerson, who greeted him "at the beginning of a great career." Whitman promptly got out a second edition, with *I Greet You at the Beginning of A Great*

Career. R. W. Emerson printed on the backstrip and the full text of Emerson's letter inside, together with a reply beginning:

> Here are thirty-two Poems, which I send you, dear Friend and Master, not having found how I could satisfy myself with sending any usual acknowledgement of your letter. The first edition, on which you mailed me that till now unanswered letter, was twelve poems — I printed a thousand copies, and they readily sold; these thirty-two Poems I stereotype, to print several thousand copies of. . . .

Here, obviously, Whitman is again embarking on one of his "stretchers." What probably disturbed Emerson more, however, was the emphasis on sex in some of the new poems. When in 1860 Whitman was on the point of bringing out a third edition, this time with a commercial Boston publisher, he and Emerson had a long talk on the Common, Emerson urging him to exercise a little restraint. Whitman's stubborn refusal to do so caused him trouble later on — getting fired from his job, having his book banned in Boston, among other things — and diverted the attention of many readers from more important aspects of his work, as well as attracting to him some odd characters, including a widow in England who wanted to marry him. In England, however, the problem of the upsetting poems was quietly solved when William M. Rossetti edited a volume of Whitman's verse there in 1868 and simply left out the poems he considered in poor taste.

The great and sobering experience for Whitman was the Civil War. He did not himself serve as a combatant; but when he heard that his brother George had been wounded near Fredericksburg, he set out in search of him. For the most part in Washington, he served as a male nurse in Army hospitals. His later prose volume *Specimen Days* gives an unforgettable account of these experiences.

The assassination of Lincoln was the occasion of "When Lilacs Last in the Dooryard Bloom'd." Interestingly enough, however, Lincoln is not mentioned in it by name: like the

Eroica Symphony, it is a work to extol the memory of *a hero*. This poem represents a high point in the writing of the elegy in modern times. Entirely free from the admixture of sectarian and personal polemics that mar *Lycidas* and *Adonais*, it has an underlying symbolic structure that is perfectly firm and amazingly integrated, as

> Lilac and star and bird twined with the chant of my soul,
> There in the fragrant pines and the cedars dusk and dim.

It worthily formulates a feeling that all — including Americans in general and the poet in particular — have on the death of a great leader.

Another of the poems that became central to *Leaves of Grass* in its later form is "Passage to India" (1871), commemorating three engineering feats of the 1860's: the Atlantic Cable, the Suez Canal, and the Union Pacific Railroad — viewed, however, not just as material facts. As from the West Coast one faced lands where the human race had its cultural and religious beginnings, now a divine plan dimly sensed by Columbus was coming to fulfillment, as the earth was being spanned and a nation with the vigor of the West and the wisdom of the East was being spiritually completed by the poet whose soul should have passage to "more than India":

> Sail forth — steer for the deep waters only,
> Reckless O soul, exploring, I with thee, and thou with me,
> For we are bound where mariner has not yet dared to go,
> And we will risk the ship, ourselves and all.
>
> O my brave soul!
> O farther farther sail!
> O daring joy, but safe! are they not all the seas of God?
> O farther, farther, farther sail!

As a matter of fact, in the early 1870's Whitman seems to have thought of his *Leaves of Grass* as a completed "epic of democracy" and to have contemplated starting another large work with "Passage to India" — more spiritual in its orientation, more nearly universal. But he gave up the project — no doubt as a result of his paralytic stroke and his mother's death in 1873. The almost twenty years of life remaining to him he spent largely in Camden, New Jersey, surrounded by a group of devotees from near and far. He supervised the later editions of *Leaves of Grass,* which more or less had reached its final state by the early 1880's, and gave directions that after his death the work be reprinted exactly as he had left it. In this form *Leaves of Grass,* then, starts from preoccupation with self, has its focal middle part in poems of the Civil War (of Lincoln, in particular), and moves on to a solemn meditation on death and eternity. It is the life of a man, the growing-up of a country, and the passage of all men from adolescence to old age.

Among many odd things that Whitman wrote in the initial preface to *Leaves of Grass* is one that has disturbed many readers: "The proof of a poet," he wrote, "is that his country absorbs him as affectionately as he has absorbed it." This sentence — worthy of an Emerson or a Thoreau — obviously cannot mean (as some have taken it to) that the test of good poetry is the number of copies sold or the standing of the poet in some sort of popularity poll. Perhaps, coming as it does at the end of the preface, it has no more significance than the *Plaudite* at the end of a Latin comedy. Or perhaps it is a diamond which one is to swallow without trying to digest. Perhaps it means that the proof of a poet is the extent to which his work has been absorbed into the very lives and fortunes of his countrymen, who may be as unaware of its being there as they are of the grass stains on their shoe soles. It suggests that ultimately art must undergo tests that are not strictly aesthetic.

In the last years of his life Whitman seems on occasion to have felt that he had failed in what he had set out to do: "I have not gain'd the acceptance of my own time," he wrote in 1888, "but have fallen back on fond dreams of the future." In the years since his death, however, his work has had something to do with the role the United States has come to play in the world. In 1919 writers in both France and Germany maintained that Wilson borrowed his "fourteen points," the basis for the termination of World War I, from Whitman. Of course, as an educated man Wilson knew Whitman's poetry. But there is also evidence that another person who had a great part in drawing up the "fourteen points" was especially interested in *Leaves of Grass* — Jan Christian Smuts of South Africa, who in 1894-1895 had written a book on Whitman and derived from the poet a philosophy which Smuts called "Holism" (emphasizing the "whole") as set forth in his book *Holism and Evolution* (1926).

In Europe *Leaves of Grass* was first widely read in England. The reviewers there in 1866 approached the book with considerable self-assurance: one wrote that the poet "had managed to acquire or imbue himself with not only the spirit, but the veriest mannerism, the most absolute trick and accent of Persian poetry"; another wrote that he had visited Whitman and found him prone on his back on the bare earth with a blazing one-hundred-degree sun overhead, "one of his favourite places and attitudes for composing poems." Gradually, the problem of properly estimating Whitman became entangled with the rivalries of certain literary coteries in London and the issue of homosexuality (as it came to the fore in the Wilde case). Whitman's deviations from normal prose usage, too, seem to have upset many British readers — whereas Longfellow's, being more circumspect, did not.

Germany was introduced to *Leaves of Grass* by the same German poet who had translated Longfellow, Ferdinand Freiligrath, then living in England as a refugee. In Germany, in 1868, he published an appreciative essay which first undertook to consider Whitman as a world poet, and by the end of the century there was a Whitman cult in Germany. After World War I interest in *Leaves of Grass* was revived, and a translation appeared that gave the Germans the opportunity they had long enjoyed with Shakespeare of having available a version that could stand alongside the original — a translation hailed by Thomas Mann in 1922 as a "great, important, indeed holy gift" which his fellow Germans could benefit from "if we are willing to accept him."

In Russia Tolstoi was interested in *Leaves of Grass*. Turgenev, in a letter of 1872, said he intended to send his publisher a translation of some poems from it, but did not get around to doing so — though this may have helped start him on his own *Poems in Prose*, begun in 1878. Early in the present century, the Symbolist poet Balmont, having translated Poe, prepared a Russian text of *Leaves of Grass* — which was not published, however, till 1911, and was then much criticized for verbal inaccuracies. Meanwhile, another translation, by Chukovsky, appeared and became the standard Russian version — the first edition in 1907, the tenth (of ten thousand copies) in 1944. Though pointing out in an introduction to the ninth edition (1935) of the Chukovsky translation that Whitman's poems were not revolutionary in the Marxist sense, Prince Mirsky emphasized the purely artistic aspects of this "last great poet of the bourgeois era of humanity, the last in the line that begins with Dante . . . a truly great innovator, the greatest that the world of poetry has known."

In the United States, the tendrils of Whitman's work have, in an odd way, entwined themselves with the very growth of modern American literature. Like Poe, Whitman had great influence on the Symbolist poets in France. Among nineteenth-century writers much influenced by Whitman were, in England, J. A. Symonds (who first encountered *Leaves of Grass* during his twenties, then wrote to ask the aging Whitman a number of rather personal questions, and in 1893 issued a book on him) and, in France, the Symbolist poet Jules Laforgue (who published three groups of translations of Whitman in *La Vogue* in 1886 and at the same time was working out a similar kind of poetry which later came to be known as *vers libre*). Thus Whitman's influence made an Atlantic round trip. When Eliot during his undergraduate days at Harvard first wrote a "modern" poem, it was in imitation of one by Laforgue.

One important influence on both Whitman and his French Symbolist followers was the literature and thought of the Orient, and Whitman in turn has not been without his influence on the Far East. Like Emerson and Thoreau, he had long been aware of such works as the *Bhagavad Gita* — interest in Far

Eastern literature being much "in the air" at the time. Late in life, he remembered having read "the ancient Hindoo" poems in preparation for writing *Leaves of Grass*. Closer to the time when he had written it in its initial version, however, Thoreau had called on him in New York and asked him whether he had read "the Orientals"; and Whitman said, "No, tell me about them" — which may indicate no more than that he was always interested in knowing more about them. More important than external borrowings from an Asiatic author, however, is Whitman's awareness of an attitude basic to Hindu thought involving an interpenetration of subject and object. At one time this attitude had been widespread in Europe as well as in Asia: Dante, for instance, believed that really to depict an angel one had first to be one. But from the Renaissance on, there was an increase in "objectivity" — or separation between subject and object. Whitman undertook to bridge this gap — a cleft which had never cut as deep in the East as it had in the West. The assumption that one is what he sees is as elemental as is the parallelism in his verse form (which appears in the Bible, in American Indian songs, and in the *Vedas*). To an Indian scholar the *Leaves of Grass* embodies the teaching of Vedanta; the "Song of Myself" is an echo of the sayings of Krishna — because all these go back to a common substructure of both Eastern and Western thought and feeling. Toward the end of the past century Vivekananda "read and re-read" *Leaves of Grass* and considered Whitman "the Sannyasin of America." When Whitman influence is reflected by as distinctly Indian a writer as Tagore, one needs somehow to understand the phrase "his country" in not too literal a sense to get the full force of Whitman's apothegm about the proof of a poet being in his absorption by "his country."

The fact that for Whitman the East largely meant India was due in part to Japan's not having been opened up to the West till 1853. Like any newspaperman, he was intensely alert to the events of the day, and when in 1860 the Japanese mission visited New York, he wrote a poem for the *Times*, "The Errand-Bearers" (published ten days after the event, and later

incorporated into *Leaves of Grass* as "A Broadway Pageant"),
beginning:

Over the Western sea hither from Niphon come,
Courteous, the swart-cheek'd two-sworded envoys,
Leaning back in their open barouches, bare-headed, impassive,
Ride to-day through Manhattan.

"To us, then at last the Orient comes," exclaims Whitman —
not just the Japanese but the whole East, "venerable Asia, the
all-mother." An anticipated visit of the Prince of Wales to the
United States meant to the poet that soon the West would also
be coming to this land of liberty, and the earth would be encircled. In lines of increasing amplitude Whitman declares
that this fulfilled the hidden purpose in the long westward migrations from man's original Asiatic home.

As early as the 1890's, essays on Whitman appeared in Japanese, and adequate translations by the 1920's; in 1953 there
was a Whitman exhibition in Tokyo; some of his poems are
normally included in high-school textbooks and hundreds of
thousands of copies of *Leaves of Grass* have been sold in Japan.
The "opening up" of Japan came too late for Japanese poetry
to exercise a formative influence on him, but it did influence
his followers among the French Symbolists. This Japanese influence manifested itself in an increased sharpness, concreteness,
and succinctness. Thus the followers of the French followers
of Whitman often objected to his being diffuse, and the American *vers librists* tended to produce a rather constricted version
of free verse (sometimes referred to as Imagism). Thus Whitman's poetry made contact with the world — to some extent
in Asia itself and to some extent in Europe. If he freed verse,
the contact with Asia to some extent confined it again — though
in a way different from Poe's efforts to make the poem a self-
contained work of art.

4. Mainly the Novel, Amateur to Professional

Twain to James

Outstanding literary achievements during the half-century between the Civil War and World War I were those of Mark Twain, William Dean Howells, and Henry James. Not only in America but also in Europe, the late nineteenth century was a great era of prose fiction, which often seriously undertook to criticize society — for example, Turgenev's *Sportsman's Sketches* (1852), Mrs. Stowe's *Uncle Tom's Cabin* (1852), Dickens' *Bleak House* (1853). When Flaubert was haled before the court to defend his *Madame Bovary* (1856) against a charge of indecency, he could but give the answer prepared by the influence of Poe and others of the early nineteenth century, that art is autonomous — though, under the influence of such opposition, the novel became more and more a covert means of disturbing bourgeois complacency.

Much of the best early nineteenth-century work had been in shorter forms or, when in longer, had been *tours de force*. Brackenridge, Brown, Cooper, Hawthorne, Melville seldom give a sense of handling fictional forms with complete technical mastery. They wrote what the nineteenth century considered romances, not novels. But by the time James had finished his work during World War I, the novel had been exemplified and discussed in as thoroughgoing a way as any other form of literature. In fact, in the development of the novel, James's work was an apparently unsurpassable culmination as, in other fields, was the work of Dante, Cervantes, Shakespeare, and Milton.

President during the early careers of such unlike talents as Twain and James was Abraham Lincoln. Though he is usually thought of in contexts other than the merely literary, he did utter words that have been heard round the world; and by what he both said and did he has assumed a special place in American literature. His speeches and other writings have a distinctive style, which to many Americans represent what writing should be, the unpretentious utterance of Man Thinking. To Mrs. Bixby in Boston he wrote: "Dear Madam: I have been shown in the files of the War Department a statement of the Adjutant-General of Massachusetts that you are the mother of five sons who have died gloriously on the field of battle. . . ." There is a late nineteenth-century factualness about the very opening of this letter — a tendency to proceed from the bald statement of actuality. As Lincoln said in another connection, "If we could first know where we are, and whither we are tending, we could better judge what to do, and how to do it." This was not only his political but also his literary creed. When someone asked him what he meant in one of his speeches, he wrote in reply:

> It puzzles me to make my meaning plainer. Look over it carefully, and conclude I meant all I said, and did not mean anything I did not say, and you will have my meaning. . . . If you will state to me some meaning which you suppose I had, I can and will instantly tell you whether that was my meaning.

This is, of course, the idea of the "plain style," consciously adopted by many of the early American colonists, reaffirmed in a spirit of eighteenth-century rationalism by some of the most influential of the revolutionary generation, and here being reasserted in an age of scientifically inspired realism.

Outstanding among Lincoln's speeches are five addresses: the two Inaugurals, the "House Divided," the "Cooper Union," and the "Gettysburg" — which has been called by Carl Sandburg "one of the great American poems." Lincoln was close to American traditions of oral literature — more those of the settled agricultural stage than those of the earlier, flamboyant hunting stage. He very frequently told folktales with direct application to immediate political questions, and on occasion used homely words and proverbs. "My young friend," he is reported to have said once, "have I hunkered you out of your chair?" This sort of thing shocked many in his day, and during his own lifetime he was one of the most immoderately criticized of American presidents. Actually, however, what he was doing went back to traditions very deeply ingrained in humanity in general and specifically in Americans — as can be observed in the writings of Bradford, for instance, or of Franklin — and was at once old in its plainness and new in its realism.

Lincoln also has a special place in American literature as the subject of writing. During his own lifetime books of "Lincoln sayings" and of stories about him (as in *Old Abe's Joker*) were in circulation. His death is at the heart of Whitman's *Leaves of Grass* — the American epic if we have one. One of the best of Melville's poems deals with him — as do scores of poems by other writers. From a campaign biography by Howells, through the ten-volume work by Hay and Nicolay, and to the six-volume study by Sandburg the life of Lincoln has been a continuing focal point of interest and his work has provided a touchstone for writing that might be considered American.

An author whom Howells called the "Abraham Lincoln of our literature" is Samuel Langhorne Clemens ("Mark Twain"). He was born in Florida, Missouri, in 1835, in circumstances not too different from those under which Lincoln had been born in Kentucky twenty-six years before. Clemens was the first major American writer born west of the Mississippi. When he was four, his family moved to Hannibal, the town he was later to make famous through his writings. His formal schooling ended when he was twelve, as the result of his father's death; and — like Franklin — he worked in the printing and newspaper office of his elder brother. His earliest humorous pieces appeared in his brother's newspaper; and when he was but seventeen, a humorous sketch of his was printed in a Boston comic magazine. After having served his apprenticeship in Hannibal, he went as journeyman printer to New York and Philadelphia. For a while he was a steamboat pilot on the Mississippi; but, with the closing of river traffic during the Civil War, he accompanied his brother, who had been appointed Secretary of the Nevada Territory as a political consequence of Lincoln's election, and for a few years was a miner and newspaperman in Nevada and California. A popular oral tale that he wrote up at Artemus Ward's suggestion and sent to New York (where it was printed in 1865) was "The Celebrated Jumping Frog of Calaveras County" — about a trained frog named Dan'l Webster whose owner was too eager to get up a contest and was overreached by the animal's being surreptitiously filled with buckshot. The story is told at some length in a deadpan manner: "Well," says the winner of the contest as he walks away, "*I* don' see no p'ints about that frog that's any better'n any other frog."

What Twain was a little prouder of having written at this time, however, was a series of travel sketches of Hawaii, dealing not merely with the anecdotal and picturesque but also the commercial and political aspects of this area, which subsequently was to become such a crucial point in the United States involvement in the Pacific. In Twain's day a native king ruled Hawaii (or, as it was then called, the Sandwich Islands). American missionaries and businessmen had long been there. The question of whether forces from the distinctly northern or southern states were to press on farther into the Pacific had been in the background of the Civil War (in which Twain had served briefly on the Confederate side).

While in Hawaii he got a "scoop" on the sea disaster of the *Hornet* and transmitted it to *Harper's*. He seriously considered going on to the Far East and working from there. In 1866 he wrote from Hawaii to his mother that Anson Burlingame, the United States minister to China, says if I will come to China in the first trip of the great mail steamer next January and make my house in Pekin his home, he will afford me facilities that few men can have there for seeing and learning. He will give me letters to the chiefs of the Great Mail Steamship Company which will be of service to me in this matter. I expect to do all this, but I expect to go to the States first — and from China to the Paris World's Fair.

Though as things turned out he did not, and instead returned to New York (to head out soon for the Near East), one must not overlook the fact that Twain was primarily a newspaperman. *Innocents Abroad* was originally a series of newspaper sketches. After his marriage, he lectured in order to establish himself as a newspaper editor in Buffalo. Most of his financial ventures were in the field of printing and publishing; and to make good his losses in that field, his lecturing round the world was means and not end. When toward the close of his life he dictated what he called his *Autobiography*, it was largely a commentary on current events in the manner of a newspaper columnist or editor. As with Franklin, Whitman, and scores of others, his background of typesetting and reporting was very different from those of Irving, Cooper, Emerson, or James.

Twain raised fundamentally journalistic forms to genuinely literary status — somewhat as Homer and Shakespeare, in other periods, had done to semiliterary activities that flourished in their day. Twain differs from Whitman in that he thought in terms of prose rather than poetry. As Whitman reopened the door between prose and poetry, so Twain reopened it between oral and written prose. Howells, a thoughtful observer, has left us a clear idea of how Twain's writing struck him as differing from his own: before I write a page, he said in effect, I have first an outline or firm skeletal structure for the whole passage in my mind; but when I read Twain I get the most uncanny sense of his moving with utter freedom:

So far as I know, Mr. Clemens is the first writer to use in extended writing the fashion we all use in thinking, and to set down the thing that comes into his mind without fear or favor of the thing that went before or the thing that may be about to follow.

After Twain's return to the Atlantic seaboard (his base of operations for the rest of his life), he projected a travel series for California and New York newspapers to be written on what would have been called in the Middle Ages a pilgrimage: from the voyage to the Holy Land of a group on the *Quaker City* in 1867, he wrote a series that ultimately became *Innocents Abroad* (1869). It is a varied account — some of it offensive to the sensibilities of some people, as are certain passages in Chaucer's account that also purports to have been written on the basis of a pilgrimage. Twain's defense (like Chaucer's) is that he has merely recorded what happened and that his purpose was

> to suggest to the reader how *he* would be likely to see Europe and the East if he looked at them with his own eyes instead of the eyes of those who travelled in those countries before him.

Though we cannot very well establish today whether what is recounted in *Innocents Abroad* really happened exactly as reported, we do know that the publisher who had agreed to bring out the series as a book grew alarmed at certain unconventional aspects of the writing and was induced to go ahead only by Twain's threat of a lawsuit. When the volume finally appeared, it proved sensationally popular.

After having written another travel book based on memories of the trip out to Nevada, *Roughing It* (1872), Twain undertook to write a novel that was avowedly fictional, and elicited the collaboration of an already established novelist, Charles Dudley Warner. The result was *The Gilded Age* (1873), notable for its central character, Colonel Sellers (who was to become well known on the stage in a dramatized version of the novel), and for the fact that the post-Civil War period in the United States is now sometimes referred to as the "Gilded Age," from Twain's use of the phrase.

The Twain works that are most highly regarded in their own right as literature, however, are three interrelated books: *Tom Sawyer* (1876), *Life on the Mississippi* (1883), and *Huckleberry Finn* (1885). In 1875, at Howells' suggestion, there appeared in the *Atlantic* a series by Twain called "Old Times on the Mississippi" — his reminiscences of experiences on the river (even as he had told of the western trip in *Roughing It*) and in celebration of river piloting (somewhat as Melville's *Moby Dick* had dealt with whaling). The first part of this "Old Times" series deals with his early ambitions and exacting training as a "cub," the last with mature piloting activities. The whole account has a remarkable fluency and liveliness. The veteran pilot, Bixby, has taken the wheel and a number of visiting pilots have expected him not to attempt a dangerous crossing ahead in the dark and have been awaiting the signal for the boat to dock, but the boat goes on:

Insensibly the men drew together behind Mr. Bixby, as the sky darkened and one or two dim stars came out. The dead silence and sense of waiting became oppressive. Mr. Bixby pulled the cord, and two deep, mellow notes from the big bell floated off on the night. Then a pause, and one more note was struck. The watchman's voice followed, from the hurricane deck:

"Labboard lead, there! Stabboard lead!"

The cries of the leadsmen began to rise out of the distance, and were gruffly repeated by the word passers on the hurricane deck.

"M-a-r-k three! M-a-r-k three! Quarter less three! Half twain! Quarter twain! M-a-r-k twain! Quarter less — "

Mr. Bixby pulled two bell ropes, and was answered by faint jinglings far below in the engine room, and our speed slackened. The steam began to whistle through the gauge cocks. The cries of the leadsmen went on — and it is a weird sound, always, in the night. Every pilot in the lot was watching now, with fixed eyes, and talking under his breath. Nobody was calm and easy but Mr. Bixby. . . .

The year after the "Old Times" series had appeared, Twain brought out his *Adventures of Tom Sawyer*, an idyll of boyhood. Starting out much as he had done in "Old Times," but in the third person, Twain recreates the carefree world of his boyhood as Tom and his playmates steal jam, whitewash the fence, release a pinchbug in church, play at pirates. Visiting a graveyard at midnight, however, they witness a murder for which an innocent man is arrested. The last part of the novel develops more serious overtones as the children testify in court, stalk the murderer, search for the treasure, and find themselves blocked by the bungling attempts of the adults to cope with the situation. Cluttered as the climax is, the work has an overall shape (derived, perhaps, from the three-act play); the characters mature somewhat in the course of the action; and some of the episodes recall those in *Don Quixote*.

Shortly after completing *Tom Sawyer*, Twain began a sequel, told in the first person by Tom's disreputable but loyal friend Huck, son of the town drunkard. In 1882 Twain revisited the river to gather more material for a book into which he wanted to expand the "Old Times" series. Among other things, he tossed a chapter of the Huck Finn material — as if it were so much lead type — into this projected book. The result was *Life on the Mississippi* (1883), a book that contains some of his best (the former "Old Times" series being now Chapters IV-XVIII) and some of his worst. It is a sort of literary collage, not helped by having been brought out by a made-up publishing company of Twain's and by his household's having been quarantined as the deadline for the manuscript drew near.

Then, in 1885, he brought out *The Adventures of Huckleberry Finn*, the most highly regarded of his works, centering squarely on the Mississippi River and all its rich, complex, and mysterious life — only now as transmuted through memory and imagination, not (as he had attempted in the last part of *Life on the Mississippi*) merely reported. On this great muddy river Huck (to escape his father) and Jim (an old Negro seeking freedom) embark together. The essential humanity of the two, set off against the grotesque forms of life they encounter, develops a wild and nightmarish quality (increased by the fact that when Twain had pulled out a section and put it in *Life on the Mississippi* he had not made any adjustment in the action or given any indication that something was missing. As a result, *Huckleberry Finn* does not quite make sense to the overly conscientious reader who might try to plot the action on a map of the Mississippi River). Inwardly, Huck is confronted throughout with a conflict between the restraints imposed on him by convention and conscience and the promptings of his intuitive morality — the latter winning out. Externally, the world of nature — in which the characters, action, and theme are so deeply imbedded — is by turns hostile and friendly.

Taking the three books as an interpenetrating complex, one sees in them a succession from the more to the less innocent — as in Dante's *Inferno*. The great natural symbols of the river, the raft, the essentially human Jim, the overly imaginative Tom, the somewhat primitive Huck formulate in dense, palpable, and moving form some intensely felt aspects of American and generally human experience and vision. Within this group of three books one can see what Hemingway meant when he considered modern American literature as having begun with Twain. The palpable, concrete, jabbing way in which Huck sometimes expresses himself was later often imitated by Hemingway:

> I took the sack of corn meal and took it to where the canoe was hid, and shoved the vines and branches apart and put it in; then I done the same with the side of bacon; then the whisky jug; I took all the coffee and sugar there was, and all the ammunition; I took the wadding; I took the bucket and gourd . . . I cleaned out the place. . . . I fetched out the gun, and now I was done.

Of course, this style is not *just* Twain's and Hemingway's: it has primitive qualities that are older than the opening of the

Book of Genesis and that have been widely cultivated in writing since World War I. James T. Farrell saw in Huck and Tom "two accusing fingers pointing down the decades of American history." Lionel Trilling once declared that Twain's style is something "almost every contemporary American writer who deals conscientiously with the problems and possibilities of prose must feel, directly or indirectly." Not only have these three books by Twain received high critical acclaim, both at home and abroad (particularly in Germany, Russia, Scandinavia, and South America), but they have been and still are being widely read — perhaps more widely, on a purely untutored choice and over the better part of a century, than any other books with any claim to literary standing. If *Leaves of Grass* is the American epic and *Huckleberry Finn* the American novel, or if — at least — both stand like pillars at the entrance to what is to be considered modern American literature, it is interesting that they have certain common qualities — both based solidly on experiences and facts distinctly American, such as those of Lincoln's assassination and of the great central river.

During the 1880's, the scene of Twain's novels extended to medieval Europe, in *The Prince and the Pauper* (1881) and *A Connecticut Yankee in King Arthur's Court* (1889) — the latter, incidentally, the source of the phrase "New Deal," which Franklin Roosevelt adopted for his national policies in the 1930's. One of Twain's works of the nineties with special features of interest is *Pudd'nhead Wilson* (1894). The title character solves a murder case through the use of fingerprints (years before the institution of the Bertillon system) and straightens out a situation like that explored romantically in *The Prince and the Pauper*, but here transferred to the Mississippi region. As the result of miscegenation, a mulatto slave Roxana is able to substitute her white baby for the infant heir of the plantation, and the child thus benefited, having grown to manhood, defends his status by selling his own mother to a slavetrader. Twain, having earlier written of *Innocents Abroad*, was now dealing with some not-so-innocents at home.

The character of the books that Twain wrote during the so-called Gay Nineties is varied: his anonymous book on *Joan of Arc* (1896) venerates the saint; *Tom Sawyer Abroad* (1894) and *Tom Sawyer, Detective* (1896) revive figures created in earlier works; *Following the Equator* (1897) recounts experiences on his lecture tour to Australia and India. Having forgone the opportunity to go to the Far East in his thirties, he eventually got there.

Before the end of his career, in 1910, he had been showered with honors round the world. One that he regarded highly was his honorary doctorate from Oxford in 1907. Much of his very late work, however, is quite somber. *The Mysterious Stranger* (posth. publ. 1916) deals with the medieval equivalent of Tom Sawyer's gang, now confronting Satan in a version of Hannibal set in Austria and called Eseldorf. It could be called religious in the sense of "dealing with ultimate rather than proximate matters," and often runs on the theme of vanity of vanities. This sort of concern by an author as he draws toward the close of his career is not unprecedented — witness Cooper, Melville, Howells.

Two years Clemens' junior, William Dean Howells (1837-1920) had a similar background of limited formal education and of early typesetting and reporting experience — in the shop of his father, an editor of Welsh birth and Swedenborgian persuasion, and in various small towns in Ohio. By 1860 the future novelist had established himself in the capital of Ohio as reporter for the state legislature, had contributed some verse to the *Atlantic*, and he and a friend had brought out a volume of poems. In consequence of writing a campaign biography of Lincoln, Howells was appointed consul in Venice, and held that post during the Civil War. Some prose sketches that he had written while abroad for the Boston *Advertiser* were reprinted as his first published volume, *Venetian Life* (1866). Soon after his return to the United States he joined the staff of the *Atlantic*, became editor-in-chief in 1871, and continued in that office for ten years, after which he resigned and moved to New York.

Through his editorship Howells made a great contribution to American literature. It is hard to imagine Twain as having been able to focus on the river as he did without Howells' suggestions, and James later wrote that Howells' agreement in advance to serialize his first novel "was really the making" of him. Howells was a staunch friend of many writers at the turn of the century; and when the American Academy of Arts and Letters came into being in 1904, he was elected its first president and was continuously reelected until his death — "manifestly," as Edmund Gosse wrote in 1912, "the leader of American literature" — or, as was often remarked, with a play on his middle name, the "dean of American letters."

Much of Howells' work during the sixties and seventies was essentially a transcript of personal observation and experience, often joined by rather unobtrusive dramatic elements. From very early in his life he had written little plays; and in Italy he had discovered the sharp, witty, relaxed work of the eighteenth-century playwright Goldoni. Throughout his long career, Howells wrote many attractive little skits — mostly one-act comedies or farces. Elements of the travel sketch and light drama appear in his early works: *Italian Journeys* (1867), *Suburban Sketches* (1871), *Their Wedding Journey* (1871), *A Chance Acquaintance* (1873), *A Foregone Conclusion* (1875), *The Lady of the Aroostook* (1879) — localized in Italy or America, usually *en route*, often with elements of conscious contrast or interaction between two cultures, anticipating the "international" situation which James was to exploit in his novels.

Modest as Howells' early books are, some of them made a distinct impression abroad. Coming across a battered copy of *Venetian Life* left by some traveler on the edge of the Indian desert, Kipling spent most of the night reading it, and decades later when he went to Venice recalled automatically "phrases and sentences from the pages read so long ago." Turgenev in Paris wrote Howells' friend Boyesen:

> I have read *Venetian Life* and *A Chance Acquaintance* and like both books very much indeed. I think I even

prefer the former. There is in both a delightful freshness and *naturel,* and a gay, subtle, artless, elegant humor which I enjoyed thoroughly.

Turgenev's interest in Howells' work was part of his general awareness of American writings — Hawthorne's, Whitman's, Bret Harte's — as, vice versa. Howells was aware of Turgenev's (with its tendency on the part of the author to stay out of the scene, as in a play, and with its restricted number of characters and general unity of theme); for as Howells later wrote:

> Life showed itself to me in different colors after I had once read Turgenev; it became more serious, more awful; and with mystical responsibilities I had not known before my gay American horizons were bathed in the most melancholy of the Slav, patient, agnostic, truthful.

But "I was," Howells said, "a traveller before I was a noveller."

By the eighties Howells felt it safe to embark on a career of living from his fiction, most of which was by now going into new editions each year. Oscar Wilde, in one of his usual overstatements, declared publicly that no living English novelist could be named with James and Howells. Howells had a strong conviction that the British novels of the mid-century generation were really unworthy — that the gaudy claptrap of Dickens and the sleazy confidences of Thackeray, like the long-windedness of Richardson and the "dirtiness" of Smollett, were truly inferior to the qualities of serious Continental European and American fiction of his day. Such an attitude, of course, brought storms of protest from many British critics, who tried to make out that Howells was merely puffing himself up. But he was not: personally, he was one of the most unassuming of mortals, as preternaturally gifted as Emerson had been in recognizing others' merits. The point at issue was not just Boston vs. London: Howells was as quick to recognize the worth of a Meredith or a Hardy as he was a Twain or a James. The point was that by the eighties a new generation was coming to the fore and — like Huck on the Mississippi — had to get away from Pap.

If some of Howells' and James's attitudes toward literature are to make sense, one has to assume that a particular kind of literature in successive historical periods may improve or deteriorate — an assumption not made by all people: Stevenson, for instance, thought Howells a "zealot" who "dreams of an advance in art like what there is in science." One also has to assume that bad fiction can drive out good fiction and work positive harm. As one of Howells' readers wrote him: "Whatever in my mental make-up is wild and visionary, whatever is untrue, whatever is injurious, I can trace to the perusal of some work of fiction." Howells himself declared: "We believe fiction in the past to have been largely injurious" — an attitude that would have been appreciated by Thomas Jefferson. Howells' further point, however, is that in his own day the novel was making a breakthrough, and he wished to devote his full efforts toward furthering this — despite the fact that poetry and drama had personal attractions for him. Whether one made the assumptions he did about the novel seemed to him to boil down to a question of how seriously one took it — whether one's interest was only amateur or truly professional.

During his lifetime Howells wrote some thirty-five novels. In one, *The Undiscovered Country* (1880), set in Boston, a newspaperman undertakes to expose a spiritualist and his daughter, who flee and find refuge in a Shaker community, where the spiritualist dies and his daughter and the reporter are married. It is an odd novel, somewhere between Hawthorne's earlier *Blithedale Romance* and James's later *Bostonians* — a work, H. G. Wells later observed, "in which the leading character so to speak is a *topic*" — a sort of "problem novel." *A Modern Instance* (1882) deals with the runaway marriage of headstrong Marcia Gaylord and an unscrupulous newspaperman Bartley Hubbard; in Boston she suffers greatly from his dishonesty, and eventually she obtains a divorce and he is killed in Arizona; but although her faithful friend the young minister Ben Halleck wishes to marry her, even at the cost of giving up his calling, the question remains whether —

scruples of New England conscience considered — this would be a possible solution.

In 1882 Howells went abroad; in Edinburgh he supervised the printing of a twenty-one-volume edition of his works; and in Florence he began a new novel, *Indian Summer* (1886), based on a fictionalized version of some aspects of his own situation: a middle-aged American editor from the Middle West returns to Florence, where he had been years before, and meets the widow of an American he had known there. In this Turgenev-like novel the editor and the widow ultimately marry.

Meanwhile having returned to Boston, Howells issued his perhaps best-known novel, *The Rise of Silas Lapham* (1885), in the same year as *Huckleberry Finn*. Howells and Twain, in very close touch with each other, reached the high point in their careers together somewhat as Hawthorne and Melville had done at mid-century. *Silas Lapham* is the first major American novel about a businessman. In the opening pages, Silas has arrived at the height of his material prosperity and is being interviewed by Bartley Hubbard, the newspaperman in *A Modern Instance*: the resulting write-up serves not only to fill in the antecedent action but also establishes a contrast between conventional accounts of such men and actuality. The novel deals with Silas' building a house on the fashionable "water side of Beacon Street" and his initial contacts with Boston "society," for the son of one of the old Boston families ultimately marries one of his daughters. Silas' bragging about his paint business, as the young man explains to his father, "might have been vulgar, but it wasn't sordid. And I don't know that it was vulgar." Presented more sympathetically than the big businessmen in later naturalistic novels by writers such as Norris and Dreiser, Silas, having lost both his wealth and his almost completed house, exhibits the admirable side of his character; thus his moral rise is counterpointed against his material fall. If the nobility of Silas and the indirection in the courtship of his daughter by the young Brahmin sound to some readers today unrealistic, like the tinkle of an old music-box tune, these aspects do not therefore diminish the literary value of the work. The increasing prevalence, with time, of a less blunt type of businessman and a more blunt type of courtship only throws into sharper relief the purely structural aspects of the novel, as writing; and one sees it today, perhaps, less as if it were life and more as what it is, literature. Boston families old and new at the beginning of the last quarter of the nineteenth century are precisely set off against each other. As in Turgenev, the novel is highly unified in scope and theme. In recommending that his publisher issue a French translation, the French critic Taine wrote:

> it is the best novel written by an American, the most like Balzac's, the most profound, and the most comprehensive. Silas, his wife and his two daughters are for us new types, very substantial and very complete.

The second most highly regarded of Howells' works appeared five years later, *A Hazard of New Fortunes*, set in New York City. This is much more inclusive, dealing with characters of all social classes and backgrounds, focusing on a magazine *Every Other Week*, which Basil March, a character vaguely resembling the author, has come from Boston to edit. There is a less sympathetic presentation of the newly rich character in the novel, Dryfoos, and his wife and daughters. Also there is an old German socialist named Lindau, refugee from the Revolution of '48, who plays a role in this work similar in some respects to Father Zosima in Dostoievsky's *Brothers Karamazov*; Lindau ultimately is killed in the New York streetcar strike of 1888. In this novel the influence of Turgenev has been succeeded by that of later Russians, particularly Tolstoi. A Dostoievsky-like concern with abnormal mental states appears in some of Howells' novels of the nineties. Among the better of his late novels are *The Quality of Mercy* (1892), *The World of Chance* (1893), *The Landlord at Lion's Head* (1897), *The Kentons* (1902) and *The Son of Royal Langbrith* (1904). *A Traveler from Altruria* (1894) and *Through the Eye of the Needle* (1907) explore utopias. To the end of his life, also, Howells continued to write in other forms than the novel — poems, plays, essays. He conveyed his firm belief in realism and the moral purpose of art through his "Easy Chair" articles in *Harper's* as well as through volumes such as *Criticism and Fiction* (1891), *My Literary Passions* (1895), and *Literature and Life* (1902). Notable autobiographical volumes are *A Boy's Town* (1890), *My Mark Twain* (1910), and *Years of My Youth* (1916). Like Twain, he was honored by a degree from Oxford, as well as by degrees from other universities — symbols little anticipated by either author in his unacademic youthful career in the Middle West. Increasingly during his later life Howells was concerned with questions of social justice and the role of the United States in the world, as well as with certain spiritual questions that perhaps brought him closer, in an oblique way, to the concerns of his Swedenborgian father.

Half a dozen years younger than Howells, Henry James, Jr. (1843-1916) brought the novel to unprecedented heights of richness and virtuosity. An earlier phase of his work, in which, having adapted certain technical procedures from painting, he followed the lead of Hawthorne and Turgenev, culminated around 1880 in *Daisy Miller* and *The Portrait of a Lady*. A later or "major" phase, in which he worked in larger compass and more in terms of procedures from the theater, reached its height at the beginning of the present century with *The Ambassadors*, *The Wings of the Dove*, and *The Golden Bowl*. Thus James enlarged the structural, psychological, and mythic potentialities of the novel. Much of his work depends on nuance, on what is called in painting "values" — the relative degree of definiteness and of light or dark in different parts of the composition. Much of it involves the possibility that the meaning of a given situation is indefinite or questionable, as if the incidents were actual happenings and not mere fiction. Any attempt to deal with his works briefly runs serious danger of oversimplifying them.

The family to which James belonged was of northern Irish ancestry, and the financial substructure of their nineteenth-century intellectual achievement was laid by the novelist's grandfather, a prosperous and rather strict Presbyterian merchant in Albany. His son, Henry James, Sr., rebelled against the narrowness of his upbringing and became a New York colleague of the Emerson group. Distrustful of dead forms and mere conventions, he wished to get to the spiritual realities behind them and, like Howells' father, had high regard for the writings of Swedenborg.

To him and his wife — also from an upstate New York family of Irish Protestant ancestry — were born five children: William (1842), Henry (1843), Garth (1845), Robertson (1846), and Alice (1847) — their place of residence being mainly near Washington Square in New York City and for a time in Albany and in Europe. Naturally there were rivalries within the family, a tendency for the eldest son to be looked up to and indulged, and a generally cosmopolitan atmosphere; but as families go, the James family was unusually harmonious, intellectual, and affectionate. It was important to Henry, Jr., for he outlived the other members — never married, looked after his invalid sister, and never really experienced the break with family ties that often marks the beginning of a writer's self-awareness.

Since the adolescent William became interested in painting while the Jameses were in Paris, they moved to Newport, Rhode Island, so that he could study with William Hunt and John LaFarge (Henry also did a little sketching there). After a year, however, William became interested in science, and this time the family moved to Cambridge, where he was enrolled in the Lawrence Scientific School (and, soon thereafter, Henry in the Law School). Owing to physical disabilities neither William nor Henry fought in the Civil War. Their two younger brothers, however, did: one was wounded, and neither achieved anything like the success of their elder brothers. After having accompanied Agassiz to Brazil to collect zoological specimens and having studied in Germany for a year, William received his doctorate from the Harvard Medical School in 1869, and in 1872 began a distinguished teaching career at Harvard that was to continue for some thirty-five years.

Dynamic and influential, he was a pioneer in psychology and philosophy. The James-Lange theory is that one does not feel fear and then run, but one runs and feels fear. William's *Principles of Psychology* (1890), an important text in a then new field, used for the first time the phrase "stream of consciousness" (as, during the ensuing decade, Henry's novels came more and more to focus on the stream of consciousness of the characters — a development which passed into European fiction during the decade after that). William's *Will to Believe* (1897) is a group of ten essays pointing out that we believe pretty much what we want to: we *may* wait for the confirmation of evidence that might satisfy us intellectually, but we do so at great risk, for "in either case we *act*." *The Varieties of Religious Experience* (1902), originally delivered as lectures at the University of Edinburgh, is a sympathetic treatment of a great many kinds of personal religion and a justification of them on psychological grounds (which was to have wide influence through the second quarter of the twentieth century but to lose some of its influence to existentialism in the third). *Pragmatism* (1907) and a sequel *The Meaning of Truth* (1909) present his philosophical position: a truth is whatever "proves itself to be good in the way of belief" — it is "expedient thinking" — and ideas have meaning only in relation to their consequences in the world of feeling and action.

In these works, William James wrote with great liveliness. Someone has said that William wrote psychology like a novelist and Henry novels like a psychologist. Like their father, the two brothers carried on an attack against conventional barriers between ideas.

In 1879 in the *Atlantic*, Henry James, Sr., had brought out a series of essays in which he argued for a conception of marriage that is even a little more spiritual than the one set forth in the Bible. If one partner in a marriage commits adultery — he said, in effect — the other partner should not seek divorce; for both husband and wife have been guilty of having allowed "the ritual covenant practically to exhaust and supersede . . .

the real and living one." In *The Portrait of a Lady* and in *The Golden Bowl*, Henry James, Jr., presents such marriages — and in *The Golden Bowl* a seemingly impossible situation has a reasonable outcome. When, in 1885, William edited a volume of his late father's writings and sent a copy to Henry, then in London, the novelist replied:

> It comes over me . . . how intensely original and personal his whole system was, and how indispensable it is that those who go in for religion should take some heed of it. I can't enter into it (much) myself — I can't be so theological nor throw myself into conceptions of heavens or hells, nor be sure that the keynote of nature is humanity, etc. But I can enjoy greatly the spirit, the feeling, the manner of the whole thing . . . and feel that poor Father, struggling so alone all his life, and so destitute of every worldly or literary ambition, was yet a great writer.

To be sure, both William and Henry relied more on intuition than had their father — but in the end it all comes out about the same. One is reminded of the way Hawthorne's attitudes ultimately confirm older Puritan ones: with William and Henry James, however, it is a later stage of New England thought and feeling — the Transcendental phase — that is confirmed.

The Jameses and the Howellses moved to Cambridge at about the same time, and Henry soon became acquainted with the new member of the *Atlantic* staff who had lived for five years in Venice. Henry's studies at Harvard seem not to have meant much to him; but his friendship with Howells did. His first signed short story and his initial attempt at longer fiction, *Watch and Ward* (1871), appeared in the *Atlantic*. His first novel to appear as a book, *Roderick Hudson* (1875), develops some suggestions from Hawthorne's *Marble Faun* in the "realistic" method of Turgenev — with a minimum of comment by the author, no sharply defined hero or villain, each character doing what he does under his own impetus. Though, in comparison with Turgenev, the result may seem a little melodramatic, James's novels of the seventies show that he was doing the same sort of thing in prose fiction in the late nineteenth century as Longfellow had been doing largely in poetry earlier in the century — bringing America up to date on new Continental modes of sensibility.

Up to 1875 — that is, till James was in his thirties and well established as a writer — he lived largely in New York or New England. Then, for some forty years from 1875 on, he lived largely in Europe — though retaining his American citizenship and occasionally revisiting America. He was, of course, highly honored in England, ultimately receiving an honorary degree from Oxford and the Order of Merit from the British government. After World War I broke out and the United States delayed in entering, he — as a gesture of public acknowledgment of his sympathy with the Allied cause — became a British subject. But before his death the next year — at the age of seventy-two — he directed that his ashes be returned to the family burial place in Cambridge, Massachusetts. In terms of the influences that molded his writing, however, he seems to have had more in common with Continental work, particularly French and Russian.

The first of his so-called international novels — and in fact the first clear-cut full-length one in world literature — was *The American* (1877). It is about an American businessman who wants to marry the daughter of a corrupt and snobbish French family but is prevented by them from doing so; later, when he has it in his power to revenge himself on them, he refrains, the object of his affections having meanwhile entered a convent. Though both Howells and James, in shorter fiction, had worked previously with the idea of a clash between two cultures, here is clearly the extended development of a situation in which a character from one culture enters another and each changes and is changed by the incidents that ensue.

One of James's shorter pieces of fiction on the international theme is *Daisy Miller: A Study* (1878). Winterbourne, an American who has been long abroad, meets an innocent and artless American girl fresh from Schenectady who goes around in Rome with a scandalous freedom that proves fatal to her;

after her death, he realizes that he has done her an injustice, that the relationship between them had further potentialities, and that he has

> lived too long in foreign parts. . . . Nevertheless he soon went back to live at Geneva, where there continue to come the most contradictory accounts of his motives of sojourn: a report that he's "studying" hard — an intimation that he's much interested in a very clever foreign lady.

In other words, everything reverts to the *status quo ante*. A conventional romantic story might have shown Winterbourne dedicating himself to her memory. To many late nineteenth-century readers James seemed insensible in *Daisy Miller* — particularly, too, as it is really a succession of four quasi-dramatized scenes, with scarcely a word in it that is not presented from the point of view of the actors in the little drama. What James meant by calling it a study, he later explained, was the deliberately flat presentation of the title character. Perhaps also it was a study in the characterization, through dialogue, of other members of the Miller family, who are brilliantly presented — the bratty little brother and the complaining mother. Many readers assumed that Winterbourne was James, and thought of Daisy Miller as a stereotype and the book as an "outrage on American girlhood." "Daisy Millerism" became a widely used term for something that Twain had touched on earlier in his account of some "innocents abroad." Later, James insisted that he had not intended Daisy Miller as a typical character, but as a highly individual one, as an antidote against stereotyping, as "pure poetry."

The suggestion that James may have been following in the footsteps of Twain as well as those of some other American authors should not be dismissed offhandedly as preposterous. More than once James came along after Twain and undertook to do with more subtlety something that the older writer had done rather crudely. Toward the end of the century, Twain wrote an answer to the anti-American French novelist Paul Bourget, and James soon presented a much more subtle and intricate answer in *The Golden Bowl* — though, of course, that is but one aspect of this masterpiece. Also the idea of a modern American finding himself transported to an earlier historical period, which underlies Twain's *Connecticut Yankee*, was the subject of the novel James was working on at his death, *The Sense of the Past*. Twain's and James's personal opinions of each other, however, were no higher than Poe's and Emerson's of each other.

The novel which brought to a culmination the early phase of James's career is *The Portrait of a Lady* (1880-1881). It centers on the character of Isabel Archer, who at the beginning of the action is an independent, self-sufficient, idealistic American girl. Becoming an heiress, she is engineered by a designing European woman into marriage with the latter's lover Osmond, a corrupt European, in order to enable him to establish a proper home for his illegitimate daughter Pansy. Isabel renounces her desire for independence and voluntarily accepts suffering for the sake of the child. *The Portrait* is one of the most unified of James's "big" novels, the central character one of the most appealing, and the relationship between the foreground figure and the various background figures most carefully calculated.

In 1885, the year of *Huckleberry Finn* and *Silas Lapham*, James brought out a somewhat Zolaesque novel, American in setting, *The Bostonians*, which had taken its immediate inception from Howells' *Dr. Breen's Practice* (1881) but is also related to other works of fiction, such as *The Blithedale Romance*. The reform movement, once New England's glory, was presented here as having degenerated into neurotic feminism. Also charged with substantial content of incident, characters, and ideas are *The Princess Cassamassima* (1886), hinging on the suicide of a young man who has become involved with a group of anarchists and is told by them to assassinate a certain duke but cannot bring himself to do so, and *The Tragic Muse* (1890), focusing on life in the artist's studio and on stage in London and Paris.

The latter work reflects James's preoccupation with play-

writing during the early nineties. He had always been interested in the theater, having written reviews and short dramatic
pieces. *Daisy Miller*, so nearly a drama already, he adapted for
the stage in 1882; and *The American*, in his theatrical version,
ran for some hundred performances in 1890. Four original
plays were brought out in a volume *Theatricals* (1894). *Guy
Domville*, a play set in eighteenth-century France, was produced in 1895, but was not successful: James was much upset
when he was booed on his stage appearance at the end of the
first performance, and after a month's run the play closed. A
full-length play of his, revealing Ibsen's influence, *The Prom-
ise*, did not find a producer and was reworked as a novel *The
Other House* (1896). Now and then James continued to write
for the stage, but he never found the theater an entirely satisfactory vehicle — though after his death many pieces of his
fiction have been turned into effective stage works by others.

Important in James's work are his pieces of shorter fiction,
over a hundred in number. One that shows the deepened dramatic sense that emerged from his efforts actually to write for
the theater and that has been effectively adapted by others for
stage, screen, air, and opera is "The Turn of the Screw"
(1898). It is related to the ghost story, a kind of tale that he,
like Hawthorne before him, had always favored and that many
Far Eastern peoples had developed to a high art. A governess
on a lonely British estate tries to protect two children from the
attempts of spirits to reach and further corrupt them, and in
the resulting struggle the boy dies in her arms.

As the nineteenth century drew to a close, James returned
to long fiction, but more as a dramatist than as a portraitist.
The Spoils of Poynton (1896) hinges on the rivalry between
mother and prospective daughter-in-law over the furnishings
of an English country house; but the physical objects involved
are only suggested by James, the emphasis being on the effect
they exert upon the emotions and the dramatic tensions they
create between the people in the novel. *What Maisie Knew*
(1897) focuses on the corruption in human relationships
that ensues on the divorce of parents and the preternatural ef-

fect of aging this produces in their six-year-old daughter, from whose point of view the situation is seen: as Maisie enters her teens, she has left her childhood behind, and the unusual technical feature of the novel is its being conceived in terms of the developing consciousness of a child from six to thirteen. *The Awkward Age* (1899) takes up the same general theme only with different characters: the daughter of corrupt parents here, Nanda Brookenham, is older than Maisie but similarly surrounded by unsavory intrigue, from which she is finally rescued by an old gentleman who long ago loved her grandmother; technically, this novel is an adaptation into English of what is called in French the *roman dialogué* or novel treated in discontinuous "panels" or scenes as in a play.

The first of the three novels that mark James's early twentieth-century "major phase" is *The Ambassadors* (1903), which, according to the author, had its "germ" in a remark made by Howells to an art student in Paris about the importance of really living while one is young: thus James acknowledged his indebtedness for this work to Howells, even as at mid-century Melville had acknowledged the inspiration of Hawthorne in *Moby Dick*. Lambert Strether, the central figure in *The Ambassadors*, is sent by a wealthy widow to Paris to bring back her son Chad, who is detained there by his infatuation with a Frenchwoman. Strether arrives, and is so taken by the fineness of the relationships that Chad has available to him there that he cannot find it in his heart to advise him to leave them. Meanwhile the widow, impatient of results, sends her daughter and son-in-law to replace Strether in his "embassy." Though Strether must ultimately renounce further involvement in the world that has suddenly opened up for him and must cut himself off from the world closing behind him, he is by the end of the novel a finer and more perceptive individual than he was in the beginning, and much more self-possessed. In and through its humanly psychological aspects, this novel formulates what an older culture (that of Paris) means to a younger (that of the United States).

The Wings of the Dove (1902), focusing on the saintly

character of Milly Theale, an American heiress destined shortly to die but during her last days in the hands of a predatory "English gang" (to whom she rises superior by her nonresistance), is usually taken as a tribute by the novelist to a cousin of his who died young, Minny Temple. The title and the names of some of the characters have religious suggestions: certainly Milly is the secular counterpart of a saint — as is Beatrice in Dante's great work.

The Golden Bowl (1904) has as its central figure Maggie Verver, whose father Adam — a retired American businessman now collecting art — has brought her to England. There she marries the Italian Prince Amerigo, whose mistress marries Maggie's father. Thus Maggie faces the possibility of there being continued adultery within both marriages (exacerbated by the Prince's undeveloped moral sense and her new stepmother's eagerness for this particular form of human activity) — a problem increased by the birth of the *principino*. Her father finally decides to go back to America, and Prince Amerigo matures morally. As in *The Wings of the Dove*, there are Biblical and other overtones here, and the suggestion of a conception of marriage enunciated by the author's father.

In all three of the "major phase" novels the central figures conquer by resisting not evil — a course recommended by Tolstoi on the basis of his reading of the New Testament. The comparatively passive role of the protagonist, with the action in the novels occurring largely as a result of surrounding factors, is handled with a virtuosity unequaled in the kind of domestic and psychological novel which James had thus brought to a full realization of its potentialities. James's novels stand opposed to many influential works of the late nineteenth century. The Nietzschean *Übermensch* and the Marxist class struggle are rejected as sharply as they are by Tolstoi and Dostoievsky. There is little place in James for Richard Wagner's attitude of "give me love or give me death," for Nora's door-slamming in *A Doll's House*, or for the bizarre double suicide in *Rosmersholm*. The writers nearest in thought, maturity, and stature to Twain, Howells, and James as they reach the height of their careers are their contemporaries among the Russians rather than those among the West Europeans.

James discussed those of his novels that he considered his best in his prefaces for the twenty-four-volume New York edition (1907-1909), for which he revised the texts and in general established the canon of his writings — somewhat as Whitman did toward the end of his life for *Leaves of Grass*. Also earlier — in 1888 — James had written an essay "The Art of Fiction," in which he insisted that the writing of novels was a serious matter and that many of the distinctions and rules that had been urged for it were without much basis:

> A novel is a living thing, all one and continuous, like any other organism, and in proportion as it lives will it be found, I think, that in each of the parts there is something of each of the other parts. . . . As people feel life, so they will feel the art that is most closely related to it. This closeness of relation is what we should never forget in talking of the effort of the novel. Many people speak of it as a factitious, artificial form, a product of ingenuity the business of which is to alter and arrange the things that surround us, to translate them into conventional, traditional moulds. This, however, is a view of the matter which carries us but a very short way, condemns the art to an eternal repetition of a few familiar *clichés*, cuts short its development, and leads us straight up to a dead wall.

"No man of our time," declared Pound in 1918, "has so labored to create means of communication as did the late Henry James." T. S. Eliot, in 1924, wrote:

> The example which Henry James offered us was not that of a style to imitate, but of an integrity so great, a vision so exacting, that it was forced to the extreme of care and punctiliousness for exact expression. James did not provide us with "ideas," but with another world of thought and feeling. For such a world some have gone to Dostoievsky, some to James; and I am inclined to think that the spirit of James, so much less violent, with

so much more reasonableness and so much more resignation than that of the Russian, is no less profound, and is
more useful, more applicable, for our future.

Graham Greene in 1936 concluded an essay on James by
speaking of him as "a solitary in the history of the novel as
Shakespeare in the history of poetry." Though there has been
continued interest in James's works ever since they appeared,
in the 1940's there occurred what has been termed a James
"revival" — comparable in intensity to the Melville "revival."
Using language in ways that outwardly look like prose, Melville, Whitman, Twain, James — each in his way — combined
the aims of poetry and prose in a reintegrated purpose that is
perhaps best characterized as simply literary.

As the James family figured prominently in late nineteenth-
century writing, so also did the Adams family. Earlier, the
Adamses had led in politics, furnishing the republic with its
second and sixth presidents. President John Quincy Adams'
son Charles Francis was American minister at the Court of St.
James during the Civil War. The interests of the latter's sons
Henry and Brooks — friends, incidentally, of the James brothers — ran more to historiography. Their attitude was different
from the Jameses', however, in stressing determinism rather
than free will — thus perhaps confirming attitudes endemic to
their family.

After studying at Harvard and in German universities,
Henry Adams (1838-1918) was secretary to his father in London. Returning to Harvard to teach (1870-1877), he edited the
North American Review and brought out his *Essays on Anglo-
Saxon Law*. Going on to Washington, he completed a nine-
volume *History of the United States of America during the
Administrations of Thomas Jefferson and James Madison.* Two
novels that he wrote, *Democracy* (1880) and *Esther* (1884) —
the latter under a pseudonym — are today of slight literary interest. After his wife's suicide, he traveled widely, particularly
in the Orient. His poem "Buddha and Brahma," written in
1891, undertook to formulate the implications of Buddha's si-

lence on whether mind and matter were ultimately real: we must seek, the poem says,

> To live two separate lives: one, in the world
> Which we must ever seem to treat as real;
> The other in ourselves, behind a veil
> Not to be raised without disturbing both.

Having been adopted into a tribe in Tahiti, he wrote a book tracing the history of royal intrigue in that island, *Memoirs of Arii Taimai* (1901), under his Tahitian name Tauraatua I Amo.

In 1895 his younger brother Brooks published a study, *The Law of Civilization and Decay*, in which the decline of Western civilization, particularly of the United States, is seen as far advanced, having been intensified by the capitalists, whom Henry called in his letters the "gold-bugs." Both Henry and Brooks seem to have momentarily expected the collapse of the world as they knew it — an attitude with which one is familiar from previous Christian writings.

The most widely admired work of Henry Adams is *Mont-Saint-Michel and Chartres* (1904). The title refers to the eleventh-century abbey and thirteenth-century cathedral in northern France, in which the spirit of the First Crusade and the veneration of the Virgin Mary are most palpably expressed — evidence, according to Adams, of the highest degree of concentration and integration of power in the history of man. In prose of undeniable charm, Adams goes into cathedral construction, stained glass windows, poetry, and scholastic philosophy — all of which, to him, mean something very much his own:

> Of all the elaborate symbolism which has been suggested for the Gothic cathedral, the most vital and perfect may be that of the slender nervure, the springing motion of the broken arch, the leap downwards of the flying buttress — the visible effort to throw off a visible strain — never let us forget that Faith alone supports it, and that,

if Faith fails, Heaven is lost. The equilibrium is visibly delicate beyond the line of safety; danger lurks in every stone. The peril of the heavy tower, of the restless vault, of the vagrant buttress; the uncertainty of logic, the inequalities of the syllogism, the irregularities of the mental mirror — all these haunting nightmares of the Church are expressed as strongly by the Gothic cathedral as though it had been a cry of human suffering, and as no emotion had ever been expressed before or likely to find expression again. The pathos of its self-distrust and anguish of doubt is buried in the earth as its last secret. You can read out of it whatever else pleases your youth and confidence; to me, this is all.

As if conducting a party of girls through the northern French "Gothic" region, he has in this work celebrated the power of woman, as embodied in the Virgin. In his "Prayer to the Virgin of Chartres," he imagines himself a twelfth-century monk, anxious over the possibilities of science and technology:

> Seize, then, the Atom! rack his joints!
> Tear out of him his secret spring!
> Grind him to nothing! though he points
> To us, and his life-blood anoints
> Me — the dead Atom-King!

Under the title *The Education of Henry Adams*, his autobiography was privately printed in 1907 — variously described by him as a plea for educational reform, a twentieth-century counterpart to St. Augustine's *Confessions*, and a pendant to the *Chartres* book to show how far the concentrated energy of the thirteenth century had been dissipated by the twentieth. A third-person autobiography by an intellectual and a neurasthenic upset by current problems, it has much in common with the writings of Nietzsche and later of Spengler. It is a precious record of the impact of the nineteenth century on at least one highly sensitive and articulate individual, then approaching seventy, who expressed himself in extraordinarily felicitous prose.

As the writings of Henry Adams and Henry James represent highly individual responses to developments involved in the oncoming twentieth century, so too there were widespread group responses to the late nineteenth-century situation among writers — notably a movement usually referred to as "local color," which reached its height after the Civil War. In painting, the "local color" of an object is its color when seen in ordinary daylight as distinct from its color when seen in indirect or unusual illumination. Originally the intention of the "local colorists" was realistic. But later in the century, certain writers came more and more to specialize in the features and peculiarities of particular localities and their inhabitants and to concentrate on the depiction of them for the sake of depicting them — with a resultant gain in technical facility and loss in larger significance.

From the literary point of view, the best writing with local-color emphasis was that in New England. The type of the rural tale was established by Rose Terry Cooke of Hartford, one of whose stories appeared in the first issue of the *Atlantic* in 1857 — under the editorship of the author of the *Biglow Papers*, who made his magazine a local-color stronghold. Some of Mrs. Cooke's best stories were brought together in *Huckleberries Gathered from New England Hills* (1891). A younger writer, Mary E. Wilkins Freeman of Randolph, Massachusetts, wrote approximately two hundred rather grim New England stories, some of which appear in *A New England Nun* (1891) and reflect Turgenev's influence as well as a tendency toward a more incisive type of realism than did the work of major American writers of the period.

The best of the New England local colorists is Sarah Orne Jewett of South Berwick, Maine, who cannot be charged with mere concentration on detail for detail's sake. Pinned to her writing desk were two of Flaubert's sayings, which might be translated: "To write everyday life as one writes history" and "Not to make one laugh, but to act in the way nature does — that is, to make one dream." Some precedent for the forms she early practiced is to be found in Hawthorne, and for her concentration on the New England scene in Mrs. Stowe's *The*

Pearl of Orr's Island. At twenty, she placed a story, "Mr. Bruce," in the *Atlantic*. Howells urged her to collect some of her sketches in a first volume, *Deephaven* (1877).

The outstanding volume among some twenty she issued, however, is *The Country of the Pointed Firs* (1896), a connected group of sketches tracing the writer-observer's growing awareness of the diverse and highly individualized life in the imaginary Maine coast town of Dunnet. As in a Vermeer interior there is often a map on the wall, so in a Jewett story there is sometimes a suggestion that her provincial figures are participating in situations like those in the larger world. Toward the end of the *Pointed Firs* volume, for example, the narrator visits a woman who thinks of herself as Queen Victoria's twin:

> "Yes," said Mrs. Martin again, drawing her chair a little nearer, " 't was a very remarkable thing; we were born in the same day, and at exactly the same hour, after you allowed for all the difference in time. My father figured it out sea-fashion. Her Royal Majesty and I opened our eyes upon this world together; say what you may, 't is a bond between us. . . .

Mrs. Martin recounts her marrying a man named Albert, having two children, Victoria and Edward, going with her husband to sea, and actually getting a glimpse of Queen Victoria, "and she looked right at me so pleasant and happy, just as if she knew there was somethin' different between us from other folks." Of this volume, Kipling wrote her: "It's immense — it is the very life. . . . I don't believe even you know how good that work is!" Her disciple Willa Cather rated it with *The Scarlet Letter* and *Huckleberry Finn*. There is about Miss Jewett's writing a strange resonance which, if one is unable or unwilling to perceive it, one can dismiss as merely "genteel." She wrote, as Alexander M. Buchan in *Our Dear Sarah* observes, "not like a man, subduing the objects of the earth to his arrogant purpose and recording them vaingloriously, but like a woman, guarding and perpetuating within herself the essential human values."

The regionalist impulse manifested itself in the South more traditionally than in New England. Thomas Nelson Page perpetuated a glamorous picture of the antebellum South in *In Ole Virginia* (1887), a group of tales of which the best known is "Marse Chan," in which an old Negro explains in dialect how he is guarding the faithful dog of his late master, killed in the war. James Lane Allen dealt with the Lexington region in *A Kentucky Cardinal* (1894) and other novels. A lesser counterpart to Miss Jewett in Tennessee is Mary Noailles Murfree ("Charles Egbert Craddock"), who wrote a series of stories on the poor whites in the Cumberlands and Great Smokies, beginning with the volume *In the Tennessee Mountains* (1884).

In the Deep South, outstanding authors were Joel Chandler Harris and George Washington Cable. Harris, a journalist on the Atlanta *Constitution*, began a series of volumes of Negro dialect versions of animal fables with *Uncle Remus His Songs and Sayings* (1880). Harris also wrote many volumes about Negroes other than Uncle Remus, set in his native Georgia region — such as *Mingo* (1884) and *Free Joe* (1887). Cable was more closely associated with New Orleans (where he was for a while a reporter on the *Picayune*) and wrote stories of the inhabitants of that region, originally French, notably in *Old Creole Days* (1879) and *The Grandissimes* (1880). On the lecture circuit Cable teamed up effectively with Twain — the two men presenting a physical and temperamental contrast to each other, but both, though ex-Confederate soldiers, wholeheartedly in favor of the recognition of Negro rights. Two women writers of regional fiction that focused on New Orleans were Grace King (*Tales of Time and Place*, 1892) and Kate Chopin (*Bayou Folk*, 1894, and *A Night in Acadie*, 1897) — the latter writer apparently influenced by Maupassant.

The regional writing in the Deep South during this period has perhaps not quite as simple a relationship to its background as might at first seem. To a great extent it represents the expression of the Reconstructed or "New" South. The price paid by southern writers for the privilege of reaching a national and international audience through the big northern magazines and publishers was an acceptable attitude toward a "sane and earnest Americanism." The myth of the glamorous antebellum South or the acceptance of Reconstruction were all right. But a too forthright expression of discontent, a probing into the extent to which human rights were being recognized in the South, or a debunking of some of the local myths was not. Cable, for instance, had to spend the latter part of his life in Northampton, Massachusetts, because of his outspoken stand against Jim Crowism. Also it should be realized that much of this regional writing was also eagerly read in Europe: Miss Jewett, Mrs. Freeman, Miss Murfree, Cable, Harris, and others were brought out on both sides of the Atlantic.

The Middle and Far West had, of course, its regional developments too. A trailblazer for Twain was Bret Harte (1836-1902). Born in Albany, he went to California shortly after mid-century, where after teaching school, reporting, and serving as secretary of the mint, he became editor of the *Overland Monthly*, a far western rival of the *Atlantic Monthly*. "The Luck of Roaring Camp," "The Outcasts of Poker Flat," and "Tennessee's Partner" are among his better-known short stories — the best-known collection of them being *Tales of the Argonauts* (1875). Twain was associated with Harte during the California phase of his career. The *Atlantic* secured Harte for their pages by offering him a $10,000 blanket contract for anything he would write for a year; accordingly, he was for a while in New England. Eventually he became American consul in Crefeld, Germany, and spent about the last third of his life in Europe, the greater part in London, where he died. His stories were sensationally popular — in fact, their popularity was what induced Tauchnitz in Germany to publish Twain.

In Europe there were many readers who had become uncritically enthusiastic about American literature — the more outlandish the better. A flamboyant Westerner like Joaquin Miller, for example, with his red shirt, ten-gallon hat, and heavy boots, wrote a rather incredible autobiography *Life among the Modocs*, a play *The Danites of the Sierras*, and some gusty *Pacific Poems*. In California he had been taken as a joke, but in London he was received more seriously by some of the same people who had welcomed Whitman's work. Though the bubble of Miller's reputation has meanwhile floated off into space and he is known today, if at all, only as the writer of a poem "Columbus" included in anthologies, he serves to remind us that one of the extremes to which late nineteenth-century regionalism in the United States could easily go was the production of something for foreign export.

A figure prominent in the development of regional writing in the Middle West was the Indiana author Edward Eggleston, a Methodist minister, editor of numerous church papers. He had come to local color through reading Taine's *History of Art in the Netherlands*, and hoped to achieve in words what the Dutch *genre* painters had through paint. His best-known work is *The Hoosier Schoolmaster* (1871). From him stems the so-called Hoosier School of writing, including such works as Maurice Thompson's *Hoosier Mosaics* (1875), Booth Tarkington's *The Gentleman from Indiana* (1899), and Meredith Nicholson's *The House of a Thousand Candles* (1905) — not to mention a good deal of homely middle western verse like that of Will Carleton ("Over the Hills to the Poorhouse") and James Whitcomb Riley ("When the Frost Is on the Punkin"). Originally from Indiana but early establishing himself as a newspaper editor in Atchison, Kansas, E. W. Howe was the author of one of the first novels to present a highly disillusioned view of small town life: *The Story of a Country Town* (1883).

One continuing development during the later years of the nineteenth century is the publication of work by Negro writers, such as Charles W. Chestnutt of North Carolina, whose stories appeared in the *Atlantic* (a volume of seven of them being published as *The Conjure Woman*, 1899), and Paul Laurence Dunbar of Kentucky, who was encouraged by Howells to bring out a volume of poems, *Lyrics of Lowly Life* (1896), and of short stories, *Folks from Dixie* (1898). Another development with regional or local color implications is the appearance of work by cowboy novelists: Owen Wister, *The Virginian* (1902), for instance, and Andy Adams, *The Log of a Cowboy* (1903).

A special development of the southern or southwestern oral tale or local color story, grafted onto traditions deriving from Irving and Poe, is the work of William Sydney Porter ("O. Henry"), born in Greensboro, North Carolina, in 1862. At the age of twenty he went to Texas, became a bank teller, and conducted a humorous weekly, *The Rolling Stone*. Sentenced to five years in an Ohio federal penitentiary for embezzlement, he wrote more than a dozen stories that appeared in national magazines; and after his release in 1901 until his death in 1910 he lived in New York City, writing under his pseudonym some three hundred stories, ultimately collected and brought out in thirteen volumes, of which the earliest are *Cabbages and Kings* (1904) and *The Four Million* (1906). About half of his stories deal with incidents in New York, and practically all of them avoid disturbingly problematical aspects of human experience. He did not appreciate his admirers' calling him the "American Maupassant," for he said he had never tried to write anything dirty.

During the first quarter of the present century his popularity skyrocketed: by 1920 nearly five million copies of his books had been sold in the United States, and de luxe editions of his complete works were being issued and eagerly bought. An annual volume of the best current short fiction has been named in his honor, the "O. Henry Memorial Award Prize Stories"; and many of his works have been adapted for stage, movies, radio, and TV (where the "O. Henry Television Playhouse" had a long run). The French particularly have prized O. Henry's stories for their compactness, "exactness of measures and proportions" (as Raoul Narcy has phrased it), and avoidance of heavy-handed moralizing. Despite their complete innocence of Marxism, they have reached a wide audience in Russia, where stories with the "O. Henry twist" were being as assiduously cultivated by short story writers as, at the same time, in America were stories in the Chekhov manner. Between 1940 and 1955, reprinting rights were granted in twenty different countries. Enthusiasts for O. Henry have pointed out that his contribution — like Poe's — concerns technique as well as content, and that the trick ending, the informal tone, and the calculated use of telling phrases constitutes an "O. Henry style."

In such brief fictional sketches, of course, there could be little attempt to analyze social problems and urge reform — which before the Civil War fiction had begun to do. The latter purpose, however, was carried out by a utopian novel, *Looking Backward* (1888), by a New Englander, Edward Bellamy. It is set in the year 2000 in Boston as Julian West awakens and finds that society has been reorganized on a system of cooperation and shared wealth — a state of things that has come about gradually through the extension of the idea of equality from the political to the economic sphere. Though he at first feels out of place in this new world, he ultimately finds his mate, Edith Leete, and all is well. The nineteenth-century past exists for him only as a nightmare which he experiences briefly toward the end of the novel, but from which he awakens. This novel had considerable influence on both sides of the Atlantic, inspiring William Morris' *News from Nowhere* (1890) and other utopian writing such as Howells' and H. G. Wells's, and gave rise to Bellamy Clubs, to a national political party, and to a journal under Bellamy's leadership. He also wrote other social novels, such as *The Duke of Stockbridge* (1879), about Shays' Rebellion, and *Equality* (1897), a sequel to *Looking Backward*.

More upsettingly, Harold Frederic carried on the social debate in *The Damnation of Theron Ware* (1896), about a spiritually inadequate Methodist minister who feels trapped in the insincerities of his clerical profession. Sensationally popular in England under the title *Illumination*, this novel was for a time banned from the United States mails. Later in his career Frederic was London correspondent for the *New York Times*. David Graham Phillips, originally from Indiana but later a reporter on the New York *Sun* and *World* and protégé of Joseph Pulitzer, started his novel-writing career with a book about journalism, *The Great God Success* (1901), and in the ensuing ten years wrote twenty-six full-length books, mostly attacking one thing or another in the spirit of muckraking. Perhaps his best book is about a prostitute, *Susan Lenox: Her Fall and Rise*, completed in 1908. Robert Herrick, originally from Cambridge and Harvard but associated later with the University of Chicago, where he was for a while the head of the English department, began his novel-writing career with *The Man Who Wins* (1897), influenced by Strindberg's idea of the inevitable hostility and clash over supremacy between the man and the woman in marriage; possibly the best of his novels is *The Common Lot* (1904) — technically a little like Howells', only more astringent and consciously antiphilistine.

Thus, as the century drew toward its close, the simple realism of local color gave place to a stronger, more sensational emphasis. A leader in this development, Hamlin Garland (1860-1940), claimed to be practicing "Veritism" — a form of Impressionism, or emphasis on the moment of experience as it is acutely felt and immediately expressed, without much attempt to go beneath the surface. Much of his writing has the melodramatic air of oratory, a subject which he was teaching at the Boston School of Oratory at about the time that he was launching his writing career. As he wrote in his autobiographical *A Son of the Middle Border* (1917), his father, originally from Maine and a soldier in the Civil War, tried unsuccessfully to establish a homestead for his family in various parts of the Middle West, moving always farther on and encountering at each move new frustrations at the hands of nature. Hamlin himself gave up this Westward quest and returned to the Atlantic seaboard — took, as he called it, the "back trail." Thus his writing served to formulate a development in the course of the frontier within the United States, and the "back trailer" movement was to be an increasingly evident phenomenon.

One of Garland's important early books is *Main-Travelled Roads* (1891), a group of six Mississippi Valley stories that aroused criticism from people who considered him "a bird willing to foul his own nest." In answer, he said, he would give a "blunt statement of facts," and then proceeded to orate:

> My answer to all this criticism was a blunt state-
> ment of facts. "Butter is not always golden nor biscuits
> invariably light and flaky in my farm scenes, because
> they're not so in real life," I explained. "I grew up on a
> farm and I am determined once for all to put the essen-
> tial ugliness of its life into print. I will not lie, even to be
> a patriot. A proper proportion of the sweat, flies, heat,
> dirt and drudgery of it all shall go in. I am a competent
> witness and I intend to tell the whole truth."

In carrying out this intention he had been encouraged by the Chicago lawyer, Joseph Kirkland, author of *Zury, the Mean-est Man in Spring County* (1887).

Garland was not unaware of the problem of the literary, as distinct from the documentary, values in his writing. "I began to perceive," he wrote, "that in order to make my work carry its message, I must be careful to keep a certain balance between Significance and Beauty. The artist began to check the preacher." But the relation between means and ends here is significant: the aesthetic served the documentary, not the doc-umentary the aesthetic aims. A great deal of what he early wrote was really propaganda for Henry George's economic program for the single tax. Other early works of Garland's are *Prairie Folks* (1893), about his middle western boyhood, and a short novel about a woman journalist *Rose of Dutcher's Coolly* (1895), as well as a book of essays *Crumbling Idols* (1894). During the first decade of the twentieth century he wrote romances based on trips to the Rocky Mountain and Klondike regions. Then, from *A Son of the Middle Border* (1917) on, he wrote again of his boyhood, completing an ex-tensive account of his own and his family's experience.

Like Howells, he had a life span long enough to permit him to carry to fruition some of his potentialities. Three other writers, however, at the turn of the century each lived scarcely half as long and consequently do not present in their careers

quite the same sense of having fully realized their possibilities
— though what Crane, Norris, and London did complete suggests that they were far more gifted.

Standing in relation to Garland somewhat as Paine to
Franklin, Thoreau to Emerson, or Melville to Hawthorne, was
Stephen Crane (1871-1900). Fourteenth child of a Methodist
minister in Newark, he lived for a while at the Art Students'
League in New York, reported wars in Cuba and Greece for
a newspaper syndicate, and died of tuberculosis in the Black
Forest while still in his twenties. During his hectic career, he
applied in his writing some of the ideas churning around in his
day under the labels of "realism," "impressionism," and "naturalism." A sense of nervousness, of something that has not
quite jelled, is present in his early "Sullivan County Sketches"
(1892) — sharp, breezy, ironical toward both his characters
and himself. His *Maggie: A Girl of the Streets* (1893) exemplifies some aspects of the program of naturalism, i.e., pessimistic
determinism, enunciated and exemplified by Zola — an author
whose works had to a limited extent influenced Howells and
James and may or may not have actually been read by
Crane before he wrote *Maggie*. The novel opens with the rau-
cous squabbling of a slum family, in which Maggie is a flower
that has blossomed "in a mud-puddle": step by step she is beaten
down, through various levels of prostitution, till she ends up a
suicide in the East River. In this and other writing, Crane felt
strongly an urge to break through the surface aspects of a con-
ventionalized Christianity to something more spiritual underneath: on the copy of the first edition he sent to Garland he
wrote:

> . . . it tries to show that environment is a tremendous
> thing in the world and frequently shapes lives regardless.
> If one proves that theory one makes room in Heaven
> for all sorts of souls (notably an occasional street girl)
> who are not confidently expected to be there by many
> excellent people.

Here Crane was attacking the moral smugness not only of
"respectable" society but also of Maggie's Bowery environ-

ment: her betrayer, for example, insists that he's "a good f'ler. An'body' trea's me right, I allus trea's 'em right!" and her mother weeps and screams, "Oh, yes, I'll fergive her!" If one recalls that the fundamental Protestant position involves the individual's being saved not by works, perhaps one can see in the novel an attitude of rejecting — in the words of the Catechism — "the pomps and vanities of this wicked world."

The short novel of Crane's that is most widely read today is *The Red Badge of Courage* (1895). When he started to do research for it in Civil War reminiscences, he told his friend the painter Linson, "I wonder that *some* of those fellows don't tell how they *felt* in those scraps! They spout eternally of what they *did*, but they are emotionless as rocks!" The starting point for this work thus seems to have been a subliterary *genre* of war memoirs, and the intention seems to have been that of focusing not on deeds but on feelings. The third-person point of view in it is that of a common soldier, Henry Fleming, after whom the novel was originally called *Private Fleming His Various Battles;* but in the course of revision the purely individual aspects of the characters were deemphasized. As Tolstoi in *War and Peace* had played down the conventional military heroes, so Crane was here exalting the unknown soldier — that is, the one who survived. Not concrete material details are important, but psychological states. As Howells pointed out in an "Easy Chair" discussion of the novel, "A whole order of literature has arisen, calling itself psychological, as realism called itself scientific" — Tolstoi, Gorky, Ibsen, Björnson, Hauptmann, James, Maeterlinck. Thus, in literature, the objective aim had been succeeded by a more subjective one, the more documentary by a more poetic. *The Red Badge of Courage* follows the responses of the young soldier through his first battle experience, his running away and his return, and his eventually becoming a true veteran. Though there are many details throughout that suggest a primitive Christian intention, perhaps the religious aspect is but one of the many overtones, as in the late James novels. Another is the aesthetic: the color indications, for example, are handled quite carefully and sensitively. In many ways a *tour de force*, it has a spare, lithe, modern air.

Of his short stories, the one most often reprinted is "The Open Boat," based on the author's experience of having been adrift for two days off the Florida coast, in connection with his Cuban activities. Nature is here flatly indifferent to the human predicament. In the boat, however, the immanence of death has united the men; and one, Billy the oiler (a Christlike figure, comparable to Melville's Billy Budd), sacrifices himself to get his comrades ashore. Another of Crane's short stories is "The Blue Hotel": in the midst of a blizzard, an apprehensive Swede goes into a Nebraska hotel, sure that he is going to be shot, and ultimately — through the sheer operation of his own anxiety — he is. An Easterner tries to explain to a cowboy that all those present have contributed to this unfortunate outcome and that the man who pulled the trigger was but "a culmination, the apex of a human movement." The cowboy refuses to admit any share in the guilt: "Well, I didn't do anythin', did I?" In fictional guise, the story suggests the general human responsibility in the slaying of an innocent victim — as, for example, in the Crucifixion.

Crane's poems — in *The Black Riders* (1895) and *War Is Kind* (1899) — are in a rather clipped free verse, a kind of synthesis of the style of Whitman and that of Emily Dickinson. Considering all that Crane did in his twenty-nine years, one can but remark on his unusual potentialities as a writer; but, like some other of his contemporaries and like some of the early Romantics a century before, he figured in what is sometimes called in literary histories a "transition period."

Only slightly longer-lived than Crane was another novelist who had a clearer relationship to the literary movement that focused around Zola in France: Frank Norris (1870-1902), born in Chicago of rather wealthy parents, educated at private schools, the Atelier Julien in Paris, the University of California, and Harvard. His early work was rather late Romantic — short stories in California magazines, a long medievalistic poem *Yvernelle* (1892), and an article on "Ancient Armour" in the

San Francisco *Chronicle*. For this newspaper he went to South Africa to report on the Boer War in 1895, made the trip through the jungle from Cairo to the Cape, and contracted African fever in a Johannesburg military prison. Norris' approach to naturalism was thus via Neo-Romanticism rather than science. His work, though serving to domesticate in the United States the achievement of the somewhat more hardheaded, earnest, pedestrian Zola, also differs from it.

Norris' *McTeague* (1899) is an exaggerated, melodramatic example of so-called naturalistic fiction: the title character, a San Francisco "practical dentist," degenerates under the influence of various forms of animal spirits till he kills his miserly scrubwoman wife and her former lover (who has, however, in his final struggle — in Death Valley — managed to handcuff himself to his adversary and thus doom him to slow extinction under the desert sun). The figure of McTeague derives some of its aspects from the Nietzschean idea of the *Übermensch* (which had, in turn, derived some of its aspects from the Carlylean and Emersonian idea of the hero — though what Nietzsche meant by the *Übermensch* was as far from a McTeague as it was from a Hitler). Other novels of Norris' somewhat along the same line are *Moran of the Lady Letty* (1898) and *Vandover and the Brute* (1914). In *Vandover* the title character becomes, by the end of the novel, a sort of wolf, running around on all fours and howling. While these novels have aged incredibly, they represent something historically important — that certain Western European developments may be in some way assimilated into American literature and thereafter be transcended.

Norris' more solid contribution to the early twentieth-century literature of the United States is his trilogy *The Octopus* (1901), *The Pit* (1903), and (uncompleted) *The Wolf*. As he wrote to Howells in acknowledging a favorable review of *McTeague* and outlining his plans:

> My idea is to write three novels around the one subject of *Wheat*. First, a story of California (the producer), second a story of Chicago (the distributor), third, a

story of Europe (the consumer) and in each to keep to
the idea of this huge Niagara of wheat rolling from
West to East. . . .

By "East" he here apparently meant primarily Europe, not
Asia. In planning this "big epic trilogy," however, he was
starting to work his way back toward the kind of global orientation exhibited by many earlier American writers.

A third leading prose writer at the turn of the century —
one of our first internationally famous Californians and earliest
writers of proletarian literature — was Jack London (1876-
1916), who completed during less than twenty years some fifty
books. His early life in San Francisco was quite bizarre and,
as he later said, was "pinched by poverty." On one of his youthful escapades he claims to have pursued a herd of seal as far as
Japan and to have landed there and got drunk in Yokohama.
He published a prize-winning account of this trip, "Typhoon
Off the Coast of Japan," in the San Francisco *Call.* In 1894 he
deepened his social consciousness and learned of Marxism when
he started across the country to Washington with Coxey's
Army. Back in California, at nineteen, he attended Oakland
High School and, briefly, the University of California at Berke-
ley. With the discovery of gold in Alaska in 1896, he went to
the Klondike, but returned with scurvy. In 1900 his "An Odyssey of the North" appeared in the *Atlantic.* Soon a volume of
his short stories was published, *The Son of the Wolf* — hearty
action stories set in the Far North, "where men are men."
What women were there he was soon to reveal in a work of fiction, *A Daughter of the Snows* (1902). This was shortly followed by *The Call of the Wild* (1903), *The Sea Wolf* (1904),
and *White Fang* (1906).

In 1902 London had started out for South Africa to report
the aftermath of the Boer War for the American Press Association, but when he got to England he found that his assignment
had been canceled. As a result, he wrote instead an exposé of
conditions in the London slums, *The People of the Abyss*
(1903):

From the slimy, spittle-drenched side-walk, they were picking up bits of orange peel, apple skin, and grape stems, and they were eating them. The pits of green gage plums they cracked between their teeth for the kernels inside. They picked up stray crumbs of bread the size of peas, apple cores so black and dirty one would not take them to be apple cores, and these things these two men took into their mouths, and chewed them, and swallowed them; and this, between six and seven o'clock in the evening of August 20, year of our Lord 1902, in the heart of the greatest, wealthiest, and most powerful empire the world has ever seen.

In 1904 he went to Japan to report the Russo-Japanese War, and this time, despite constant harassment, managed to carry through partially his international assignment.

Rapidly London was becoming a national idol as a lecturer. In *The Iron Heel* (1908) he wrote supposedly from the vantage point of 1932 and told how capitalism would fight back against the threat of socialism — as it did in World War I and thereafter. Anatole France in an introduction to a new edition of *The Iron Heel* in 1924 attributed to London prophetic insight:

Alas, Jack London has that particular genius which perceived what is hidden from the common herd, and possessed a special knowledge enabling him to anticipate the future. He foresaw the assemblage of events which is but now unrolling to our view.

In 1909 London wrote a novel *Martin Eden,* an "indictment of individualism" in which the central character ends up by committing suicide. As London's own private affairs became more and more complicated, in 1916 shortly before his own presumably self-inflicted death he resigned from the Socialist Party "because of its lack of fire and fight, and its loss of emphasis upon the class struggle."

London's works have had and still have a very widespread appeal, both in the United States and abroad. Between 1932 and 1940 the number of published French translations of American authors runs: London, twenty-seven; Poe, fourteen; James, seven; Faulkner, five; Hemingway, four; etc. In the 1940's the chief librarian of the Royal Swedish Library wrote of London as "the most admired of all American authors in Sweden." Between 1918 and 1943 his various books were printed in over five hundred editions and ten million copies in Russian.

Although in the work of the late nineteenth-century American prose writers there is much that is essentially poetic, there is no sizable, sustained, and determined body of poetry published during the poets' own lifetime by writers of the stature of some that have previously been considered. Emily Dickinson, today generally considered next to Whitman in importance as a poet, was in her lifetime no more of a literary presence than was Edward Taylor some two centuries before: only seven brief poems of hers got into print during her lifetime, and during her later years (when she wrote comparatively fewer poems — perhaps only a dozen or so a year) she seems not to have been much interested in further publication. Although during her lifetime she sent poems to her friends in letters and after her death there ensued haphazard publication of much of her work, her letters and poems have been made available in an orderly and complete form only since her papers passed into the hands of Harvard University in 1950. There are still, however, many uncertainties about the order, dating, and "final version" of many items — something that normally does not exist to quite this extent with writers who have seen most of their own work through the press. As with Taylor one wonders whether he intended poetry or prayer, so with Emily Dickinson one often wonders whether she was writing a poem or a letter.

Born and spending practically all of her life in Amherst, Massachusetts, Emily Dickinson (1830-1886) was five years older than the oldest of the three authors considered at the beginning of this chapter. Thus she was only eleven years younger than Whitman , twenty-three than Thoreau, and twenty-seven than Emerson (that great seminal mind of the century who early influenced her as well as others). Like Whitman's, her most intense and poetically fruitful experiences occurred during the Civil War. It was during this time that she wrote almost half of her extant poems, and that she first communicated with Thomas Wentworth Higginson, who had just published an article in the *Atlantic* seeming to indicate his receptivity to new writers, asking him whether what she had been writing was "alive" (i.e., worth doing) and enclosing four samples — to which he replied that they were formally defective and unpublishable. Some of her poems clearly refer to the Civil War as being then in progress; and, although they are not her best, other of her poems about death — like Whitman's — are perhaps also to be understood against this background. Like Edwards and Franklin in the previous century, Emily Dickinson and Walt Whitman never met — despite the fact that they both influenced some of the same writers. A nice sense of the difference between the two is conveyed by a poem each wrote about a train, Whitman entitling his "To a Locomotive in Winter" and beginning "Thee for my recitative" and Emily Dickinson beginning, without title and in the first person, "I like to see it lap the miles." One worked additively, the other subtractively; one was masculine and extrovertive, the other feminine and introvertive. They exemplify a complementary relationship, like that of Poe and Emerson earlier in the century. Her poems are quick, deft, and — like Zen Buddhist work — of the essence.

Her attitude toward nature is different from that of Emerson and the English Romantics. In the following short poem (dated in the Harvard edition c. 1879 and included by the author in some half-dozen letters, where she referred to it as "a Humming Bird"), there is no explicit lesson drawn from the suggested bit of experience, no praise or blame of the natural order — simply the abstract touches of motion and color:

> A Route of Evanescence
> With a revolving Wheel —
> A Resonance of Emerald —
> A Rush of Cochineal —

> And every Blossom on the Bush
> Adjusts its tumbled Head —
> The mail from Tunis, probably,
> An easy Morning's Ride —

Her more thought-provoking poems, however, deal very often with death. One that she sent to Higginson and that was printed in 1862 (though with a different second stanza) formulates her vision of the souls of the departed, waiting in the cemetery — with no intrusive comment from the poet, but just with a sense of this being the way it is, mysterious and wondrous and vast:

> Safe in their Alabaster Chambers —
> Untouched by Morning —
> And untouched by Noon —
> Lie the meek members of the Resurrection —
> Rafter of Satin — and Roof of Stone!

> Grand go the Years — in the Crescent — above them —
> Worlds scoop their Arcs —
> And Firmaments — row —
> Diadems — drop — and Doges — surrender —
> Soundless as dots — on a Disc of Snow —

Emily Dickinson has, of course, affiliations with earlier Puritan religious thought. In Jonathan Edwards' day her part of Massachusetts had been a focal point of the Great Awakening. In her girlhood it was still more Calvinistic than Boston. Her background was Trinitarian Congregationalist. When a student at Mt. Holyoke in 1847 she was lectured at (in a manner reminiscent of Edwards' Enfield sermon) to profess her choice of "the service of God," but she could not bring herself publicly to "get religion." All her life she remained religiously unconventional and intransigent — possibly not being able to "get" religion because she had it all the time.

In her quick, darting emphasis on the vividness and unexpectedness of the color and motion suggested by the individual word or phrase, she differs fundamentally from the other major poet of the post-Civil War period, Sidney Lanier (1842-1881), who more often sought in his poetry a steady flow of sound. In this he was working in a tradition that had been at its height earlier in that great century of music, the nineteenth. The fact that the emphasis in poetry was shifting from an auditory to a visual and kinesthetic base cost Lanier any possible widespread public, as did also the fact that he was a Southerner.

Born in Macon, Georgia, he was graduated from Oglethorpe University, served in the Confederate Army, was taken prisoner while running the blockade, contracted tuberculosis in prison camp, and lived in the South during the disheartening days of Reconstruction. He wrote a rather nonrealistic novel about the Civil War, *Tiger-Lilies* (1867). Though his poems cannot be called "realistic" either, they make unmistakable reference to current problems: for example, the need for diversified agriculture in "Corn," and the prevalence of prostitution in "The Symphony" — where the Lady laments:

> O purchased lips that kiss with pain!
> O cheeks coin-spotted with smirch and stain!
> O trafficked hearts that break in twain!

Lanier was also a professional musician, and before the end of his short life was serving as flutist in the Peabody Orchestra and lecturing on English literature at Johns Hopkins University in Baltimore. A still useful book growing out of his academic activities and incorporating his knowledge of both music and poetry is his *Science of English Verse*.

"The Symphony" (1875) sets forth the thoughts and feelings of a highly articulate musician, as if in an extended piece of music. In the beginning Lanier's mind dwells on "trade" — on buying and selling. He regrets the extent to which materialism has invaded the world about him. The violins are saying that they wish trade were dead and that more human warmth and less calculating intellect prevailed. This essential theme is developed throughout the poem — as it were by different instruments and in their particular tone-colors. A passage of great delicacy, with a suave and sustained quality that Whitman and Emily Dickinson seldom attempted, occurs when Lanier's own instrument professes to speak for

> All sparklings of small beady eyes
> Of birds, and sidelong glances wise
> Wherewith the jay hints tragedies;
> All piquancies of prickly burs
> And smoothnesses of downs and furs,
> Of eiders and of minevers; . . .

The instruments and themes are brought together toward the end: the poor folks' crying, the women's sighing, knighthood, childhood, Christianity — or, to state them differently, economic exploitation, prostitution, idealism, innocence, religion (thus there is a progression from the less to the more edifying — from, as Beethoven said of his symphonies, "suffering to joy"). The poem concludes with the beautiful line: "Music is love in search of a word." Highly wrought and formal in a way that has not been in fashion during most of the present century, Lanier's poems are rich, creative, and unique — and some of them are literature of a high order.

There were, of course, other writers of verse — for example, Charles Warren Stoddard, with his *South Sea Idyls* (1873), written about some of the same areas as Melville had visited. But the late nineteenth century in the United States was not one of its really burgeoning poetic periods. Nor had drama as yet come into flower. There were theaters, actors, and audiences, but no plays that continue to be much read or performed. James A. Herne achieved widespread popularity with his *Hearts of Oak* (1879), and reflected an awareness of Ibsen's *A Doll's House* in *Margaret Fleming* (1890). Bronson Howard wrote social comedy (*Young Mrs. Winthrop*, 1882; *One of Our Girls*, 1885) and one of the first successful plays about the Civil War, *Shenandoah* (1888). From the West Coast came David Belasco, whose *Madame Butterfly* (after a story, 1897, by John Luther Long) and *The Girl of the Golden West* are the bases of operas by Puccini. From the Middle West came Augustus Thomas, whose *In Mizzoura* (1893) adapted the Bret Harte formula to the stage and whose last important play, *The Copperhead* (1918), is based on the Civil

War. Worthy of mention, also, are Clyde Fitch's *The Girl with the Green Eyes* (1902) and *The Truth* (1907).

But from the Civil War to World War I, poetry and drama lagged behind prose fiction as an object of serious public concern. Even much of the prose fiction during the first decade of the twentieth century was by older writers, and the careers of such brilliant younger men as Crane, Norris, and London were abortive. The period at the turn of the century — in contrast to those periods before the Civil War and after World War I — was not a time of literary fulfillment in America; it was what is sometimes called a "transition period." The public literature narrowed itself more to the local, regional, national, or at most Atlantic, losing its earlier sense of the whole world and dealing more with what *was* than with what *might be* — its focus becoming more and more bourgeois and this-worldly.

In the essay in the larger sense, however, there appeared stirrings which were to broaden this rather narrow focus again. Expository prose — including personal essays and writing in special and technical fields — must not be overlooked in an account of a literary period: after all, so-called imaginative literature plays a negligible role in early American literature, and it does not do to shift entirely in the course of a historical account the basis upon which examples of that literature have been selected for discussion. Particularly some writings should be mentioned that have affected — directly or indirectly — the rest of the world, East and West, and helped to restore a world orientation to American thought, reasserting a concern with matters that are ultimate rather than immediate and, if not yet "art," providing the basis for "a new art."

A continuing stratum of American prose was concerned with religion and the church. American influence in the Roman Catholic church had for some time been exerted in the direction of liberalization, but prevailing trends at the Vatican had been toward conservatism: in 1864, for example, among the "Principal Errors of Our Times" was listed the idea "that the Roman pontiff can and ought to reconcile himself to agree with progress, liberalism, and modern civilization," and in 1870 the dogma of papal infallibility was explicitly promulgated. During the twentieth century, however, the tendencies toward "Americanism" (as it was colloquially referred to in Roman Catholic circles) have received more official recognition. An example of a writer who helped in this development was John Lancaster Spalding of Kentucky, later Bishop of Peoria, with his *Lectures and Discourses* (1882), *Means and Ends of Education* (1895), *Thoughts and Theories of Life and Education* (1897), and *Socialism and Labor* (1902). Among Protestants there was much clerical and lay writing in favor of the "social gospel" — a development that still further reversed the emphasis that had, in Luther's day (with his stress on salvation by faith rather than works), separated them from the Roman Catholics. There was also, during the closing decades of the nineteenth century, a great deal of strongly American-supported missionary activity, with attendant publication.

In the somewhat technical field of philosophy there was a good deal of late nineteenth-century writing in the United States. German idealism, particularly that of Hegel, had been brought by the German immigrants up the Mississippi; and in 1867, in St. Louis, William T. Harris founded and conducted for a quarter of a century the *Journal of Speculative Philosophy*. Economics owes much to Thorstein Veblen's *The Theory of the Leisure Class* (1899), and sociology to William Graham Sumner's *Folkways* (1907).

In a more personal vein, some of the essay-writing and other activities of Americans had Eurasian influence. Many Americans were responsible for picking at the cracks that had begun to show in the imposing edifice of Victorianism. The American Henry Harland was the founder and editor of *The Yellow Book*, which brought much of the antiphilistine agitation in London to a focus. The painter, etcher, and essayist James McNeill Whistler (born of Irish stock in Lowell in 1834; educated in Moscow, at West Point, and in Paris; and settled by 1860 in London) soon came in conflict with that disciple of

Charles Eliot Norton and grand panjandrum of British art criticism, John Ruskin, Slade Professor of Art at Oxford. When
Whistler exhibited one of his "nocturnes" at the Grosvenor
Gallery Exhibition, Ruskin attacked the work in his *Fors Clavi-
gera* as "imposture. I have seen and heard much of cockney
impudence before now; but never expected to hear a coxcomb
ask two hundred guineas for flinging a pot of paint in the public's face." Whistler sued him for libel, and won. By the turn
of the century Whistler's wit and address had found a host of
British imitators. Some of the best of his remarks are included
in *The Gentle Art of Making Enemies* (1890). Oddly enough,
he sometimes was using ammunition that had been left by his
fellow West Pointer, Edgar Allan Poe.

More on the positive side, Whistler was instrumental in
spreading interest in Far Eastern art — particularly Japanese
prints. He and his circle were searching for a viable style that
would show a way out of the morass into which nineteenth-
century eclecticism had wandered. Overemphasis on certain
kinds of art had left other kinds neglected, and many of the enthusiasts for these neglected areas combined in a sort of syn-
aesthetic move under an Impressionist banner, to regain greater
public response by shock methods. Whistler's emphasis on certain effects influenced poetry: when he exhibited his "Symphony in White No. 2: The Little White Girl in the Mirror" at
the Royal Academy in 1865, for instance, there was a poem by
Swinburne "Before the Mirror" attached to the frame. Whistler's famous "Ten O'Clock" speech (1885) ends with a declaration that even if new artists were not to appear "the story of
the beautiful is already complete — hewn in the marbles of the
Parthenon — and embroidered, with the birds, upon the fan
of Hokusai — at the foot of Fusiyama."

Thus the American-Asiatic relationship took on aesthetic
emphasis. Japan and other non-European lands were to give
the kind of impulse to further American and other "Western"
artistic development during the twentieth century that Greece,
for example, had given to Renaissance Western Europe.
Though Japanese art had early influenced French Impression-

ist painting, the contribution of Americans like Whistler, Hearn, and Fenollosa was to help carry this early influence to its logical conclusions.

The way for Lafcadio Hearn had been prepared by other Americans. Percival Lowell, of the well-known New England family, after studying extensively in Japan in 1883, wrote *The Soul of the Far East*. In Korea he was counselor to the old regime, and his *Chosön* is a unique record of this older way of life as he had observed it. His interest was paralleled by that of other New Englanders, notably Sturgis Bigelow, who brought back twenty-six thousand objects of Japanese art (some now in the Museum of Fine Arts, Boston) and after extensive study in Japan became a Buddhist and wrote *Buddhism and Immortality*.

In Lafcadio Hearn, however, there appeared a peculiarly gifted writer, of mixed national antecedents (one might question whether he was an American, but — if not — what was he?). Born in 1850 on an Ionian island in the Aegean of a Greek mother and an Irish father, he came to the United States in 1869. After brief journalistic activity in New York, he went to New Orleans, and for two years was a correspondent in Martinique. In 1890, having read Lowell's books, he went to Japan for *Harper's Magazine* and taught English in governmental schools, wrote for the Kobe *Chronicle*, lectured, was adopted by the Samurai family into which he married, and spent the rest of his life there. Among the many volumes of his essays, there are about a dozen on Japan, beginning with *Glimpses of Unfamiliar Japan* (1894) and going on through the more substantial *Japan: An Attempt at Interpretation* (1904). More than mere travel books, these undertake to convey the essential spirit of the Far East. Though Hearn is said never to have learned the Japanese language very well and to have depended largely on translations and his own acute intuitions, he effectively interpreted the West and Japan to each other and, under the aegis of Buddhism, reconciled the fundamentally discordant elements of Impressionism, evolution, and nationalism by stressing the nuances, the "fugitive subtleties" of expression and personality he found in the Japanese arts:

> And what are these but the ebb and flow of life ancestral — under-ripplings in that well-spring unfathomable of personality whose flood is Soul. Perpetually beneath the fluid tissues of flesh the dead are moulding and moving — not singly (for in no phenomenon is there any single-ness), but in currents and by surgings.

Hearn's interpretation of Japan has been credited with having influenced the Japanese themselves, who as their culture became more and more industrialized have found in his image of them an idea of what they perhaps once were, might have been, or like to think of themselves as being. Thus his work has interpreted not only the East to the West but also the East to itself.

Another contribution to Far Eastern self-realization was made by Ernest Fenollosa of Salem, son of a Spanish music teacher residing there and of the daughter of a Salem shipping magnate. After graduating from Harvard, Fenollosa was appointed professor of philosophy at the then new University of Tokyo, where he campaigned intensively to save the Japanese artistic heritage from being swallowed up in an uncritical acceptance of an outmoded European culture. To this end he established an "Art Club of Nobles," and in 1886 was appointed Commissioner of Fine Arts for the Empire. He was the first director of the Tokyo Academy and the Imperial Museum, charged with registering all the art treasures of the country. "You have taught my people," the Japanese emperor told him, "to know their own art." For a while he was also curator of the Japanese section of the Boston Museum of Fine Arts. On one of his visits to Boston in 1892 he wrote a long poem *East and West* for the Phi Beta Kappa exercises at Harvard. Also he translated the texts of some fifty Nō plays in *Certain Noble Plays* of Japan (edited by Ezra Pound). His monumental *Epochs of Chinese and Japanese Art* was posthumously published. The Japanese government officially sent a cruiser to convey his ashes to Japan and place them alongside those of Sturgis Bigelow in a shrine sacred to the followers of their adoptive Buddhist faith.

The movement of reaching out to the Far East constitutes, to be sure, a minority and often overlooked movement in late nineteenth-century American literature. More in the public eye, of course, and more "literary" in the usually accepted meaning of the term, was the intense cultivation of the novel during this period, when the literature of the world was enriched by the vitality of Twain, the balance of Howells, and the fineness of James.

A Wider Range
5. of Literature
Eliot, O'Neill, Faulkner

In fields other than the novel important early twentieth-century work has been done by authors born and bred in America — poets such as Robinson, Pound, Eliot, Frost, and dramatists such as O'Neill, Anderson, Wilder, Miller, Williams. Early in the century a renewed interest in poetry and drama manifested itself in the little magazine and the little theater. Particularly during the second quarter of the century, American literature attracted international attention — even as it had done, on a more individual basis, from the second quarter of the previous century. The wider range of this interest than just the novel was pointed up by the Swedish Academy's awarding the Nobel Prize for literature to O'Neill in 1936 and Eliot in 1948.

Of course, prose fiction continued; and the Nobel selections also point to an international role in that field: Lewis in 1930, Buck in 1938, Faulkner in 1949, Hemingway in 1954, and Steinbeck in 1962. Only two novelists from England, Kipling and Galsworthy, have been so honored — neither particularly in tune with the mid-twentieth century. Though the literature of a country is a matter of more than just winning prizes, the decisions of the Swedish Academy, which operates on a world basis, suggest that twentieth-century English literary developments have been largely American — especially those which can be considered, in the words of Nobel's will, "of an idealistic tendency."

As the last chapter, starting with the Civil War, began with Lincoln, so perhaps this one, opening with World War I, might begin with the wartime President and 1920 Nobel Peace Prize recipient Woodrow Wilson. Between Lincoln and Wilson one notes the same kind of difference as between Twain and James — Wilson an intellectual of great refinement and idealism, but unfortunately not as gifted as Lincoln with the common touch. Yet each in his way was concerned with achieving the plain style. In a speech at Buckingham Palace in 1918 Wilson said:

> We have used great words, all of us, we have used the great words "right" and "justice," and now we are to prove whether or not we understand those words and how they are to be applied to the particular settlements which must conclude this war. And we must not only understand them, but we must have the courage to act upon our understanding. Yet after I have uttered the word "courage," it comes into my mind that it would take more courage to resist the great moral tide now running in this world than to yield to it, than to obey it.

It was Wilson's misfortune that he relied too much on this "great tide running in the hearts of men," and after the war found himself, like Hamlet, in a situation beyond his powers, his own country refusing to ratify the Versailles Treaty and the League of Nations. For the duration of the war, however, his words formulated a highly idealistic spirit of what he called the New Freedom.

An American poet who can be taken as reflecting a rather quieter and less political version of the same idealism is Edwin Arlington Robinson (1869-1935). Shortly after the close of World War I he wrote one of his best-known lyrics, "The Dark Hills":

> Dark hills at evening in the west,
> Where sunset hovers like a sound
> Of golden horns that sang to rest

> Old bones of warriors under ground,
> Far now from all the bannered ways
> Where flash the legions of the sun,
> You fade — as if the last of days
> Were fading, and all wars were done.

Increasingly in later life he wrote long narrative poems with strongly psychological emphasis, concentrated on a few intensely conceived characters — almost Jamesian, particularly in the book-length novel in blank verse, *King Jasper*, contemporary in setting, brought out the year after his death with a preface by Robert Frost.

Born at Head Tide, Maine, Robinson spent his boyhood in nearby Gardiner, attended Harvard for two years, and during about the last half of his life lived in New York City, with summers at the MacDowell Colony in Peterboro. His volumes of verse written at the beginning of the century attracted the attention of Theodore Roosevelt, who reviewed one of them in a magazine and obtained a job for him in the New York Customs House (1905-1910). Though Robinson tried his hand at playwriting (*Van Zorn*, 1914, and *The Porcupine*, 1915), his published work shows a consistent and intense concentration on lyric and narrative poetry. The short poems in his early volumes are mostly in fixed forms such as sonnets, ballades, and villanelles. Some are poetical exercises based on classical originals; others are about writers (Zola, Verlaine, Hood, Crabbe); and still others succinctly characterize individuals conceived of as living in "Tilbury Town" (Gardiner, Maine): Richard Cory, suicide; Aaron Stark, miser; Cliff Klingenhagen, who drank wormwood and smiled. The first long blank-verse poem of Robinson's to appear was "Captain Craig" (1902), purporting to be written by one of the young men of Tilbury who, together with a few of his friends, had discovered there an old beggar who reminded them of Socrates. Also in the 1902 volume is "Isaac and Archibald," embodying a memory of childhood when the narrator visited two kind and considerate old men — both poems encouraging in the reader a mood of thoughtful meditation.

One of Robinson's better-known poems is "The Man against the Sky" (1916). It presents simply — but with, as Professor Cestre of the University of Paris pointed out, "Dantesque majesty and grandeur" — the figure of a man on a hilltop as seen against the sunset, a symbol of mankind:

> Between me and the sunset, like a dome
> Against the glory of a world on fire,
> Now burned a sudden hill,
> Bleak, round, and high, by flame-lit height made higher,
> With nothing on it for the flame to kill
> Save one who moved and was alone up there
> To loom before the chaos and the glare
> As if he were the last god going home
> Unto his last desire.

The poet speculates on this solitary figure's attitude of mind — on his nature and destiny — in a manner somewhat autumnal and Brahmsian. But he concludes that if human life were without meaning or future, the man would not be there against the sky — but would either do nothing or commit suicide:

> If after all that we have lived and thought,
> All comes to Nought, —
> If there be nothing after Now,
> And we be nothing anyhow,
> And we know that, — why live?
> 'Twere sure but weaklings' vain distress
> To suffer dungeons where so many doors
> Will open on the cold eternal shores
> That look sheer down
> To the dark tideless floods of Nothingness
> Where all who know may drown.

Outstanding among the later long poems of Robinson's is his Arthurian trilogy: *Merlin* (1917), *Lancelot* (1920), and *Tristram* (1927). The Robinson versions differ from the medieval source material in that the characters change with the unfolding incidents and the action is clearly more realistic: Tristram becomes involved with Isolt, for example, without needing to have recourse to a love philtre.

Most of the other long poems that Robinson wrote after World War I are set in more or less modern times. In his hands the blank-verse form achieved such flexibility and naturalness that one is scarcely conscious of it as a pattern in itself. Here the late nineteenth-century concentration on prose fiction seems rather to have spilled over into the area of poetry and to have influenced even a conservative poet like Robinson.

Three of Robinson's younger contemporaries, however, were much more radical in their approach to poetry. Ezra Pound, Amy Lowell, and Gertrude Stein had in common a gift of bringing out their contemporaries, of often wishing to set them right, and of instigating experimentation — somewhat as had Franklin and Emerson a century or so before. They really wanted and expected something new, evaluating what was in terms of what might develop from it as well as of what it had been. Though much of what the three themselves wrote may in the long run turn out to be of historical interest only, a review of their careers helps outline the literary developments of the early twentieth century. The influence of these "organizers" occurred mainly through personal contacts in Europe.

The career of Ezra Pound (b. 1885 in Hailey, Idaho) carried further a tendency noted by Hamlin Garland in leading spirits of his generation to take the "back trail": coming from farther west than the Garlands had reached, Pound took the trail first back to Philadelphia, then farther back to London, then Paris, then Rapallo. Thus Pound — like some of his contemporaries — can be called an "expatriate writer" (a term often used to describe the Americans in Paris during the twenties — not, however, a wholly adequate phrase if stretched to include James and Hemingway). Pound's first move from the Rocky Mountain area to Philadelphia, a seat of culture that had flourished early in America but had been less creative in the nineteenth century, was prompted by his father's occupation as an assayer for the United States mint there. In 1906 Ezra Pound received his Master of Arts degree in romance languages at the University of Pennsylvania, where he had as friends two others who were to figure in twentieth-century poetry — Hilda Doolittle ("H.D.") and William Carlos Williams. After a brief and unhappy teaching experience at a middle western college, Pound (like Emerson after his initial pastorate) headed for Europe. Pound's first volume of verse, *A Lume Spento*, was printed at Venice in 1908 — some of it written in a Browningesque dramatic lyric style that had seen its heyday in the mid-nineteenth century. This initial volume gave at least one British reviewer an impression of "virility in action." From an essay written in 1909 we know that Pound felt that he would "like to drive Whitman into the old world. I sledge, he drill. . . ."

During some dozen years in London Pound published about forty volumes, almost all verse. *Personae* (1909) was notable, according to one reviewer, for "brusque intensity of effect" and according to another, for the absence of "the current melancholy or resignation or unwillingness to live." From 1909 to 1911 he lectured on medieval and Renaissance poetry at the Regent Street Polytechnic Institute. Adopting a Bohemian manner, he began to figure in London groups that perpetuated a type of poetic activity that had flourished in Paris after the Franco-Prussian War. "There are innumerable poetic volumes," he wrote Williams, "poured out here in Gomorrah." A particularly successful series, edited by Edward Marsh, was called *Georgian Poets* and was accompanied by semipublic meetings, or "squashes"; but after the first issue inclusion in it was limited to British contributors. A group in which Pound could play an increasingly prominent role, however, had been started by T. E. Hulme (whose "Complete Poetical Works" — consisting of about half a dozen bits, each under ten lines — Pound included as an appendix to his *Ripostes*, 1912). Hulme's idea was that to have a new poetry there must first be established a new technique of concentration on a single image. By 1910 Hulme's group came to be known as *Les Imagistes* and to be largely dominated by Pound. Whereas in prose fiction Howells and James had made the English-speaking world aware of what had been developing on the Continent, no one quite so thoroughgoing had brought to Anglo-Saxon readers the corresponding developments in poetry. Allowing for great differences in temperament and ability, one might say that Pound undertook to do for poetry what James had done for the novel.

At one of the meetings of Hulme's group, in the Soho restaurant known as the Eiffel Tower, Pound bellowed out his "Sestina: Altaforte," beginning

> Damn it all! this our South stinks peace.
> I have no life save when the swords clash.

This caused great consternation among the diners, apprehensive of a war with Germany. Viewed one way, the poem was to astonish the *bourgeoisie*; viewed another, it was a formal exercise based on a Provençal poem by Bertran de Born, with six stanzas ending in a repeated pattern of final words and an envoi (the subject matter, however, being different from that of troubadour poems, which were usually about love).

During the second decade of the twentieth century, moreover, there were stirrings of concern for the state of poetry in the United States. In 1911 Harriet Monroe in Chicago persuaded a hundred people each to pledge $50 a year for five years to underwrite a magazine; and in 1912 she launched *Poetry: A Magazine of Verse*, for which Pound was "Foreign Correspondent." Through him the early numbers of this magazine furnished a mouthpiece for the London *Imagiste* movement. Also in 1912 the *Poetry Journal* began publication in Boston; some half-dozen poetic anthologies appeared; and some dozen American poets whose names would be recognized today issued separate volumes. In New York City, moreover, a new series entitled *The Glebe*, edited by Alfred Kreymborg and published by Albert and Charles Boni, included an anthology *Des Imagistes* (1914), selected by Pound, as its fifth number. By this time the "poetic renaissance" had begun on both sides of the Atlantic. In 1916 in the United States there were almost as many volumes of poetry and drama published as there were of fiction. Proceeding as it had from France to

England to America, it proved a predisposing factor for the Allied war effort; and no one will probably know what led Pound to take such an active role in this development, operating from abroad but becoming an even greater factor in the literary situation at home.

Some unexpected consequences ensued. One was that Ernest Fenollosa's widow, having read some of Pound's contributions to *Poetry* and having noted the Chinese source of most of his poems in *Des Imagistes*, turned over her husband's notes to Pound — whom Eliot, oddly enough, has termed "the inventor of Chinese poetry for our time." Pound, in turn, interested Yeats in this material; and Yeats's later Irish plays are strangely influenced by the Nō drama — though there is no indication that he took the challenge of this material with anything like the seriousness that Pound did, for whom this unexpected stimulus from Japan and China came as confirmation of a tendency already present in his writing and deeply at work in American literature itself. Pound addressed himself seriously to the problem of finding or creating common ground between the poetry of America and Asia. His volume of poems *Cathay* (1915) reflects his work with the Fenollosa material. *Certain Noble Plays of Japan* (1916) are Nō plays. *Ta Hio: The Great Learning* (1928) deals with the Confucian classics, carried on further in *Confucius: The Unwobbling Pivot and The Great Digest* (1947). Pound has also, of course, incorporated a great deal of Chinese material in his Cantos.

Not only for Yeats but also for countless other writers of the twentieth century Pound has done much — for Frost, Joyce, Hemingway, Cummings. As a translator or imitator he has extraordinary verve, as in this "Alba" in *Lustra* (1915):

> When the nightingale to his mate
> Sings day-long and night late
> My love and I keep state
> In bower,
> In flower,
> 'Til the watchman on the tower
> Cry:

> "Up! Thou rascal, Rise
> I see the white
>   Light
>   And the night
>   Flies."

His virtues are like those of the college instructor, as Emerson's were like those of the village parson — both, of course, operating outside the expected institutional framework.

In 1920 Pound moved to Paris, and in 1928 to Italy. In 1939, on the eve of World War II, he made a hasty trip to the United States to try to head off the clash that he saw was imminent; and during the war he broadcasted over the Rome Radio on shortwave to America, attacking the capitalistic basis and the current activities of the Allied powers. As a result, in 1943 he was indicted in the federal courts for giving "aid and comfort" to the enemies of the United States "contrary to his duty of allegiance." When in 1945 the Allies invaded Italy he was arrested and taken to Washington. There, however, he was hospitalized at St. Elizabeth's, and completed the ten *Pisan Cantos* (1948 — Nos. 72-84 in the overall numbering). There too he was awarded the first Bollingen Prize for poetry by an advisory committee of fourteen well-known writers acting in the name of the Library of Congress — a decision which precipitated a storm of protest that reached the floor of Congress and the pages of numerous periodicals. The decision, the advisory committee insisted, had been made solely on "poetry achievement" and "objective perception of value." In 1958 the indictment against Pound was dismissed, and he was released. Accompanied by his wife he returned to Italy, where their married daughter and two grandchildren live in an Alpine castle. Among other things, he has been concerned with finishing his Cantos, which have become his lifework in somewhat the same way as were Dante's *canti*, known as the *Divine Comedy* and completed in exile at the castle of Can Grande della Scala.

The Cantos appeared in installments, the first three having been published as early as 1919 and the 109th in 1959 (though a 1965 reprint includes only Cantos 1-95); Pound's original plan for exactly 100 Cantos has, evidently, been abandoned. They begin directly, with Odysseus and his crew sailing to the Underworld to slaughter sacrificial animals and give the dead spirits voice:

> And then went down to the ship,
> Set keel to breakers, forth on the goodly sea, and
> We set up mast and sail on that swart ship,
> Bore sheep aboard her, and our own bodies also
> Heavy with weeping, and winds from sternward
> Bore us out onward with bellying canvas,
> Circe's this craft, the trim-coifed goddess. . . .

Time and again throughout the Cantos there are oases of expository poetry — evocative of the United States of John Adams, the Italy of Dante, the Greece of Homer, and the China of Confucius. Brought into immediate juxtaposition with these passages, however, are long stretches of distinctly less edifying material, deriving from immediate experiences of Pound in the present century. Much of this modern material is about *usuria* — the use of money to make money — which is castigated by Pound with great bitterness. The poetic method is starkly presentational — a kind of extended ideogram, a concept of writing that seems to have been influenced by Fenollosa's notes on the pictographic nature of Chinese poetry. The radical difference between this concept of writing and one that has prevailed in Europe and America since the Renaissance causes difficulties for some readers, but deserves serious consideration, particularly today when the reading public is so eye-minded and when America and East Asia confront each other at so many points. Pound's contribution to American literature (like Poe's and Whitman's in the century before him) involves not just some more writing but also the challenge of a new way, or method, or aim of writing — a heroic attempt to assimilate the artistic ideals of Confucian China with those of Poe (by way of the French Symbolists) and Emerson (by way of Whitman).

Like *Leaves of Grass*, the Cantos are a man's life, for better or worse — and are not yet completed. Any view of them is thus necessarily partial. The concern over money, which becomes increasingly strident as they succeed one another, can be taken as a normal human concern, or as a special one on the part of Pound (who was unusually generous to his fellow writers in distress). Unconsciously, it may have been prompted by the poet's urge to come to terms with his father's occupation. It involved a rejection of the whole capitalistic value system. When the Cantos are completed one will unquestionably be in a better position to talk about what they mean. From a personal point of view they have undertaken to present something like a history of the world. The roll in it of American literature as a confrontation of Europe and Asia is brought out sharply through a new method of presentation.

Eleven years older than Pound but in some respects his follower, Amy Lowell (b. 1874 in Brookline of an old Boston family) makes clear by the title of her first volume of poems, *A Dome of Many-Coloured Glass* (1912), an admiration for Keats, of whom she later wrote a biography. Having contributed to *Poetry*, she went to London for the summer of 1913 with a letter of introduction from Harriet Monroe to Pound, who included one of her poems in *Des Imagistes* and tried to persuade her to back first the *Egoist* and then the *Mercure de France* for him to edit. Meanwhile, in her second volume of poems, *Sword Blades and Poppy Seed* (1914), the title poem describes the narrator buying swords and seeds from "Ephraim Bard, dealer in words," and seeing the sun rise; and another poem, "Astigmatism," shows "the Poet" going along with his walking stick whacking off the heads of all flowers that are not roses, and she adds:

> Peace be with you, Brother,
> But behind you is destruction and waste places.

Returning to London for the summer of 1914, she eased Pound out of his leadership of the Imagists and moved the publication center of the group (minus Pound) to Boston, where beginning in 1915 there appeared an annual anthology, *Some Imagist Poets,* and other individual volumes in a "New Poetry Series." As president of the New England Poetry Club and lecturer and controversialist, she proclaimed the gospel of the "New Poetry" (*Six French Poets,* 1915, and *Tendencies in Modern American Poetry,* 1917). Toward the end of her life, she issued anonymously a witty *Critical Fable* (1922) about the poets of her day, after the manner of her granduncle James Russell Lowell.

After World War I Amy Lowell became more and more interested in Far Eastern poetry. Her *Pictures of a Floating World* (1919) include fifty-four *hokku*-like "Lacquer Prints" and seven "Chinoiseries." In the translation of 137 Chinese poems published as *Fir-Flower Tablets* (1921) she was assisted by a friend in China, the librarian of the Royal Asiatic Society. As had Pound, she found that the visual contours of Chinese characters offered unexpected stimulus for poetic composition.

A third figure as forceful — and about the same age — as Amy Lowell was Gertrude Stein, born in what is now suburban Pittsburgh but spending her childhood in Vienna, Paris, Baltimore, and Oakland. She attended Radcliffe, and there came to admire William James, under whose direction she assisted in psychological research (published in 1896) on "automatic writing," substantiating a closer relationship between the conscious and the unconscious than had been assumed earlier. At James's suggestion, she studied medicine for a while at Johns Hopkins.

But in 1902 she and her brother Leo went to London, and in 1903 to Paris, where their apartment became a focal point for the artists of the Latin Quarter, notably Matisse and Picasso. Leo was working on his art and aesthetics, Gertrude on her writing. The first novel she completed was a Henry Jamesian treatment of a Lesbian situation, published posthumously as *Things as They Are* (1951).

Her first book to be printed was *Three Lives* (1910), which she wrote after having translated Flaubert's *Trois*

Contes. The most distinctive of the three fictional biographies is the second one, "Melanchtha," in which the thoughts and feelings of a complex Negress are suggested by repetitive verbal rhythms set off against those of her simpler friends Rose Johnson and Jeff Campbell:

> Melanchtha told Rose one day how a woman whom she knew had killed herself because she was blue. Melanchtha said, sometimes, she thought this was the best thing for herself to do.
> Rose Johnson did not see it the least bit that way.
> "I don't see Melanchtha why you should talk like you would kill yourself just because you're blue. I'd never kill myself Melanchtha 'cause I was blue. I'd maybe kill somebody else Melanchtha 'cause I was blue, but I'd never kill myself. If I ever killed myself Melanchtha it'd be by accident, and if I ever killed myself by accident Melanchtha, I'd be awful sorry.

During most of the sketch Melanchtha and Jeff seem headed toward marriage and probe their own and each other's feelings in a Jamesian way (though in language as simple as Huck Finn's), but in the end they drift apart: Melanchtha is forsaken by her friends and dies in a home for consumptives — in accordance with the epigraph from Laforgue at the head of the volume: "So I am an unfortunate and it is neither my fault nor the fault of life." "Melanchtha" has been widely praised — and justly so. Richard Wright, for example, said that through it his "ears were opened for the first time to the magic of the spoken word" and that when he read it to a group of semiliterate fellow-Negro stockyard workers he found that they understood every word: "Enthralled, they slapped their thighs, howled, laughed, stomped, and interrupted me constantly to comment upon the characters."

Gertrude Stein's first published magazine article was "Three Portraits of Painters" in Alfred Stieglitz's *Camera Work*, in 1912, about Cézanne, Matisse, and Picasso — the first appreciation, incidentally, of Picasso to appear in print anywhere. She and Leo had purchased a Cézanne painting of a female head, and much of the thought and planning for *Three Lives* took place while Picasso was painting her own portrait.

Her next extended prose work, *The Making of Americans,* about her family, was not published till 1925. Meanwhile, a volume of hers appeared, *Tender Buttons* (1914), usually considered poetry — but in some ways quite free (more so than Whitman or the *vers librists*). She also published quasi-dramatic works, some of which have been performed — notably *Four Saints in Three Acts* (with music by Virgil Thomson). Through both world wars she lived in France and exerted much influence on Americans there — Anderson, Fitzgerald, Cummings, Hemingway. The popular *Autobiography of Alice B. Toklas* (1933) — a book of Left Bank gossip purporting to have been written by her companion — was actually written by Gertrude Stein herself.

Unlike Pound and Amy Lowell, she had come to authorship with scientific rather than literary assumptions. She was the center of a circle different from either of theirs. Her concentration on her own feelings as they were developing within her and her persistent attempts to get them down on paper in their actual shape, tempo, and texture, as well as her generally unsentimental approach to life, helped open the minds of her contemporaries to possible new formulations of experiences and ideas.

The outstanding writer of the period between wars who perhaps owed most to Pound was T. S. Eliot. A back-trailer and expatriate, he was born in St. Louis in 1888, took his Master of Arts degree at Harvard in 1910, and became a British citizen in 1927. "In my end," he was later to quote in the best of his poetical works, the *Four Quartets*, "is my beginning" — "my" here obviously not to be taken too literally. His moving to England on the eve of World War I completed the circle begun by a seventeenth-century ancestor who had emigrated from East Coker to Massachusetts, where he served as a juror in the Salem witchcraft trial, and by the poet's grandfather, a Unitarian minister, who had gone from his graduation at Harvard to found a church, a school, and a university beyond the Mississippi. Eliot's mother had written verse plays, and his own juvenilia — published in school magazines in St. Louis and at Harvard — were in conventional nineteenth-century British modes. As an undergraduate in 1908, however, he read Symons' *Symbolist Movement in Literature* and immediately began imitating Laforgue. A period of study at the Sorbonne enabled him to hear the lectures of Bergson and to deepen his awareness of the work of Claudel, Gide, and Dostoievsky. Back at Harvard in 1911, he did further graduate work in philosophy and Sanskrit.

In 1914 Eliot went to Europe on a traveling fellowship, and through Conrad Aiken met Pound, who found him

> the only American I know of who has made what I can call adequate preparation for writing. He has actually trained himself *and* modernized himself *on his own.* The rest of the *promising young* have done one or the other but never both (most of the swine have done neither). It is such a comfort to meet a man and not have to tell him to wash his face, wipe his feet, and remember the date on the calendar.

Intuitively Pound recognized that Eliot — with his technical knowledge of older writings — was prepared to make a contribution to world literature. On one occasion he is supposed to have told Eliot: "You let *me* throw the bricks through the front window. You go in at the back door and take out the swag." He sent Eliot's "The Love Song of J. Alfred Prufrock" to *Poetry* and browbeat Harriet Monroe into publishing it in 1915, then tried to get her to give it a prize. Though unsuccessful, he perhaps felt his vision realized when Eliot in 1948 was awarded some $40,000 by the Swedish Academy.

Eliot's manuscript version of *The Waste Land* was cut down to about half its original length by Pound and was dedicated to him as *il miglior fabbro* before it saw publication in the *Criterion* in 1922. At the last minute Eliot provided it with notes (which he later regretted) because the printer needed additional copy. Actually this fragmentation of what

Eliot may originally have had in mind and this starting point for endless exegeses was the "making" of the poem — as the expression of the "disillusionment of a generation." (This Eliot himself declared was "nonsense. . . . I may have expressed for them their own illusion of being disillusioned, but that did not form part of my intention.") It is fairly clear that Eliot's general idea was to present the immediate world of his experience as a waste land in contrast to the world that one glimpses through some of the great classics, particularly Dante's *Divine Comedy*. There is, of course, nothing new about the idea of art being long and time fleeting, or about the cult of Dante, which had enjoyed special importance at Harvard since the days of Longfellow — or, for that matter, about the Anglo-American adaptation of post-Franco-Prussian-War French styles. What strikes one as unusual in *The Waste Land*, particularly in the last part of it, is the East Indian imagery:

> Ganga was sunken, and the limp leaves
> Waited for rain, while the black clouds
> Gathered far distant, over Himavant.

The thunder enunciates, in Sanskrit, the Brahman formula: Give. Sympathize. Control. And the poem ends with a sort of threefold Amen: Shantih shantih shantih. That we are not now in nirvana is, of course, a perennial and universal observation; but the Sanskrit coloring is notable. Influenced by the East, Eliot also is said to have reinfluenced it: the British critic and professor at the University of Singapore, D. J. Enright, in 1965 remarked in print that *The Waste Land* had "left more of a mark on the postwar Japanese consciousness than the rest of the Occupation put together."

In *The Waste Land* there are five numbered sections, the first, third, and fifth bearing most of the weight and the second and fourth contrasting (the former by its juxtaposition of a baroque and a realistic passage and the latter by its brevity and elegiac tone). This layout also underlies each of Eliot's *Four Quartets* (1935-1942), the group of poems that are his most mature, the most his own. Each of the four is named after a place with personal or ancestral associations. Two fragments from Heraclitus (given in Greek at the beginning) say, in effect, that truth is one though many live as if each had his own truth and that the way up and down are one and the same — in other words, that beneath apparent diversity and contradiction there is unity. In line with this epigraph, the theme of "Burnt Norton" is stated at the beginning: that all times are interrelated and simultaneous. In the first movement the theme springs from a childhood memory of a rose garden; in the second, cosmic and terrestrial aspects of the theme are suggested, with emphasis on "the still point of the turning world"; in the third, descent is made into the modern city and the isolated individual; in the fourth the question is raised whether nature will receive us after death, and the answer is that

> . . . the light is still
> At the still point of the turning world.

In the fifth movement the poet points out that words, which must move in time, are inadequate to express the supratemporal — in other words, love:

> Love is itself unmoving,
> Only the cause and end of movement,
> Timeless, and undesiring
> Except in the aspect of time
> Caught in the form of limitation
> Between un-being and being. . . .

and the Quartet ends with an allusion to the childhood memory of the rose garden.

"East Coker" has as theme that end and beginning are one. "The Dry Salvages" has a remarkable movement at its center in which Krishna urges Arjuna to "fare forward." "Little Gidding" is remarkable for a Dantesque conversation between the poet and a restless spirit with whom he had early been associated in trying to "purify the dialect of the tribe" and for a climax which draws upon the late medieval English mystics and upon Dante in his vision of the heavenly rose: the last movement begins with a passage in which the poet explicitly states his poetic ideal, and ends:

> And all shall be well and
> All manner of thing shall be well
> When the tongues of flame are in-folded
> Into the crowned knot of fire
> And the fire and the rose are one.

From 1934 on, when Eliot wrote *The Rock*, a propaganda play for a Church of England building fund campaign, he turned more to verse drama: *Murder in the Cathedral* (1935), based on the moral and psychological crisis involved in St. Thomas à Becket's martyrdom; *The Family Reunion* (1939), based on the *Oresteia*; *The Cocktail Party* (1949); *The Confidential Clerk* (1954); and *The Elder Statesman* (1959). These are plays of increasing fineness, and entailed the poet's actually working with the theater — and for *Murder in the Cathedral*, ultimately the movies. Of course, to many of his early admirers who thought of him as an iconoclast, some aspects of his later career seemed disappointing. There is, to be sure, less tension, less acidity in *The Elder Statesman* than in "The Love Song of J. Alfred Prufrock," and Eliot obviously mellowed in his later years. But the early and the later work relate to each other as negative and positive print, and Eliot remained pretty consistent.

An important element in this consistency was his affirmation of a quite catholic religious position: on one occasion, he said that he was a Tory in politics and an Anglo-Catholic in religion. He was an active layman within the Church of England, and in some of his prose (for example, *The Idea of a Christian Society*) was quite explicit in his advocacy of definite ecclesiastical organization. In his poetry, however, he is quite inclusive in his spiritual ideas — tending more toward a mystical than a dogmatic type of religiosity.

Any consideration of Eliot's writings takes one beyond the area of poetry. As essayist in various magazines, editor of *The Criterion*, member of the publishing firm of Faber and

Faber, and lecturer at Cambridge and Harvard universities, he had a critical influence that was worldwide. His first prose volume was *The Sacred Wood* (1920), and in the course of time he came to occupy in British and American letters as respected a position as did some of the Victorian essayists in the nineteenth century or Dr. Johnson in the eighteenth. Eliot also received honorary doctor's degrees — from some eighteen leading universities in the world — as well as other international honors.

No less highly honored was Robert Lee Frost, born in San Francisco as early as 1874 — but certainly one of the outstanding twentieth-century poets of the world. His father, a newspaperman who had had to leave New England because of his prosouthern sympathies, named him after the Confederate general, Robert E. Lee. After spending the formative first ten years of his life on the West Coast, the boy — following the death of his father — was taken by his mother to Lawrence, Massachusetts, where he went to high school and began writing poems, some of which appeared in school publications. After brief college attendance and working at various jobs, he married and in 1900 moved to a farm in Derry, New Hampshire, where he raised chickens, did some teaching, and wrote poems which now and then were printed in magazines.

In 1912 Frost sailed with his wife and four children to England for a stay of a little over two years. During that time his first two volumes of poetry were published in London: *A Boy's Will* (1913) and *North of Boston* (1914). When Pound heard that the first volume was coming out, he rushed with Frost to the publisher's, got a copy, and fired off a review to *Poetry*. Thus, from the relatively more compact situation in London, influence was exerted on the less easily compassable American public, and via Chicago there was launched a Californian who on the "back trail" had written a book of verse more or less about New England. During the last nine months of his stay abroad, Frost and his family lived in Gloucestershire, in close touch with a number of poets whose work appeared in *Georgian Poetry*: Abercrombie, Gibson, Thomas, and Brooke. Both Abercrombie and Gibson urged the editor to include Frost in the second issue, but the editor wanted no Americans in it. When in 1915 the Frosts returned to the United States, the poet was encouraged by several developments in his public relations: a laudatory review by Amy Lowell, good arrangements with an American publisher, and invitations to lecture, teach, and serve as college "poet in residence." Every several years thereafter another volume of his poetry appeared — *Mountain Interval* (1916), *New Hampshire* (1923), *West-Running Brook* (1928), and so on right through to the year before his death when *In the Clearing* (1962) came out.

What gave Frost's poetry remarkable consistency was its firm base in classical Latin and the realistic handling of New England subject matter. Actually, Frost's attitude toward Latin was comparable to that of writers a century and more before. In terms of classical works, one might characterize his early poetry as tending formally toward that of Catullus, Horace, and Vergil, and philosophically toward that of Lucretius. Some of it is presented as taking place in New Hampshire and Vermont — an area dealt with by the poet for purposes not merely of local color but also of delineating by implication (as being like or unlike) the larger world — somewhat as Sarah Orne Jewett had done earlier in prose. In *New Hampshire*, for instance, he wrote that the local setting of his poems "is no proof that I aimed them at New Hampshire":

> I may as well confess myself the author
> Of several books against the world in general.

In this respect he offers an interesting comparison and contrast to Pound (whose release from St. Elizabeth's, incidentally, he was perhaps more immediately responsible for effecting than was any other one person).

Perhaps the most intelligent of the twentieth-century American writers, Eliot and Frost relate to each other as do — to move into a higher echelon of poet for purposes of a simile — Dante and Shakespeare, the one writing more in terms of a system, the other less. Both originally from beyond the Mississippi, Frost was one of the first writers born on the West Coast to attain international fame.

Some half-million copies of Frost's books have been sold; and, whatever the ultimate estimate of his work may be, it is clear that he has reached a very wide audience — as did, in the previous century, Longfellow (to one of whose poems the title of Frost's first volume is an allusion). Such poems as "Mending Wall," "Stopping by Woods," and "Birches" are well on their way to being as generally familiar as any poems in the language. One of the most popular attitudes Frost assumed in his poems is that embodied in "The Pasture," which has more than once been used as an introduction to volumes of his collected verse:

> I'm going out to clean the pasture spring;
> I'll only stop to rake the leaves away
> (And wait to watch the water clear, I may):
> I sha'n't be gone long. — You come too.
>
> I'm going out to fetch the little calf
> That's standing by the mother. It's so young
> It totters when she licks it with her tongue.
> I sha'n't be gone long. — You come too.

Frost's first volume was predominantly lyric and in the first person; as he wrote in a letter a couple of months before it was issued: "It comes pretty near being the story of five years of my life. In the first poem I went away from people (and college); in the one called A Tuft of Flowers I came back to them. . . ." In his second volume there are a number of dramatic monologues and dialogues, such as "The Death of the Hired Man." All his life long Frost was attracted to the presentation of dramatic tensions, and — though he never became deeply involved with the theater as such — he did write a few one-act plays, published a long pastoral dialogue modeled on the first eclogue of Vergil but set in New England, and during the late 1940's issued a pair of quasi-dramatic philosophical poems (*A Masque of Reason*, about Job, and *A Masque of Mercy*, on the Jonah episode in a New York setting). Increasingly in his later years he wrote a rather astringent and basically philosophical or epigrammatic type of verse with no very specific localization geographically — like "Fire and Ice" in the *New Hampshire* volume:

> Some say the world will end in fire,
> Some say in ice.
> From what I've tasted of desire
> I hold with those who favor fire.
> But if I had to perish twice,
> I think I know enough of hate
> To say that for destruction ice
> Is also great
> And would suffice.

In addition to being an able writer, Frost was a real personality on the platform and in private. With his some forty honorary degrees from American universities and half a dozen from British (including Oxford, Cambridge, and Dublin), he no doubt established some sort of world record in this department. He won the annual Pulitzer Prize in poetry four times. In the late 1950's he was sent by the State Department to Brazil, England, and Israel, making public appearances that were quite as winning as those he had long been making at home. By the end of his life he had become a sort of poet laureate: in 1960 Congress gave him a gold medal, and in 1961 he read a poem at the inauguration of President Kennedy. In 1962 — at the age of eighty-eight! — on the invitation of the Soviet Writers' Union, he flew to Russia, where he was visited by Premier Khrushchev and urged magnanimity and rivalry between Russia and the United States on larger matters than the Berlin Wall — one of the more unusual espisodes in literary history, comparable perhaps to Goethe's talk with Napoleon.

The global aspects of Frost's poetry are more personal and selective than those of some other American writers. It is primarily a matter of America and Europe, not Africa and Asia — though, of course, Russia does extend to the United States across the Bering Strait. Frost's world thought was framed within the overall outlines of the classical humanist and Hebraeo-Christian tradition, as well as within those of pre-Einsteinian science. Hard as it may be to believe, at least for one who thinks of the Yankee turn of phrase as the essence of Frost's poetry, his poems have been effectively translated into many languages — Russian, German, French, Japanese — in addition to being read abroad in the original. Though not as directly concerned with Far Eastern literature as Pound, he occasionally used some of the techniques exploited in the *haiku* — for example, at the end of "A Boundless Moment":

> We stood a moment so in a strange world,
> Myself as one his own pretense deceives;
> And then I said the truth (and we moved on).
> A young beech clinging to its last year's leaves.

In his final volume of poems, Frost refers to his times as

> A golden age of Poetry and power
> Of which this noonday's the beginning hour.

Any account of American poetry during this period is bound to seem crowded. Three poets associated with Illinois are Edgar Lee Masters (1868-1950), with his *Spoon River Anthology* (1915); Vachel Lindsay (1879-1931), who went about the country reciting his own poems — particularly "The Congo" — and preaching his "gospel of beauty" with evangelistic fervor; and Carl Sandburg (1878-1967, born in Galesburg, Illinois, of semiliterate Swedish parents), who wrote free verse (though with a more impressionistic style than Whitman and with increasing fineness, witness his volume *Honey and Salt*, 1963). In the course of an active career devoted partly to journalism Sandburg achieved much in a number of different fields — *Rootabaga Stories* for children, a collection of folk songs *The American Songbag*, an autobiography

Always the Young Strangers, a novel *Remembrance Rock*, and a magnificent six-volume biography of Lincoln.

Formally enrolled under the Imagist banner were two poets born in 1886: Hilda Doolittle ("H.D."), originally of Bethlehem, Pennsylvania, and John Gould Fletcher, of Little Rock, who early wrote some impressionistic "color symphonies" and whose autobiography *Life Is My Song* (1937) is of documentary interest. A number of outstanding women came forward on the poetic scene during the twenties: Sara Teasdale (1884-1933) of St. Louis, who wrote mainly love lyrics; Elinor Wylie (1885-1928), author of some Shelleyan poems and rather fragile novels; Edna St. Vincent Millay (1892-1950) of Rockland, Maine, prominent among Greenwich Villagers in New York City and notable for her sonnets; and Marianne Moore. Miss Moore, born near St. Louis in 1887 shortly before Eliot and graduating from Bryn Mawr in 1909 in the same class as H.D., was also a Greenwich Villager for a while and from 1925 to 1929 editor of one of the most distinguished of the little magazines, *The Dial*. She has steadily written a type of precise, objective, alert poem (often about animals, such as the jerboa or the pangolin) celebrating values of independence, courage, and endurance which may easily be related to her Protestant religious background.

During this time also, of course, a great many men wrote substantial bodies of poetry — William Ellery Leonard, Louis Untermeyer, Robert Hillyer, Mark Van Doren, Conrad Aiken, E. E. Cummings, John Wheelwright, Dudley Fitts, William Rose Benét, and his younger brother Stephen Vincent Benét, whose *John Brown's Body* (1928) celebrated the Civil War in a poem of epic proportions. Active in New York at this time were a number of Negro poets: James Weldon Johnson, Langston Hughes, Countee Cullen — in fact, a term sometimes applied to one of the developments of the twenties in New York is the "Harlem Renaissance."

A poet regarded by many as the greatest of this period is Hart Crane (1899-1932). After an unhappy childhood in Ohio, he came to New York in 1916. His first major poem was

"The Marriage of Faustus and Helen" (1923), in which he expressed the yearning for a union between aspiration and ideal beauty as he perceived intimations of it about him — in a streetcar, at a dance, in war. *The Bridge* (1930) is a more extensive work, of over a thousand lines, embracing episodes from the whole history of America beginning with Columbus, going on to the Indians, explorers, and settlers, and including the great authors of our literary classics. The symbol linking the actual and ideal is the Brooklyn Bridge:

> O Thou steeled Cognizance whose leap commits
> The agile precincts of the lark's return;
> Within whose lariat sweep encinctured sing
> In single chrysalis the many twain, —
> Of stars Thou art the stitch and stallion glow
> And like an organ, Thou, with sound of doom —
> Sight, sound and flesh Thou leadest from time's realm
> As love strikes clear direction for the helm.

According to his letters, this work was intended as an affirmation of experience to counteract the negativism of *The Waste Land*. Among some of the best of Crane's shorter poems is a set of six love lyrics of the sea, "Voyages."

A quite different poet, tending as definitely to the realistic as Crane did to the idealistic, yet intransigently modern and author of one of the outstanding long poems of our time *Paterson*, is William Carlos Williams (1883-1963). By profession a physician in Rutherford, New Jersey, he wrote several volumes of comparatively plain style poetry and of prose — fiction, essays, memoirs.

A more abstract and purely musical type of writing — quite different from that of the two just mentioned — was the poetry of Wallace Stevens (1879-1955), educated at Harvard and by profession a lawyer and official in a Hartford insurance company. With great distinction he wrote in the style of the French Symbolists: from *Harmonium* (1923) on, he issued several volumes of firm, assured poetry that invites interplay between lightly suggested objective details and poetic

order supplied to them by the reader's imagination — a
superb poetic achievement of great integrity.

In some respects opposite to him was Robinson Jeffers
(1887-1962), who after graduation from Occidental College
in Los Angeles settled on the shores of the Pacific, at Carmel,
in a stone house built largely with his own hands. His *Tamar*
(1924) is an extensive verse narrative, set in California, which
has as its central character a wild figure who — as in many
ancient myths — pursues her course through multiple relationships of incest, ending with the destruction of her house:

> God who makes beauty
> Disdains no creature, nor despised that wounded
> Tired and betrayed body. She in the starlight
> And little noises of the rising tide
> Naked and not ashamed bore a third part
> With the ocean and keen stars in the consistence
> And dignity of the world.

Works like this and subsequent ones remind us that the genteel, introverted, subjective lyric is not the whole of poetry.
With the continuing Depression and the outbreak of World
War II (which he did not wish his country to enter), he lost
popular favor but kept on writing (in *The Double Axe*, 1948,
he declared himself an advocate of Inhumanism). The last
volume of his poems to appear during his lifetime, *Hungerford*
(1954), includes some moving and personal poems, autumnal
in mood.

An influential and quite various group of writers, whose
work included much poetry, began to take shape early in the
century in Nashville. The originating spirit was a man of international Jewish background, Sidney Hirsch, who had delved
into Buddhism and Taoism in the Far East and had come into
contact with Gertrude Stein in Paris. About him there assembled at Vanderbilt University a group that from about 1915
on held fortnightly meetings and from 1922 to 1925 published
a magazine *The Fugitive* (from which an anthology was
published in 1928). An influential member of the group was a

former Rhodes scholar, John Crowe Ransom, whose poetic practice and precept — like Hulme's in London — called for the avoidance of abstraction. The group ultimately came to include Donald Davidson, Merrill Moore, Allen Tate, and Robert Penn Warren. Among their students were Cleanth Brooks, Randall Jarrell, and Robert Lowell. The original idea behind the Fugitives was not specifically regional; in fact, they definitely opposed sentimentalizing over the "Old South." But by the end of the twenties the activities of the *Fugitive* group as such were over; and Ransom, Davidson, and Tate were among the twelve Southerners who contributed essays to a volume *I'll Take My Stand* (1930), which advocated the preservation of an agrarian South against the industrialization of the North. Thus one offshoot of the originally progressive and international *Fugitive* impulse took a regional and reactionary direction — which was, of course, to figure in the great activity of southern writers at mid-century.

A notable poet of northern background who has become a prominent public figure is Archibald MacLeish, with his *Tower of Ivory* (1917), his Laforguean *Hamlet of A. MacLeish* (1928) written during a five-year sojourn in France, and his long *terza rima* work about Cortez and Montezuma, *Conquistador* (1932), evoking the clash of two death-marked civilizations. In 1939 he was appointed Librarian of Congress, and helped set up UNESCO: in his essay "The Irresponsibles" (1940) he insisted that the poet must be concerned with *all* experience and must take sides in the current totalitarian-democratic conflict. From 1949 to 1962 he was a professor at Harvard, and has been awarded many honors (including the Pulitzer Prize three times). Some of his later work has dealt with Biblical material (*Songs for Eve*, 1954, and a play based on the Book of Job, *J.B.*, 1958) or has been critical and expository (*Poetry and Experience*, 1961). At mid-century he expressed his conception of the mission of poetry thus:

> Poets, deserted by the world before,
> Turn round into the actual air;
> Invent the age! Invent the metaphor!

Certainly no one could maintain that there was any interruption in the need for poets or in the desire on the part of writers to fill this need. Many of the poets already mentioned continued active beyond mid-century. But a number of developments — the Depression, science, totalitarianism, World War II — seriously curtailed the kind of aesthetically oriented and freely creative experimental literary activity that had flourished in the twenties. W. H. Auden, the most influential British poet of this period, moved to the United States in the late 1930's and exerted his influence toward regard for form and avoidance of the obviously histrionic. By mid-century the literary climate had changed, and the creative work of a great many outstanding poets had been virtually completed.

For all their number and vitality, however, they were at most maintaining a tradition in which notable work — some of world significance — had been done in America during previous centuries. With drama, however, the situation is different. The first American dramatist of world significance is Eugene O'Neill (1888-1953). He rose to prominence by way of a literary development parallel to that which took place in poetry from about 1912 on — the "little theater" movement. In the late nineteenth century there had been a good deal of "little" or "experimental" theater activity in Europe — Antoine's Théâtre Libre, Stanislavsky's Moscow Art Theater, and the Abbey Players in Dublin. In the second decade of the twentieth century, however, it suddenly emerged in the United States — a settlement house group in Chicago at Hull House, a privately sponsored Toy Theater in Boston, and considerable activity in the Greenwich Village section of New York City. By 1918 there were fifty, by 1924 two thousand little theaters in the United States. In 1915 a group had begun to present original plays in Provincetown, and soon thereafter moved to Greenwich Village: through them O'Neill had a chance to try out his early plays — at first one-act and then longer. Also in 1915 the Washington Square Players were organized, and during the twenties some of their members reorganized as the Theatre Guild, which became a "big" theater production group, undertaking O'Neill's longer works.

Probably no previous American writer had reached a world audience quite so quickly and on so many levels. His almost fifty plays came into being over a comparatively short time — about a quarter-century. Less than a decade after he had begun to come before the public with substantial plays — actually, from about *Beyond the Horizon* and *The Emperor Jones* (produced and published 1920-1921) on — the response to his plays became international. By 1923 a writer in the *Dublin Magazine* rated him above "Shaw, Synge, . . . and all the Continentals," and by 1929 an Australian book on his plays considered him alongside Aeschylus and Shakespeare. The Nobel Prize awarded him in 1936 brought, of course, world recognition; his *Long Day's Journey into Night*, on which he began working about 1940, had its world premiere in Stockholm (later being performed in the United States and winning for O'Neill his fourth Pulitzer Prize and the Drama Critics' Award — though he had died three years before); and between 1952 and 1962 more full-length studies of his plays appeared in foreign languages than in English. Obviously he is not just part of American literature or of literature in English but of literature.

Born in New York City, son of an Irish immigrant who had become a sensationally popular actor, O'Neill began his early formal education in Roman Catholic schools and spent a year at Princeton. After a hectic youth (involving a hasty marriage, some experience at sea, a number of jobs, and attempted suicide), he spent six months in a tuberculosis sanitarium and there began to write plays. His first volume of one-acts was privately printed in 1914, and during the ensuing school year he attended the "dramatic workshop" at Harvard. The summer after that he went to Provincetown and participated in the production of some of his plays there and in Greenwich Village — particularly some one-acts of the sea, such as *Bound East for Cardiff*, *Thirst*, and *The Long Voyage Home*. By the 1920's, O'Neill's plays were full-length productions, increasingly concerned with rejecting the philistine world of American society and business. *The Hairy Ape* (1922) — though starting out on shipboard and reintroducing a character from one of his one-acts — presents the illiterate stoker's sense of not belonging in the world of the fashionable passengers and ends with his fatal embrace of the ape in a zoo. The means by which the action is presented is what is sometimes referred to as "expressionism" — according to which events are acted out on the stage as they are conceived of within the somewhat disordered mental world of one of the characters. As a result, expressionistic stage settings and action tend to be mechanical, automatic, stylized; and at its best, values are stressed that are more visionary and poetical than utilitarian and prosaic. In *All God's Chillun Got Wings* (1924), a promising Negro intellectual married to a white girl regresses to infantilism under the resulting tensions. *Desire under the Elms* (1924) presents the conflict in a hard-bitten New England family between the old, lustful, tightfisted father and his sons — a sort of *Brothers Karamazov* situation, but with an old man who is no buffoon. In *The Great God Brown* (1926), O'Neill uses masks to symbolize the personality of man, split between the artist Dion Anthony and his stodgy friend William A Brown. After Dion's career has ended in disaster, his friend William takes over his mask (together with his wife, his creativity, and his uncompromising attitude) — with the same result, leaving the wife to console herself with her sons and the mask of Dion. Also an attack on the materialism of the West is *Marco Millions* (pub. 1927, prod. 1928), in which the business-oriented Marco Polo is set over against Kublai Kaan's grand-daughter, who dies of love for him.

The juxtaposition of the Occident and the Orient in *Marco* points to an awareness on O'Neill's part of the wisdom of the East, as integral to his approach as it had been to that of Eliot — or, earlier, of Emerson and Thoreau. This awareness had come to him partly through Nietzsche (whose best-known work purports to be the sayings of Zoroaster) and through Strindberg (whose *Dream Play*, for example, presents the temptation of Brahma by Maya); early in his career, moreover, ONeill had been greatly moved by a theosophical book *Light on the Path*, and over his door at Provincetown he had inscribed a quotation from it: "Before the eyes can see they must be incapable of tears. . . . Before the soul can stand . . . its feet must be washed in the blood of the heart." His Nobel Prize money went to the building of a house in California which he called "Tao House." His whole life-work, intended for the "theater of tomorrow," was devoted to an end which might be characterized as the dispelling of the illusions of Maya and the achieving of Nirvana.

By 1927 O'Neill had embarked upon a succession of dramas very ambitious and rich in emotional and symbolical over-tones, and quite unique in dramatic literature. *Lazarus Laughed* (pub. 1927, prod. 1928) carries the New Testament episode of the raising of a man from the dead on through his subsequent life-affirming career, during which he proclaims a message at first Christian (in Judea), then Dionysian (in Greece), and finally Oriental (in Rome). The play makes fantastic demands on the theater, calling for seven masked choruses (each representing a period of life and each consisting of seven types of character) and, of course, for an elaborate historical background. The Theatre Guild finally decided it could not produce it, and actually it has been played in the theater only as a very special event. But it is a great work of literature — one of the touchstones, if there have been any in our time.

Strange Interlude (1928), a nine-act play utilizing "asides" which constitute a sort of stream of consciousness, deals with the psychological tensions caused in the lives of several men by a neurotic woman, Nina Leeds. At first glance this might also seem unsuited to the stage; but the original Theatre Guild production played to capacity houses for 414 performances, and other productions have elicited enthusiastic responses. Less grandiose, more inward than *Lazarus*, this play contributes to the disillusionment of the characters in the drama and of the audience: as the man with whom Nina is married in the end says,

> Let's you and me forget the whole distressing episode, regard it as an interlude, of trial and preparation, say, in which our souls have been scraped clean of impure flesh, and made worthy to bleach in peace.

Mourning Becomes Electra (1931) is a thirteen-act trilogy which derives some of its characters and incidents from the Oresteian dramas of the classical Greek tragedians — the locale having been transferred to post-Civil-War New England. The motivation, however, is analyzed in terms of modern psychology, and the purport of the trilogy — unlike Aeschylus — is one of disillusionment. Instead of a final procession celebrating the transmutation of blood guilt into orderly process of law, O'Neill's trilogy ends with the withdrawal of the protagonist into her shuttered house, to remain there with her tormented memories. "Love isn't permitted to me," she says. "The dead are too strong!" The situation in this trilogy is an involuted one of considerable darkness, hate, and revenge; and it represents a kind of dead end within the sequence of these three oversize dramatic works.

Thus O'Neill seemed in 1931 to have concluded his career as a significant dramatist; and although he continued to be honored and to write plays, they did not make any statement comparable in power to that of his trilogy. *Ah, Wilderness!* (1933) represents an excursion into comedy, focused on adolescent rebelliousness. In 1939, however, he began work on a serious play, *The Iceman Cometh*, which was produced in 1946; and during the forties he wrote *Long Day's Journey into Night* and *A Moon for the Misbegotten* — plays much more spare in action, background, and characters, closer to O'Neill's personal experience, and written with the superlative mastery one sometimes finds in the very late work of many great artists. *A Moon for the Misbegotten* (prod. 1947, pub. 1952), *Long Day's Journey into Night* (1956), and *A Touch of the Poet* (1957) form a sequence from dark to light in somewhat the same way as the three powerful works produced and published between 1927 and 1931 form a sequence from light to dark.

The emphasis in O'Neill's dramas is not particularly on external conflict but rather on inner emotion. In 1922 he wrote:

> It seems to me that man is much the same creature, with the same primal emotions and ambitions and motives, the same powers and the same weaknesses, as in the time when the Aryan race started toward Europe from the slopes of the Himalayas.

Many of the traditional aims of poetry are realized through his dramas, and the prevailing tone has often been characterized as one of mysticism.

Of the same generation as O'Neill and devoting some of his best efforts to the writing of verse tragedy was Maxwell Anderson (1888-1959). His early life in Pennsylvania, North Dakota, and California was spent in teaching and journalism, but he came to New York for his mature writing career. His first success in the theater was the result of his collaboration on a rather deglamorized prose war play, *What Price Glory* (1924), later published in a group of *Three American Plays* (1925). Continuing to write in a number of *genres*, he turned in 1930 to verse drama with *Elizabeth the Queen*, and gradually adapted his method to include American and contemporary material. One of his distinctive works he derived from the Sacco-Vanzetti case of 1920, collaborating on working up the material into a prose play *Gods of the Lightning* (1928) and finally into the verse drama *Winterset* (1935), in which the son of an unjustly executed Italian radical tries to establish the guilt of a gangster who has just been released from prison but who shoots him. Traditional dramatic features are here adapted to a contemporary setting: for example, the hero and heroine say:

> *Miriamne:* You won't forget?
> *Mio:* Forget?
>   Whatever streets I walk, you'll walk them, too,
>   from now on, and whatever roof of stars
>   I have to house me, you shall share my roof
>   and stars and morning. I shall not forget.

The dramatic situation in each of his *Eleven Verse Plays* (1940) is conceived of in terms of individual human problems of guilt, revenge, justice — man in direct and personal conflict with political and social forces. In this respect, both he and O'Neill — like Frost — distrusted group solutions to essentially human problems. Though not as original as O'Neill, Anderson practiced his art with integrity over a long career. During the thirties, when "socially conscious" drama was at its height, O'Neill temporarily retired from the theater but Anderson kept the curtains up with his verse dramas. During the forties and fifties, Anderson wrote verse and prose dramas on historical and contemporary subjects, and on occasion dramatized outstanding current novels —notably Alan Paton's *Cry, the Beloved Country* under the title *Lost in the Stars* — and expressed himself on the subject of drama (*The Essence of Tragedy*, 1938, and *Off Broadway*, 1940).

Of course, there were many playwrights other than these two giants. Elmer Rice, with *The Adding Machine* (1923), was one of the first successful exponents of Expressionism. Sidney Howard, Philip Barry, and S. N. Behrman were responsible for notable plays, rather on the light side.

During the thirties, under the growing weight of the Depression, there was a good deal of realistic and propagandistic social-protest drama, fostered particularly by the Theatre Union and the Group Theatre in New York. From the ranks of their actors a playwright distinctive of this era emerged, Clifford Odets (1906-1963, b. in Philadelphia). In 1935 — in addition to going with a group to Cuba to protest violation of civil liberties — he had three plays produced: *Waiting for Lefty*, *Awake and Sing!*, and *Till the Day I Die*. The first one has actors planted in the audience, and by the end of the last act the whole theater is shouting "Strike! Strike!"; the second broods over the hopelessness of a complicated family situation; and the third is an anti-Nazi play. Soon, however, Odets was shuttling between Hollywood and New York, and his later plays — such as *The Flowering Peach* (1954), which is about Noah — have not elicited the widespread response of his earlier plays.

Another somewhat unexpected appearance on the theatrical horizon of the thirties was the novelist Thornton Wilder. Born in 1897 in Madison, he spent part of his childhood in Hong Kong (where his father was consul general), studied in California, at Oberlin, Yale, and the American Academy in Rome, and taught French at Lawrenceville School. Among his novels are *The Cabala* (1926), *The Bridge of San Luis Rey* (1927), and *The Woman of Andros* (1930). Ever since his late teens, however, he had been writing short plays (*The Angel That Troubled the Waters*, 1928, and *The Long Christmas Dinner*, 1931). A lecturer at the University of Chicago, he was largely responsible for Gertrude Stein's coming there to lecture in 1935, and he has acknowledged his indebtedness to her. In 1938 his full-length play *Our Town* was produced, and has subsequently been performed round the world. With only the bare stage and the Stage Manager fulfilling the role as a Chinese property man might, the plays deals with the daily life, with the love and marriage of two young people, and with death in a typical small town, Grover's Corners, in New Hampshire. It implies too that the apparently commonplace happenings there have potentially wide and even eternal significance. In 1952 his equally successful *The Skin of Our Teeth* suggests through incidents in the lives of the members of a family the whole development of man from the Ice Age to the present. A third play of Wilder's, *The Merchant of Yonkers* (1938), is lighter — an adaptation of an early nineteenth-century comedy — and was reworked as *The Matchmaker* (1954);

still further reworked, it opened on Broadway as a musical comedy *Hello! Dolly* (1964). Having served as an Air Force Intelligence officer in North Africa and Italy during World War II, he seems not to have resumed quite the same easy relationship with the theater public since. His *Alcestiad*, a tetralogy performed at the Edinburgh Festival in 1955, was first published in German translation; and in 1962 three one-act plays, part of two projected cycles on the Seven Deadly Sins and the Seven Ages of Man, were performed in New York.

An author prominent — like Wilder — around 1940 is William Saroyan, who wrote informal and casual plays, beginning with *My Heart's in the Highlands* and *The Time of Your Life*, in which odd, impulsive, and basically good-hearted characters manifest a gentle *joie de vivre*.

Toward the middle of the century two playwrights, Williams and Miller, came to the fore much as O'Neill and Anderson had done earlier. Tennessee Williams (b. 1914 in Columbus, Mississippi) spent part of his early life at various places in the South with his grandparents (his grandfather being an Episcopal minister) and in St. Louis with his parents and his sister. Tensions within the family and the growing illness of his sister figure in the background of *The Glass Menagerie* (1945): in this evocative, tender, and poignant work Amanda Wingfield, a dominating mother deserted by her husband, insists that her son Tom bring home a prospective suitor for her daughter Laura, who appears about to retire into her own private world of concern for her collection of little glass animals; an attempt is made and seems on the point of succeeding when the prospect explains that he is already engaged. This poetic play stands — as O'Neill's plays also do — at a far remove from the conventional so-called realistic drama, many of the devices of expressionism being utilized here to give a sense of an incident totally recalled.

A somewhat bolder drama with much more overt and sustained conflict is *A Streetcar Named Desire* (1947): of a once proud southern family, one sister, Stella, has married a very earthy character, Stanley Kowalski, while the other,

Blanche, has tried to maintain the pattern of her gentility — with complete moral disintegration. Stanley so resents Blanche that he attacks her; and she is led off to a mental hospital, still preserving the external form of her gentility. In England (where the production was directed by Olivier) and France (where an adaptation by Cocteau was staged) the play was a great box-office success, but encountered some official disapproval. To be sure, there is in it a great deal that is harsh: instead of some kind of romantic rescue for Blanche, with whom one feels great sympathy, a conclusion is unflinchingly presented that the wages of sin are — if not death, then the next thing to it, commitment to an insane asylum; and at the end Stella is faced with a bitter conflict — for all of what Williams calls her "Chinese" passivity.

Also a substantial drama with considerable action is *Cat on a Hot Tin Roof* (1955). Like *Streetcar* it won a Pulitzer Prize and aroused much the same response as the earlier play both in the United States and abroad. The action takes place on the birthday of a Delta planter who is soon to die of cancer — a hard, virile, unsentimental male character, set against his too solicitous family (who have their particular strengths, but of different kinds) — and introduces motifs of love, pride, reticence, alcoholism, homosexuality, and opportunism.

Williams' *Period of Adjustment* (1960) turns more in the direction of comedy, emphasizing tolerance and reconciliation. Also somewhat gentler in its implications is *The Night of the Iguana* (1961), set in a "rather rustic and very Bohemian hotel" beside the Mexican rain forests. The central male character, an ex-clergyman, is on the verge of a breakdown, placed between the sensual Mexican proprietress and a spiritual, understanding New England artist (whom on occasion he calls "Miss Thin-Standing-Up-Female-Buddha"). She has devoted herself to her aging grandfather, an indomitable but pathetic poet, with whose death the play ends. Some of the issues raised in previous plays — gentility vs. vulgarity, body vs. soul — are here raised again, but with greater depth, complexity, and mellowness; and the struggles of the various characters to attain freedom are symbolized by those of a captive iguana, which the protagonist ultimately releases.

Undoubtedly Williams has helped in his plays to widen the range of literature by sympathetically presenting many characters who deviate from the norm and by using symbolism to dramatize basic human conflicts. Unlike O'Neill and Eliot, he has not based his plays on ancient dramatic classics, and his aim seems less to arouse admiration for his protagonists than to urge understanding.

Unlike Williams', Miller's plays have been from the start in the realistic Ibsen-Shaw tradition — in fact, in 1950 he adapted *An Enemy of the People* for Broadway. After growing up in Brooklyn and working during the Depression at a variety of jobs, Arthur Miller (b. 1915) attended the University of Michigan, where he won several undergraduate playwriting prizes. His full-length plays reached New York with *The Man Who Had All the Luck* (1944), *All My Sons* (1947), and *Death of a Salesman* (1950). Enjoying a phenomenally long run, *Death of a Salesman* presents the pathetic life and ultimate suicide of a traveling salesman who has been "riding on a smile and a shoe-shine" — a family drama, charged with a great deal of sympathy for the victims of an entirely bourgeois set of values.

The Crucible (1953) — a quasi-historical drama (somewhat as Shaw wrote ostensibly historical plays) — deals with the Salem witchcraft trials and presents the leading accused female character Abigail as really evil, really a witch, but even more evil are the prosecutors, who become more and more corrupt as the trial proceeds. The modern implications of the play arise from the fact that during the thirties and forties there had been widespread sympathy among American intellectuals with Communist Russia, but in the fifties the investigation of possible Communist infiltration in Hollywood and Broadway sometimes bore the marks of a witch-hunt. Miller denied being a Communist and vigorously opposed the methods by which the investigation was being carried on, nevertheless, by 1956 he too was being intensively investigated by Senator McCarthy. In that year he divorced his first wife and married the film star Marilyn Monroe — a marriage which lasted four years. His playwriting career — so comparatively cautious in its earlier phases — was understandably jarred by these highly publicized developments.

In 1955 he brought out a powerful play set in the Italian section of Brooklyn, *A View from the Bridge,* in which the central character, Eddie Carbone, because of emotional ties with his ward Catherine, betrays two relatives who are unauthorized immigrants (and with one of whom Catherine is in love). In violating the mores of his community Carbone brings destruction upon himself. This is clearly tragedy in the classical sense — something that many commentators on *The Death of a Salesman* felt the earlier play lacked. Thus Miller showed that if he wanted to he could write classical-type tragedy using an American setting.

His *After the Fall* (1964), however, is more personal and experimental, taking place "in the mind, thought, and memory" of the central character, who gives his side in the painful experience of being married to a popular celebrity.

Varied, intense, and lively, drama has had an amazing period of flourishing on American soil during the second quarter of the present century — as also has poetry, with which it is closely related. During the century before, prose fiction had come into its own, and at the turn of the century was carrying out various forms of realism.

Theodore Dreiser (1871-1945), born in Terre Haute, Indiana, of immigrant German parents and early attending parochial schools, went to Indiana University for a year, served as a reporter in Chicago and St. Louis, and became editor of several New York magazines. The manuscript of his first novel *Sister Carrie* (1900) was accepted for publication and printed but not distributed — except for some copies smuggled out by the publisher's reader Frank Norris — and thus was not really published until another firm took over the work in 1907. It tells of a small-town girl, Carrie Meeber, who comes to Chicago, falls in first with a salesman, Charles Drouet, then with the manager of a saloon, George Hurstwood. She and Hurst-wood ultimately end up in New York, she a stage star and he a suicide. Possible equation of virtues and rewards — or vices and punishments — is thus canceled out: the detailed realism of the presentation, however, and the careful preparation of each incident until it seems just "what such a person in such a situation *would* do" arouses in the reader great pity for the figures thus caught in a web of circumstances. Sympathy is also aroused for the central female character in Dreiser's second novel, *Jennie Gerhardt* (1911), who experiences a fate somewhat opposite to Carrie's: instead of constantly advancing her own fortunes, Jennie is completely loving and self-effacing. A group of novels which Dreiser called a "Trilogy of Desire" — *The Financier* (1912), *The Titan* (1914), and *The Stoic* (1947) — is based on the career of the banking and transportation magnate C. T. Yerkes, which Dreiser studied in great detail, slightly disguising the names and incidents (the great central *Übermensch*-type character being called Frank Cowperwood). When Dreiser's novel *The "Genius"* (1915) ran into trouble with the Society for the Suppression of Vice, many authors on both sides of the Atlantic sprang to his defense, asserting its high literary quality (though, actually, it was not one of his best works).

The most popular of Dreiser's novels was *An American Tragedy* (1925): Clyde Griffiths, a weak and confused young man who has emerged from a sordid background to glimpse possibilities of success by marrying into a wealthy family, finds himself blocked from doing so by the pregnancy of Roberta Allen, takes her out in a rowboat and, after their boat is accidentally upset, abandons her to drown. Clyde is tried for first-degree murder and executed.

In addition to novels, Dreiser wrote much in other forms, such as short stories, essays, plays, poems, and so on. One of his most attractive books consists of a number of character sketches, *Twelve Men* (1919) — including a heart-warming account of his brother Paul, who was a popular-song writer. The novelist's active writing career extended over almost half a century. One novel at which he worked on and off during much of that time was *The Bulwark* (1946), a somewhat spare story of a Quaker, Solon Barnes, who experiences great disappointment in his children, but who in his last days is comforted by one who returns and recognizes his sterling qualities. As Dreiser approached his seventies, there were many indications of his having achieved some degree of resolution to the conflicts in his earlier life: in 1939 he edited *The Living Thoughts of Thoreau*; in 1941, he wrote an essay *America Is Worth Saving*; and in 1945 — less than six months before his death and no doubt mainly as a public gesture — he applied for membership in the Communist Party. In accepting the Nobel Prize in 1930, Sinclair Lewis said that Dreiser deserved it more than he:

> Usually unappreciated, often hounded, he has cleared the trail from Victorian Howellsian timidity and gentility in American fiction to honesty, boldness, and passion of life. Without his pioneering I doubt if any of us could, unless we liked to be sent to jail, seek to express life, beauty, and terror.

By 1930 neglect of Dreiser in America had set in — partly because, by the second quarter of the twentieth century, American fiction had begun to adopt a poetical rather than a historical, reportorial, or documentary aim. Interest in Dreiser, however, continued abroad: the publication of a complete edition of his works in Russia was regarded as the literary event of 1930. Another writer who suffered similar loss of favor in his homeland was Upton Sinclair, born in 1878 in Baltimore of a southern family but educated in New York City. Early he organized a cooperative dwelling across the Hudson from Manhattan, Helicon Hall (in which Sinclair Lewis, then a college boy, participated); later, he was largely responsible for the establishment of the American Civil Liberties Union and the League of Industrial Democracy; and during the Depression he campaigned for the governorship of California on the Democratic ticket with the program known as EPIC (End

Poverty in California). The most sensational of his novels was
The Jungle (1906), about the Chicago stockyards and meat-
packing factories (where, on occasion, a man might slip into a
vat and get rendered into lard) — a work of fiction that resulted in a governmental investigation and the passage of the
Pure Food and Drug Act. Among Sinclair's better-known
works are *King Coal* (1917), a fictionalized account of a strike
in the Colorado coal mines; *The Brass Check* (1919), a study
of American journalism that resulted in its becoming organized professionally; *Oil!* (1927), about the oil scandals of the
Harding administration — the Teapot Dome affair — focusing
(as in *The Jungle*) on a central character who turns Socialist;
Boston (1928), based on the Sacco-Vanzetti case; and *Mental
Radio* (1930), partly responsible for the establishment of an
institute within Duke University to investigate extrasensory
perception. In 1940, with *World's End*, there began to appear
a series of eleven novels in which the central character, Lanny
Budd, travels about and participates, at a high level, in the main
events of international politics from the beginning of World
War I through World War II (one of the novels, *Dragon's
Teeth*, 1942, was awarded the Pulitzer Prize).

Of some hundred books by Sinclair, there exist over a
thousand published translations. In the USSR — though he has
never been a Communist — between 1918 and 1943 almost as
many (some three million) copies of his works were sold as
of Mark Twain's. In Japan, twenty-four of his books had been
translated by 1930 and this period of the twentieth century in
American literature is often referred to as the "Upton Sinclair Era." When in 1960 Japanese students seemed eager for
alignment with the USSR, Sinclair — at the urging of his Japanese translator — helped forestall it by cabling an open letter to the major newspaper in Japan, *Shimbun*. Gandhi, in jail,
read a number of Sinclair's books, as did other prominent Indians such as Tagore. As the Lanny Budd series appeared, it
elicited high praise from many intellectual leaders of European background — Shaw, Mann, Einstein.

Contemporary with this significant development of documentary fiction there was also continued writing of the quasi-dramatic realistic novel that Howells and James had firmly established. Edith Wharton (1862-1937), born in New York City and growing up there in the midst of the social changes that followed the Civil War, is today perhaps best known for her short and grimly ironical novel set in New England, *Ethan Frome* (1911). It differs, however, from her novels of manners dissecting the New York society of her girlhood when the *nouveaux riches* were "invading" the older society: *The House of Mirth* (1905), with its central character Lily Bart caught between the clash of the old and the new New York society; *The Custom of the Country* (1913), with Undine Sprague, a climber who cuts her way through the social strata of old New York and even, in Paris, the Faubourg St. Germain; and *The Age of Innocence* (1920), with Newland Archer, a dilettante bachelor, from whose point of view the story of his acceptance of a conventional marriage in the New York of the seventies is recounted, in somewhat the mood of Proust's remembrance of things past. Some of her shorter pieces of fiction are justly celebrated — notably a series in the volume *Old New York* (1924), each set in one of the decades from the forties to the seventies. Episodes in her novels often carry the action to Europe, where she spent increasingly long periods in her later years, becoming practically an expatriate in France during and after World War I. Comparable in novelistic ability but coming from and often dealing with Richmond, Virginia, was Ellen Glasgow (1874-1945). She regarded *Barren Ground* (1925) as her best book, the story of a betrayed girl, Dorinda Oakley, who "learned to live without joy" and resolutely turned her father's run-down acres into a prosperous dairy farm. *The Romantic Comedians* (1926), *They Stooped to Folly* (1929), and *The Sheltered Life* (1932) are social satires compassionately ironical in tone. Some of her best work deals with old upper-class Virginia families faced with — and succumbing to — pressures from modern life. Though also born in Virginia, Willa Cather (1876-1947) was brought up in Nebraska, attended the state university, and was a jour-

nalist and teacher in Pittsburgh, becoming managing editor of
McClure's Magazine in New York — a position which she
resigned (on the advice of Sarah Orne Jewett) with the publication of her first novel, *Alexander's Bridge* (1912), to devote her entire attention to writing. Though some of her early
fiction was rather Jamesian, her novels most highly regarded
today diverge from that tradition and deal with the Nebraska
of her girlhood, the land being almost personified, treated lyr-
ically and scenically, the plots being allowed to emerge or-
ganically from the material rather than being imposed on it:
O Pioneers! (1913) focusing on the strong character of the
daughter in a Swedish family, Alexandra Bergson, who is able
to envision the future of the land; and *My Ántonia* (1918),
on the Bohemian immigrant, Ántonia Shimerda, who survives
disappointments to become the mother of a large farm family. After World War I, however, some of Miss Cather's novels
dealt increasingly with an earlier and more remote past: *Death
Comes for the Archbishop* (1927) and *Shadows on the Rock*
(1931) — one a kind of legend about the founder of the Santa
Fé cathedral and the second about a "philosopher apothe-
cary" in seventeenth-century Quebec. In addition to other
full-length novels and essays, she wrote many short stories;
particularly noteworthy are the three in *Obscure Destinies*
(1932).

Poetic possibilities of the novel, moreover, such as Twain
at his best had suggested, were also being explored further,
notably by Sherwood Anderson (1876-1941). Born in Camden, Ohio, he became a businessman, writing on the side, but
in 1912 he abandoned his business career and went to the Chicago counterpart of Greenwich Village. There he came in
close touch with such writers as Floyd Dell, Carl Sandburg,
and Margaret Anderson, editor of the *Little Review*, and there
he first read and was influenced by Gertrude Stein's *Three
Lives* as well as other new work then being done in Paris. Anderson's *Winesburg, Ohio* (1919), a set of sketches about frus-
trated individuals in a small town, is held together by the central observer, George Willard, a young man growing up.

(1959) is more extroverted again: a central character with a Gargantuan appetite for experience goes to Africa — as Hemingway had done — and though he comes back chastened, does not lose his lust for life. *Herzog* (1964) continues the strongly fictionalized autbiography of which *Augie March* had been an early portion: the central character is a university professor, buffeted by circumstances but maintaining his own perverse personality. (Both novels received the National Book Award, and the latter the International Literary Prize.) His *Last Analysis* (1964), a play which had a short Broadway run, is about a psychiatrist who undertakes to analyze himself on television. Trained as a social scientist, Bellow has been acutely aware of the inadequacies of the social and behavioral sciences in their report on man. Using his own experience as a basis, he has achieved a rich, palpable, and nondogmatic presentation of life — often quite messy, but a recognizable world irradiated by the author's protesting (one might almost say Protestant) spirit.

A third writer, also of Jewish background and still more cautious in his novelistic approach than Bellow, is Bernard Malamud (b. in Brooklyn in 1914, educated in New York City and teaching there, as well as in Oregon and at Bennington later). After a first novel *The Natural* (1952) — about a baseball pitcher, Roy Hobbs, who (with overtones of the Arthurian Holy Grail legend) comes to grief and loses the pennant race — Malamud wrote *The Assistant* (1957), somewhat Dostoievskyan (only on a more limited scale and without, of course, the "holy Russia" aspect of the earlier novelist). Here the central character, Frank Alpine, a second-generation Italian-American, who has been given some idea of St. Francis in the orphanage where he has been raised, elects — because of a series of frustrating incidents — to follow the pattern of life provided by a Jewish grocer, Morris Bober, and to become a Jew. In this novel as a whole and at many moments within it Malamud achieves magnificent simplicity, as when Frank asks Morris why he suffers so:

"I suffer for you," Morris said calmly.

Frank laid his knife down on the table. His mouth ached. "What do you mean?"

"I mean you suffer for me."

Since *The Assistant*, Malamud has issued two novels. In *A New Life* (1961) the central character has gone from New York to a West Coast college to teach English and with self-sacrifice follows the pattern of his predecessor. This novel enlarges Malamud's geographical scope and makes clear some of his reactions to the Far West. In *The Fixer* (1966) the material derives from an actual court case of 1913 in Kiev involving charges of ritual murder; as dealt with by Malamud, it also comes to suggest the kind of situation faced by Dreyfus, Vanzetti, many Negroes; the central character, imprisoned for three years and awaiting trial, grows spiritually stronger through suffering and rejects a false confession, suicide, despair. Interviewed shortly after completing *The Fixer*, Malamud declared: "My work, all of it, is an idea of dedication to the human. That's basic to every book. If you don't respect man, you cannot respect my work. I'm in defense of the human." His abilities are often to be seen at their best in his short stories, which have been compiled in two volumes, *The Magic Barrel* (1958) and *Idiots First* (1963).

There have, of course, been authors of Jewish family background in the United States before the mid-twentieth century, just as there have been Negro authors. But normally, before then, their writings either were confined largely to matters of concern to their immediate circle or else conformed to the prevailing mode. Since the mid-twentieth century and even earlier there have been many writers of fiction who have come to the fore with work that concerns itself with fundamentally human experience but who maintain particular emphases and insights that are a part of their special group heritage. As we have seen that three particular novelists — out of many who could be considered — have given a Jewish cast to their work, so we might also single out three whose novels have sprung from their distinctively Negro experience.

Native Son (1940) by Richard Wright (1908-1960) is a powerful naturalistic novel: Bigger Thomas, a Chicago Negro, commits murder, is tried, and is sentenced to the electric chair. Also by Wright is an autobiographical volume, *Black Boy* (1945), other novels *The Outsider* (1953) and *The Long Dream* (1958), as well as some fiction that had been published posthumously.

Ralph Ellison (b. 1914 in Oklahoma City), however, is much subtler and more flexible in his novel *Invisible Man* (1952), the unnamed central figure of which — though Negro — could be any ignored and victimized human being in the modern world. He is involved in a series of imaginative episodes which flow as sinuously as those in Voltaire's *Candide* or Dostoievsky's *Notes from Underground*. Ellison's volume of essays, *Shadow and Act* (1964), shows the breadth of his interests and the generally human orientation of his thinking.

James Baldwin (b. 1924 in New York City), son of a preacher in Harlem and in his early adolescence himself a preacher, came to the fore with his first novel, *Go Tell It on the Mountain* (1953), about the religious conversion of a fourteen-year-old Harlem youth and — through flashbacks — the experiences of his immediate ancestors of the past three generations. The action is highly concentrated and unified, covering but a Saturday and Sunday, and the writing has a strongly poetic quality deriving from the Bible. In *Giovanni's Room* (1956), set in France, the narrator is torn between his involvement with both a man and a woman, and finally botches both relationships. In *Another Country* (1961) the scene is largely in Harlem and Greenwich Village, where a half-dozen interrelated characters grope for love and meaning in a situation complicated by long-standing Negro-white hostilities. He has also written two volumes of essays, *Notes of a Native Son* (1955) and *The Fire Next Time* (1963), as well as a play *Blues for Mister Charlie* (1964).

A full account of the brilliant fictional work by southern writers at mid-century is here hardly feasible. Faulkner was, of course, the giant. Eight years his junior and born in the hill

country of Kentucky near the Tennessee border, Robert Penn
Warren was one of the *Fugitive* group in Nashville during
the early twenties. Writing poetry has been a continuing
concern of his, from his initial contributions to *The Fugitive*
through a historical verse novel *Brother to Dragons* (1953),
a prize-winning volume *Promises* (1957), *You, Emperors, and
Others* (1960), and *Selected Poems* (1966). His conception
of poetry favors the generation of inner tensions within the
poem that push hard against the regularity of its formal aspects
— an idea of poetry basic to Dante, the baroque, and Eliot. As
we have seen before, the original Fugitives were internationally
oriented. Ransom, Warren, and Cleanth Brooks were Rhodes
scholars. While at Oxford Warren wrote his first important
short story "Prime Leaf," about violence among the Kentucky
tobacco growers — the basis of his first novel *Night Rider*
(1939); and the association of Brooks and Warren as
Rhodes scholars was doubtless important in the formulation
of their influential textbooks, *Understanding Poetry* (1938),
Understanding Fiction (1943), and *Modern Rhetoric* (1949).
Warren's best-known novel is *All the King's Men* (1946,
Pulitzer Prize). Many readers have taken it as a novel about the
career of a political leader in Louisiana, Huey Long. It is,
however, something much subtler than a quasi-journalistic
report. Its main emphasis is on the psychological and spiritual
meaning of the incidents for the observer-narrator-historian
Jack Burden, who undergoes during the action an archetypal Night Journey or Death-and-Rebirth experience. *World
Enough and Time* (1950) is based on the early nineteenth-
century Sharp-Beauchamp case which had been dealt with in
drama and romance by earlier authors such as Poe and Simms.
Band of Angels (1955) is also set in nineteenth-century Kentucky and is about the daughter of a planter and a slave. *The
Cave* (1959) and *Wilderness* (1961) are symbolical, the latter
reaching its climax in the Civil War. Southern in subject matter
(note also his expository writing such as *Segregation*, 1957;
The Legacy of the Civil War, 1961; and *Who Speaks for the*

Negro?, 1965), his imaginative work is in form and mood neo-baroque.

Katherine Anne Porter, born in the nineties, has come from a very different part of the South, Texas — or from what is more properly called the Southwest. She has maintained in her work a primary allegiance to the shorter forms of prose fiction, which she has cultivated with a conscious artistry that is in the Flaubert-James tradition. Her stories have appeared in volumes *Flowering Judas* (1930), *Pale Horse, Pale Rider* (1939), *The Leaning Tower* (1944), and *Collected Stories* (1965). In addition to literary essays, she has written a single long novel, *Ship of Fools* (1962), which she began work on when she sailed from Mexico to Germany in 1931 but in which she utilized some aspects of Sebastian Brant's *Narrenschiff* (1494): a shipload of first-class passengers make a display of themselves — symbolizing of course the world, the "pomps and vanities" of which Christians from early times have been enjoined to eschew. On and off for the past thirty years she has also been working on (and has published portions of) a study of Cotton Mather.

Toward mid-century several outstanding authors from the Deep South appeared: Eudora Welty (b. 1909, Jackson, Mississippi) whose books from *A Curtain of Green* (1941) through *The Bride of Innisfallen* (1955) are concerned in one way or another with love, and present a sympathetic picture of the author's fellow Southerners; Carson McCullers (1917-1967, b. in Columbus, Georgia) with fiction also sharply presenting the anomalies in the operations of this emotion but often tending more to the grotesque, as in *The Heart Is a Lonely Hunter* (1940) and subsequent work, notably *The Ballad of the Sad Cafe* (1951); Truman Capote (b. 1924 in New Orleans) with *Other Voices, Other Rooms* (1948), about a thirteen-year-old boy who comes to a nightmarish region of Mississippi in search of his father, finds him paralyzed, and comes under the influence of a homosexual relative, on through *In Cold Blood* (1965), a "nonfiction novel" about a 1959 murder case.

Capote's much-publicized debut as a novelist — which occurred, like Mailer's, while both authors were still in their mid-
twenties — has caused understandable difficulty in the subsequent development of solid literary achievement. More solid
work can be credited to Flannery O'Connor (1925-1964, b. in
Savannah) with her novels *Wise Blood* (1952) and *Violent
Bear It Away* (1960) as well as her unforgettable short stories, almost like Maupassant in their sharpness, each focused on
a cataclysmic moment of moral or spiritual awareness. Another
distinguished southern writer who has appeared since mid-
century is Shirley Ann Grau (b. 1929 in New Orleans) with
her initial volume of short stories *The Black Prince* (1955) and
three novels, *Hard Blue Sky* (1958), *The House on Coliseum
Street* (1961), and *The Keepers of the House* (1964), dealing
forthrightly and respectfully with people in the Delta region
—white, Negro, and mixed.

Among writers from farther north, one whose fiction
has stood out during the fifties and sixties is Louis Auchincloss
(b. 1917 in Lawrence, New York), professionally a lawyer
and in his writing a professed disciple of Henry James: one of
the more recent of his novels is an evocation of a strong character, headmaster of a boy's school, *The Rector of Justin*
(1964). Also quite conscious of the James tradition is Frederick
Buechner (b. 1926 in New York City), with his first novel *A
Long Day's Dying* (1949) and subsequent novels, as well as
(since he is a Presbyterian minister) a volume of sermons *The
Magnificent Defeat* (1966).

J. D. Salinger (b. 1919 in New York City) achieved sensational success with *The Catcher in the Rye* (1951), about a
prep-school student, Holden Caulfield, in flight from a world
of "phonies" and almost ready to take out for the West with his
little sister Phoebe, but experiencing a last-minute change of
heart as he feels the need of protecting her innocence, and
returning home. *Franny and Zooey* (1961) brings together
episodes in the life of the Glass family. Though Salinger's
background is Jewish, these fictional works move far on — or,

perhaps rather, out — into the spiritual world of Christian mysticism and Zen Buddhism.

Though dealing with a very different social level from Salinger, Jack Kerouac (b. 1922 in Lowell, Massachusetts) has written a number of volumes that are also — in an odd sort of way — saints' lives. His best-known novel is *On the Road* (1957), narrated by a "Beat Generation" vagabond writer Salvatore Paradise, for the purpose of conveying a sense of an enthusiastic, affirmative, and experience-hungry character Dean Moriarty. The book also evokes, with much geographical detail, a feeling of the whole country, East and West, and, eventually, of Mexico. Kerouac's *The Dharma Bums* (1958) moves into the Zen spiritual area; his *Visions of Gerard* (1963) is more Roman Catholic in its orientation; and *Desolation Angels* (1965) includes travels through London and Tangier as well as the United States.

John Barth (b. 1930 in Cambridge, Maryland), professor of English in the State University of New York at Buffalo, has written a number of novels which remind one of discursive earlier works like *Tom Jones* or *Tristram Shandy* — or, to cite American examples, *Modern Chivalry* or the Knickerbocker history. Barth's original idea seems to have been to do a series of books each concerned with "some sort of bachelor, more or less irresponsible, who either rejects absolute values or encounters their rejection." *The Floating Opera* (1956) deals with a middle-aged lawyer, full of opinions about things, who reasons himself into suicide and back out again. *End of the Road* (1958) is about Jake Horner, psychosomatically paralyzed and unable to decide anything, who is taken by a Negro specialist in immobility to the Remobilization Farm and given Mythotherapy; later, as a teacher, he gets into a bitter conflict over prescriptive grammar. *The Sot-Weed Factor* (1960) is based on Ebenezer Cook's poem of the same name (1708), with a great deal of solemnly comic surrounding incident. *Giles Goat-Boy* (1966) is a satire on the modern university. Actually, the ostensible subject matter of these novels is secondary; the main thing is the wit and intellectual vigor of the author. They are what he calls "nihilistic comedy," novels of ideas with serious issues lurking not far beneath the absurd surface.

James Purdy (b. 1923 in rural Ohio) also represents a kind of odd sophisticated-simple approach to the novel. Having completed his M.A. at the University of Chicago, he studied at universities in Mexico and Spain and taught at Lawrence College in Wisconsin. At present living in Brooklyn, he reads a little Greek and Latin each day, and polishes his writing. In addition to two miscellanies (*The Color of Darkness*, 1957, and *Children Is All*, 1962) and a volume of poetry, he has published four novels: *Malcolm* (1959), about a teen-ager waiting for his father to turn up but meanwhile being led into situations of increasing corruption by a strange Negro undertaker; *The Nephew* (1960), in which a well-meaning retired schoolteacher undertakes to write a memoir of her soldier nephew reported missing in action, but as she begins to collect material for it she discovers certain sordid aspects of his life and finally decides to drop the matter; *Cabot Wright Begins* (1964), about a compulsive but mild-mannered rapist; and *Eustace Chisholm and the Works* (1967), which relates the disintegration and destruction of two homosexual lovers as observed by the title character, a would-be writer. All this is presented in a "deadpan" manner (such as Twain was master of in the previous century), and the effect depends much on the nuance of the actual writing and the author's skill in giving his ridiculous characters and incidents an odd vitality of their own. Purdy's work, incidentally, won high critical acclaim in England before it did in the United States, where some readers undoubtedly feel about it the way others did about Twain's when it first appeared. This "black humor" has not only American but also Continental roots: a writer who has made a notable transition from his native Russia (where he was born in 1899) to the United States (where he was naturalized in 1945) is Vladimir Nabokov, best known for his novel *Lolita* (1955).

One writer who has moved out from certain features of humor to include many ideas developed by such theologians as Karl Barth, Paul Tillich, and Reinhold Niebuhr is John Updike (b. 1932 in Shillington, Pennsylvania). At Harvard he edited the *Lampoon,* for a year thereafter studied art at Oxford, and on his return to America joined *The New Yorker* staff. Much of his early published writing was light verse, which he has issued in two collected volumes; and some of his initial assumptions about prose are carried over from his practice of the visual arts — the importance of medium and of nonlocal color. His first novel, *The Poorhouse Fair* (1959), is set in an old people's home, where the inmates — constantly aware of the proximity of death — are as unmanageable as little children; and the "Prefect," trying to handle them in a spirit of Christian humanism, is stoned for his pains. Probably the best of his novels so far is *Rabbit, Run* (1960), its central character "Rabbit" Angstrom (suggesting *Angst,* or anxiety), a "humor" character in the sense not of being funny but of having an overdeveloped character trait, that of running away from his problems. A feeling somewhat akin to awe underlies the portraits of the narrator's high-school-teacher father and strongminded mother who appear in, respectively, *The Centaur* (1963) and *Of the Farm* (1965). A straight autobiographical account of Updike's boyhood and other of his nonfictional writings are collected in a volume of his *Assorted Prose* (1965). His novel *Couples* (1968) shows a suburban group in a community he calls Tarbox, Massachusetts (between Boston and Plymouth), much ravaged by evil, particularly adultery and indifference to the church — perhaps the sort of novel, except for the style, that William Bradford might have written if he had been born three centuries later.

Another author (from New England) who has also developed the possibilities in his humorous writing and much of whose work has appeared in *The New Yorker* is John Cheever (b. 1912 in Quincy, Massachusetts). After publishing short stories collected in two volumes, *The Way Some People Live*

(1942) and *The Enormous Radio* (1954), he wrote several novels, the best known of which are *The Wapshot Chronicle* (1957) and *The Wapshot Scandal* (1964) — the Wapshots being a somewhat seedy old New England family in the imaginary run-down town of St. Botolphs, the whole tragicomic account presenting episodically a panorama of the activities of some colorful characters, from Colonial beginnings to the present (the "scandal" of the latter volume being a run-in over the income tax).

Still another author (from the Middle West) who has written fundamentally comic novels long and intensively enough to suggest a possible outcome, at a high level of literary excellence, is Wright Morris (b. 1910 in Central City, Nebraska), educated at Pomona College, and now teaching at San Francisco State College. Since the 1940's he has produced works of great freshness and maturity. *The Field of Vision* (1956), which involves a group of odd characters at a bullfight in Mexico, is an answer to issues raised in Hemingway's first major novel. *Ceremony in Lone Tree* (1960) is widely considered Morris' best book so far: the diverse, scattered, and human members of the same family which had figured in the previous novel return to Lone Tree, Nebraska, to celebrate the ninetieth birthday of the patriarch of the clan, and — though the old man does not live quite long enough for the celebration — life goes on, in this moving, intricate novel, with the intense individualism of its characters and yet with the larger implications of the sharply outlined action and the overtones of a deeply human wisdom on the part of the author. The two books have received important national awards, and are presumably to be rounded out into a trilogy by a forthcoming volume. Morris' *One Day* (1965) is circumscribed by the "day" on which John F. Kennedy was assassinated, the plot centering on a gratuitous public gesture by one of the characters, the mixed-up daughter of a prominent, mixed-up family in the California town where the story is set. She has had an illegitimate baby in Paris by a Negro who is involved in the civil rights movement; she returns to leave it anonymously at the animal hospital; but the intended effect of this contrived gesture is swallowed up in the actual events of the day. A book of Morris' literary criticism, *The Territory Ahead* (1958), takes its title from Huck Finn's last speech, in which he declares, "I got to light out for the territory ahead." Morris' dozen or more novels represent "an effort to build, out of the given raw material, an acceptable house of fiction."

In a fuller discussion of the twentieth-century American novel there should also be consideration of Conrad Richter, Henry Miller, J. P. Marquand, Gerald Warner Brace, Erskine Caldwell, John O'Hara, Jessamyn West, Frederic Prokosch, Walter Van Tilburg Clark, Nelson Algren, Josephine Johnson, Hortense Calisher, Mary McCarthy, Ray Bradbury, Vance Bourjaily, William Styron, Gore Vidal, Philip Roth, and many others — each quite individual and distinct, all adding up to a strong affirmation of vitality still exhibited by this literary form, despite a draining-off of much of its popular support to mass media that have had a fantastic development by mid-century.

Also, as in all periods of American literature, there has been vitality in expository and reflective writing. Two divergent trends in criticism have been led by John Crowe Ransom with his *New Criticism* (1941), according to which literary work is to be explicated *in vacuo*, with much attention to its tone, texture, and tensions, and by Oscar Cargill with his *Toward a Pluralistic Criticism* (1965) — two antithetical tendencies, it may be noted, that have been manifested in American thought from the very earliest times but that have manifested themselves in a certain time sequence.

There has been a great deal of writing about American history — by Bruce Catton, for example, on the Civil War and by Arthur Schlesinger, Jr., on the Roosevelt and Kennedy administrations. A highly readable over-all history of the United States is Samuel Eliot Morison's *Oxford History of the American People* (1965). Social and intellectual history —

notably Barbara W. Tuchman's *The Proud Tower* (1965) and her other studies of the early twentieth century — cuts across the boundaries of previously discrete disciplines.

In presenting psychological and sociological matters, mid-twentieth-century American writers have tended to eliminate artificial distinctions between fiction and scientific report. Margaret Mead, Rachel Carson, and Isaac Asimov have popularized scientific material, and F. S. C. Northrop has written of the sciences and the humanities and of the East and West. At mid-century, too, there was substantial work that has gained world-wide recognition in some fields that had not figured so largely before in American writing: during the 1930's refugee scholars brought in whole new disciplines such as musicology and art history and, by the 1940's, stimulated work by native Americans — for example, Gustave Reese's *Music in the Middle Ages* (1940) and *Music in the Renaissance* (1954).

American literature as it passed mid-century took on at times a character that was not exclusively verbalistic. Like the Roman Empire and The Reformation, this is an age of martyrs (not merely Christian: witness Mohandas Gandhi). It is an era of violent death in public, and this chapter, which began with *Profiles in Courage* (1956) might appropriately close with *Stride Toward Freedom* (1958), *Strength to Love* (1963), and *Why We Can't Wait* (1964) by the American recipient of the 1964 Nobel Peace Prize, Martin Luther King, Jr. (1929-1968), as well as with *The Enemy Within* (1960), *Just Friends and Brave Enemies* (1962), and *Pursuit of Justice* (1964) by Robert Francis Kennedy (1925-1968).

Viewing this development as a whole, we note that from its beginning the literature fostered by Europeans on American soil has had a pronouncedly global orientation. A Columbus could tell his Catholic Majesties that he hoped to reach the Grand Khan; and Mistress Bradstreet, for all her eight chicks and burning house, could celebrate the four monarchies of the world. Thoreau, from Walden Pond, could communicate effectively enough with his fellows in India. During most of the time that there has been any American literature, American authors have had not just an Atlantic but also a global orientation.

But by the end of the nineteenth century a kind of professional specialization had crept in. Literature came to mean belles lettres. The best writers concentrated on prose fiction. As Christianity had spread round the world, in some places it had thinned out spiritually; and animal behavior (with its emphasis on the physical present) became the disguised subject matter in place of human behavior (with its potential sensitivity to the not physically present). As the sensory experience of people grew, the inner vision reflected in their literature declined.

In some ways American literature during the half-century ending with World War I was better than it had been, and in some ways worse. The same thing can be said of it during the succeeding quarter-century, and during the past decade. But within these latter periods the writings of Americans have again manifested a potentially world vision — a concern with man — characteristic of literature during its great times of flowering. Within this manifestation, also, there is a rhythmic or dialectic sequence such as normally appears in the history of the arts.

Index

WILLIS WAGER is Professor of Humanities at Boston
University, on leave as Fulbright Lecturer in
Turkey and Iran, 1966 to 1969. Born in Kansas, he
received his A.B. from Washington University in St.
Louis, was an exchange student at the University
of Frankfurt in 1933-1934, and took his Ph.D. at
New York University, where he taught for ten years
while also serving as literary editor for a publishing
firm. He edited the Heritage Club edition of Mark
Twain's *Life on the Mississippi* and has written many
scholarly articles in the medieval field as well as
a two-volume history of the Arts, *From the Hand of Man*.

PS
92
.W25
1968
c. 2

Wager, Willis
   American literature: a
world view.

Date Due

OCT 25 '93			

Concordia College Library
Bronxville, NY   10708